Also by James Alison:

Faith Beyond Resentment
On Being Liked
Knowing Jesus
Raising Abel
The Joy of Being Wrong

undergoing god

dispatches from the scene of a break-in

———◄o►———

James Alison

DARTON · LONGMAN + TODD

For the purposes of conversation regarding *Undergoing God*, James Alison can be reached at **cgfragments@btinternet.com**

Further material by James Alison can also be found on the website www.jamesalison.co.uk, set up and maintained by Ihar Ivanoo

First published in 2006 by
Darton, Longman and Todd Ltd
1 Spencer Court
140–142 Wandsworth High Street
London   SW18 4JJ

ISBN 0-232-52676-1

A catalogue record for this book is available from the British Library.

Unless otherwise stated, the Scripture quotations in this publication are taken from the Revised Standard Version © 1971 and 1952 by the Division of Christian Education of the National Council of the Churches of Christ in the United States of America.

Typeset by YHT Ltd, London
Printed and bound in Great Britain by
Page Bros, Norwich, Norfolk

CONTENTS

————◄○►————

# of concavities and tent poles

Imagine two different groups of scientists. One group, armed with a set of encyclopaedic guidebooks which are constantly being annotated, takes turns to look at a distant star or galaxy through an extremely powerful telescope. The scientists offer comments from what they see, and in the light of what they see, or deduce, further annotations are made in the guidebooks, and their deliverances are passed on to anyone who is interested. The other group of scientists is standing round the rim of a huge concavity in the surface of the earth, or maybe they are in submarines, gazing at the rim of a huge concavity which has been detected as giving form to the sea bed. They are trying to work out what has happened, what force, what dimensions, what speed, produced this impact, and what the consequences have been, or are, or will be, for life on the planet as a result of whatever it was that produced this concavity.

Of the two groups of scientists, the one which offers the closer analogy to the discipline of theology is the second group. For the discipline of theology, a distinctively Christian discipline, presupposes a happening, an impact, an interruption, having already happened, and offering a shape which can be detected as the consequences of its having happened spread further. Furthermore, it presupposes that that happening, that impact, is not only a blind collision, of the sort produced by a meteor in the vicinity of the Yucatán peninsula, but is an act of communication. This means that the theologian is involved not merely as an outsider, commenting about something having happened, but is on the way to becoming part of the act of communication from the inside. Is on the way to becoming a shock wave from the impact, which is part of the impact itself.

Over the last five years or so, my main work as a theologian has been to prepare an adult introduction to Christianity. So far this has taken the form of a course (tentatively titled 'The Forgiving Victim: an induction into Christian vulnerability') given to small groups, one evening a week, over three months. Different hosts have generously trusted me to give this course in various locations. Lack of resources has so far hindered my aim of developing this course into material that can be used independently of my being there to deliver it. Instead, I have had the privilege of being invited to give talks, lectures, retreats and workshops on different theological subjects to different groups in four continents. These invitations have done me the very great service of stretching me into thinking about different dimensions of the happening and the concavity somewhat less glibly, I hope, than would have been the case if I had simply had the time and resources to 'write up' the course after its first or second giving.

The result of this is that I am here offering you, not yet the course, but something more like an interim report. If the course is a tent that I am learning to put up, then most of the chapters of this book are something like explorations of the shape and size of the different poles, some fixed, some telescopic, which need to be extended this way and that so as to fill out the structure of the narrative and enable the tent to become taut, spare and rainproof.

So here I would like briefly to introduce you to four of those poles, four elements of shape which I have discovered important in transmitting the happening and its concavity, echoes of which elements you will detect in the chapters of the book on which you are embarking.

undergoing

The first 'pole' is the notion of 'undergoing'. This is the corollary of the Christian claim that we are talking about a happening irrupting into and upon the world. Something happening 'at' us, or 'upon' us, or 'towards' us. But something which cannot be described except in terms of the undergoing it produces in those in whose midst it is happening. The concavity to which I referred earlier is primarily human.

The Gospel refers to the coming of the Son of Man as like that of a thief in the night. But here we are talking not about a *Deus ex machina* who simply moves us from without, as we move each other, but the appearance among us, and at our level, of the Creator. So someone who not only interacts with us, as we interact with each other, but gives us the 'selves' that are there to be interacted with, and provides the whole context and parameters within which that interaction occurs. I rather think that it is only when we are comfortable with the oddness of this 'place of undergoing' that we will find ourselves able to receive the Good News as the divine break-in it really is.

My more systematic texts, in the first section of the book, look at the themes of Monotheism, Worship, Atonement, Transubstantiation, Evil and Reconciliation. In each of these, my attempt is to show how the place from which we find ourselves talking about, or understanding these things, is not obvious, and needs more careful exploration if we are to be caught up in the living dynamic of what is going on. That is, I'm trying to sketch the shape of that sort of 'undergoing' where we find ourselves on the receiving end, and as one of the symptoms, of a process.

This sense of 'undergoing', both personal and ecclesial, is something I have found difficult both to understand myself and to get across to those whom I teach. Many of us are so used to ideas as things grasped, to a longing for boundaries and clear belonging, that 'undergoing' can be quite a perplexing notion. When we say of someone, 'She underwent a transformation', we don't mean, 'There's an object called a transformation which is hanging around out there, and it kind of fell on her.' The very word 'to undergo' is an oddity, an active verb with a passive meaning. It is more active than 'suffering', more passive than 'confronting', more objective than 'experiencing' and more involving of subjectivity than 'being handled'. So, what we can describe as we undergo something is more akin to what a slow-motion surfer might describe of what she can see from the constantly shifting position of the waves on which she finds herself as she heads for shore than it is to someone standing stably on a mountaintop with a clear vision all round. With the difference that when someone is undergoing something, it is not only what they see, but who they are who is doing the seeing, which is in a process of change.

In attempting to put shape to this undergoing, I hope I am being faithful in handing on what my Jesuit Systematic Professor in Brazil, Ulpiano Vázquez Moro, taught me when he explained that Thomas Aquinas, borrowing from Dionysius the Areopagite, held that doing theology implies a certain *pati divina* – an undergoing of 'divine things'. With, of course, the obvious consequence that it is this sort of *passio* which gives creative form to the Passion, from within.

something out of nothing

The second of my tent poles is the discovery of dimensions of the undergoing prompted by the ancient Hebrew realisation that God is not one of the gods, and thus that far from God being an object in our universe, we, and all our universe, are undergoers of God. This for me is the challenge of being a theologian, as opposed to a student of religious ideas. For a theologian's vocation requires participating on the inside of an act of communication coming from someone who is not an object in the universe. And the notion of the Creator, far from being bad science concerning the beginning of the universe, involves us in undergoing a sense of 'something coming out of nothing'. The wonderful verses of Isaiah 55:1–2,

> "Ho, every one who thirsts, come to the waters; and he who has no money, come, buy and eat! Come, buy wine and milk without money and without price. Why do you spend your money for that which is not bread, and your labour for that which does not satisfy? Hearken diligently to me, and eat what is good, and delight yourselves in fatness'',

are the signposts to the discovery of the inscape of God who is not one of the gods: and that inscape shouts: 'Something out of nothing'!

The difference, then, between belief in the Creator and atheism is that between a dynamic of finding ourselves over time with a stretched and stressed openness to 'something from nothing' tending to 'and you will receive everything', on the one hand. And on the other, the attitudinal pattern, lived over time, which says 'nothing comes from nothing' tending to 'so I may as well shore up what I can from encroaching oblivion'. This difference by no means always coincides with a person's public profession of faith or of atheism.

Now 'something from nothing' is not simply a rhetorical assertion of meaning. Nor is it simply an assertion similar to, but merely the opposite of, 'nothing comes from nothing'. It points, if true, to something of which *we* and all that we know could only be a peripheral reality and we could not at any stage possess *its* reality. We will always be to it as something in the process of receiving, as ones undergoing. We will always be contingent to it, and yet not it to us. And here the space where theology might be born is adumbrated.

In the case of all of us, our discourse is learned from others, the tools given to wield it are given by others, and we inherit, appropriate and create with what we are given. And we learn who we are, we learn to forge our belonging, our togetherness, our identity, as individuals and as groups by comparison with others. This comparison can mean (especially in infancy and childhood, when we are scarcely aware of it) 'appreciating what I am shown of myself by the other', and it can also mean, and often tends to mean (especially in adolescence and adulthood), 'defining myself over against what the other is'. And what this usually means is, 'I pick up in the other what I do not see that I dislike about myself and use it to define who the other is, and who I claim that I am not.' This leads to self-definition over against the other, and works equally in the case of individuals, and of groups of whatever size.

My point is this: self-definition over against the other is, at root, nihilistic. It is a grasped form of being which says, 'I must define myself over against the other, since if I don't, I may well find that I go out of being.' So, rivalry with the other becomes the only readily accessible source of being. By contrast with this, belief in the Creator, in 'something out of nothing' which seems to leave the believer hanging perilously over the abyss of nothing, says, 'It is only if I dare *not* to define myself over against the other that I can be nudged into learning how to trust that I will be given being over time, and that there is a purpose and a sense and a meaning to this identity whose discovery-from-within will be my joy.'

Now this is very delicate indeed, since daring *not* to define myself over against the other is always lived as a form of power-lessness. And powerlessness, being ignored, and having no status can corrupt just as absolutely as power, being sought after, and high office. The corruption can take the form of rage, rebellion and conspiracy theory, and it can take the form of fatalism, apathy and frivolity. If the one temptation is to shots of cheap, sharp meaning, the other is to no meaning at all, or any old meaning, which is the same thing. But discovering oneself on the inside of a meaning and a power which is simply not in rivalry with any power, or pow-erlessness, meaning or meaninglessness, this is something entirely different. And it is in our bearing witness to having been found by *this* that we are involved in the transmission of the ancient Hebrew discovery of, or by, the Creator.

the priestly criterion

The third of my tent poles is the question of the criterion for God. One of the corollaries of having been discovered by God who is not one of the gods, is the realisation that the principal threat to our being held in that discovery is the human tendency to idolatry. The threat lies in our capacity to project onto transcendence forms of behaviour and ideology which are merely functions of our social belonging, so that we are constantly trapped in fictions of our own production. The danger to us is that even if we are right about there being one God who is not one of the gods, effectively much of the time what we call 'God' is merely a disguised form of the social other, and not 'Another' other at all.

With God who is not on the same level as us in any way at all, and therefore whose mode of access to us is through 'something coming from nothing', we would have no obvious criterion *at our level* for discerning whether something approaching us, moving us, changing us from within, is from God or is simply another function of the social other. So a key question in all monotheistic disciplines has been, 'What is the criterion *at our level* for what is genuinely of God, what genuinely comes from "Another" other? And how do we distinguish it from our own idolatry?'

There have been different and long-developing answers to this question of criterion. Of the two most resilient answers over time, one has been, 'This Text has been given to us' – different variations on the theme of inlibration – and the other has been, 'This Person has been given to us' – incarnation. The fundamental shape of our undergoing is in each case entirely different. In the first case, 'this Text' must be hedged around so that it alone becomes the criterion for reality, and is not itself subject to human hermeneutic, since if it were, then it would no longer be a criterion, but merely another piece of the ebb and flow of human criterionless-ness. This hedge becomes problematic wherever we begin to become capable of detecting in the text signs of 'meaning derived over against the other' rather than 'meaning coming out of nothing'.

The second response requires attempting to understand a whole human life as itself the making present of 'something out of nothing' such that not only the fact of being among us is from 'elsewhere', but so also is the whole direction, acting out and shape of the life lived out. This reality must be hedged around by a very clear insistence that the physical body of the person came from 'nowhere on earth' (hence a virginal conception) and went to 'nowhere on earth' (hence an empty tomb). This hedge, obliging the mind, as it does, to rest on 'something out of nothing' in a very acute form, at least has the benefit of being coherent with the criterion it is seeking to protect.

What has become clearer to me as I have struggled to give my course is the sense in which the overall shape of the incarnation is priestly. That is to say, because we are talking about a person, prior to a text, and a happening, prior to a message, the shape of that person's acting out is the criterion for 'something out of nothing'. And the shape of that person's acting out is a certain deliberate entrusting himself to be put to death.

The criterion is then sacerdotal in this sense: the irruption of something out of nothing takes the form of a person occupying the place of sacrifice, which is discovered to be central to the human construction of meaning. However, this person occupying the place of sacrifice is coming at it from an entirely different perspective from that which had hitherto been possible for us: giving himself to it so as to undo our need ever to do such things again. In other words, this sacerdotal act is the fount of the creative interpretation of reality rather than an example of a particular participation in an act whose meaning is derived from the human ebb and flow.

I want to stress this, since it is difficult nowadays to imagine and remember that Christianity is essentially a priestly religion, and the Happening, the concavity, has essentially the form of a sacrifice in our midst, a sacrifice in which God sacrifices himself to us, and we discover that we are the wrathful divinity in the equation. Shock waves go out from that particular sacrifice, in which God proved[1] his goodness to us, and show us about ourselves and how we can be free. God 'proving his goodness' involves a certain form of acting out, a certain shape of making his point, giving us a demonstration – what I have called the Happening – which is itself the shape of 'Another' other, and thus not part of the ebb and flow of human interpretation. It is more like an invasion and conquest of our reality by another reality than it is a new insight into God from within our reality.

Now this only makes sense if what we are talking about when we talk about the incarnation, the life of Jesus, is God becoming God's living, human, criterion for us at our level, and in that 'coming into the world', being an act of communication from elsewhere. In other words, Jesus is God's living interpretation of himself to us at our level, not *over against us* in any way at all, but *for us* in the way that only God can be, as something coming out of nothing. Thus, it is through our learning to receive the shape of the sacrifice as the essential criterion for who God is, that the criterion which is not from us interacts with, undoes and reconstructs us.

---

1. cf. Rom. 3:24–6.

the living hermeneutical protagonist

So, the one who brings something out of nothing has given us a living, human acting out as criterion for what God is really like, and has interacted in our structure of meaning and being in such a way that it will never ever be the same again. The narrative of this interaction-having-happened is much stronger and more inter-pretation-resistant than a mere text. The story of Jesus and the woman taken in adultery and the parable of the good Samaritan are, for example, comparatively resistant to our inversions of their meaning in a way in which legislative texts are not. The narrative of the Passion, with its central Icon of God revealed in an innocent human being handed over to torture and death by the religious and political authorities of the time, has a power which tends to put into question all political and religious authority. Yet the stories and the parables are not entirely resistant. Even the Passion nar-rative can be captured back by the ebb and flow of human meaning, can be deflected from revealing the full shape of a benevolence and a power coming out of nothing, and turned instead into just one more variation on the theme of nihilistic definition by contrast with a wicked other.

And so, as the fourth 'pole', we begin to get a sense of the irruption into the world of the presence of the Spirit which we call Holy. This is the same protagonist as the One who brings out of nothing, and who came into the world as a specific, dated, human criterion, but who now exercises protagonism as living inter-pretative principle. The benevolence and the power of the Hap-pening would be nothing if it did not include a permanently contemporary interpretative protagonism. Contemporary not merely in the sense of re-enacted by us after the event in ways which make it seem contemporary. Contemporary in the sense of the whole dynamic of the Happening-already-having-happened being made permanently alive for us by its protagonist now.

This means that when we are faced with the question of criterion for whether something really is of God or not, whether it really does come from 'Another' other, or whether it is simply a projection, a function of our group belonging, we do not answer:

'We have this text' or even 'We had this person who did something', but 'No, we are not immune to even the very best things
that we have been given succumbing to our own fear and violence
and need for security. But the protagonist who brought about
the Happening has come among us as Spirit, as protagonist who is
on our level, but does not displace us, and will continue to face
us down, and therefore build us up by keeping alive his interpretation of himself for us, and his interpretation of us with relation to him.'

It is for this reason, I take it, that we trust that the Spirit will
lead us into all truth, and that the truth will make us free. Because
the Spirit will constantly recreate the Happening in our midst,
involving us in that recreation, the priestly shape of which we
looked at. And it will do so because the priestly shape of the
Happening was the turning inside out of a typical human lynch-
death. Because of the priestly Happening we know what falsehood
looks like – it looks like the build-up of whispers and lies tending
to the death or expulsion of an innocent victim, it looks like the
failure to speak out, to overcome convenient self-censorship, it
looks like battening down the hatches in case worse happens. And
we are constantly reminded, 'convicted' is the word often used in
the New Testament, of how easily we can reproduce that lynching,
and, by contrast, what the shape (and cost) of our extending the
Happening is.

For this reason the shape of Jesus' giving of the Spirit, at which I
look especially in Chapter 13, is so important. It is because of it
that we can say that there are two sorts of monotheism. The
monotheism of the victims and the monotheism of the victimisers.
The monotheism of the victims is wherever a group acquires its
criterion from its own sense of itself being victimised, which then
justifies the group in being over against whatever other it needs in
order to spice up its identity, its meaning and its excitement.
Whatever may happen in the interior of the group gets covered up,
and corrupt elements expelled, since the unanimity of the group-
as-holy-victim must not be threatened. Such a group can never
recognise itself as a victimiser, can never become self-critical. It is
because, at the heart of this group, there is no 'other' other, that

the group-given criteria must become tighter and tighter, and holier and holier.

The monotheism of the victimisers is just the reverse. This is the monotheism held to by people who are beginning to become aware that they are victimisers, and must be so no longer. And what is making them aware is the living spirit of the self-giving victim acting as protagonist, which is producing in their lives the shape of the Happening such that they are undergoing being brought into an entirely new space. In other words: the sign of the 'other' other in the midst of the group is the undergoing proper to people realising that they have been involved in something terrible, and yet, because of that, and without their noses being rubbed in it, they are being empowered to walk differently.

It should, I hope, be obvious that when I describe the two sorts of monotheism, I am describing two modes of being which can be present *whatever the religious or secular label and whatever the outward religious forms, or their lack.* I would hope that it is also obvious that, whatever it calls itself, there is only Christianity where the monotheism of the *victimisers* is being lived out.

And it is here that the Spirit, our living hermeneutical principle as protagonist, brings together the liturgical, the ethical and the creative. For the liturgy is our being enabled to share in the Happening-already-having happened by our being brought face to face with the self-giving priest who is also lamb and altar in heaven, and who enables our stories and our narratives to be interrupted by our victim, speaking to us in the tones of the stranger, the resident alien,[2] who comes upon us and leads us into truth. The ethical is our being empowered to recreate that for others, loving each other in exactly the same way as he loved us, enabling the Happening to become further enfleshed in us, allowing ourselves to become the concavity. And the creative is the way in which *through this process* of our learning not to lynch, our learning to detect what we are doing when we treat the social other in certain ways, our learning to distinguish between that which is of the social other, and that which is of the 'other' other, *through this process* the frontiers of

---

2. cf. Luke 24:18ff.

what *is* are stretched open, and we become more aware of what it is that is being brought into being out of nothing. We become able to undergo creation as we learn to lose our fear of falling into nothing if the social construction of our reality doesn't hold up.

a laboratory of grace

I hope I have given you here a sense of the single monotheistic dynamic to which I am pointing in the pages that follow. I have, as in my previous writing, worked out a fair amount of this from the space of that laboratory of grace which is being a gay man (who is, as it happens, a priest) in the Church at the current time. If it is really true that the Happening has come upon us, and is God communicating with us in the person of the Son and summoning us into communion with God's life, in the person of the Spirit, then the process by which we can learn to distinguish between certain violent and depraved forms of conduct which can never be justified, and the forms of love over time which are appropriate to a parti-cular variant of humanity which *just is* that way, is a process which is proper to the normal shape of the Happening-having-happened as it is kept alive in our midst. And if it is not true that the Happening has come upon us, then the result we could expect would be a group of monotheists looking for a new way to give themselves pure group boundaries by having a convenient other who, by definition, can never be brought inside or learned about, since his or her role as wicked other is too important for the well-being of the whole.

For this reason, in the second section of the book the occasion for theological discussion is the process of *pati divina* as a gay Catholic in today's Church. When I am asked to speak to gay-related issues I usually take advantage of the title I am given to engage in an exploration of some major element of Catholic doc-trine. So all the systematic elements hinted at in my discussion of the 'poles' are to be found in these texts as well. I use the occasion of attempting a reading of a passage of St Paul, one regularly abused by its being pressed into service as a sacred weapon, to set out some parameters for a living Catholic hermeneutic of Scripture. When looking at the characterisation of gay people current in the

Roman congregations, I sketch out a scholastic argument showing that the Catholic doctrine of original sin has implications for our capacity to learn what is true about humans, and about a proper understanding of natural law, which we fail to follow through on at our peril. When looking at issues of human sexuality, I try to explore how the socialisation of our language is the key issue in creating and sustaining Church. And when examining the working of the 'closet' I spend time looking at the way in which St Paul's understanding of Jesus' having become a curse for us is intimately related to his giving to us the Holy Spirit.

My argument here is cumulative: the overall shape of Catholic faith itself, a living interpretative tradition understood through a recognisably conservative reading of its sources, provides its own instruments of self-criticism. These will enable us to get out of the current double-bind produced by a sacred definition which has not been able to withstand the gradual emergence of truth which sets free, and yet which has trapped so much of our clerical structure into a series of contortions. The only way out of this mess is when people dare to ask what is really true in this sphere, and stick with their question, however inopportune it seems. But this requires a sense of being undergoers of 'Another' other who is leading us to courage in gently facing down immediate group belonging. Such a sense has been very little in evidence amongst our church leaders so far. I hope my texts will serve as resources to show both that the emergence of reality need not be as frightening as it seems, and that learning to deal with it is something intrinsic to the very shape of Christianity, and cannot be put off forever.

As a member of the long-term unemployed I depend entirely for my income on those who do me the honour of inviting me to speak in different venues. These hosts not only provide me with my material sustenance. As I mentioned at the beginning of this introduction, they push me into the study and thought necessary to address the questions which they put before me. I cannot say how grateful I am to them for both the sticks and the carrots which have nudged this donkey into production. I would particularly like to thank those who were the hosts for, and direct occasions of, chapters of this book: Fr John Julian OJN, Rev. Alan McCormack,

Dean Graeme Lawrence, Draško Dizdar, Catherine Pepinster, Marlin Brenner, Cesáreo Bandera, Sally Jakobi, Roberto Solarte, Rev. Mark Richardson, Sr Mary Aquin O'Neill RSM, Diane Caplin, Fr Brian McDermott SJ, Julian Filochowski, Xavier Martí, Rev. Tim Macquiban, Fr Gerry Blaszczak SJ, Martin Pendergast, Brenda Wall and the Foster Place Gang, Fr Bert Thelen SJ, and Fr Carlos Mendoza OP.

I have the extraordinary good fortune to count among my friends people who read and help me better my texts while they are still being forged. I prefer not to tell you how much worse these texts would be without the input of Andrew McKenna, Brendan Walsh, Paul Ford, Sebastian Moore OSB, Angel Méndez OP, Timothy Radcliffe OP and Stephen Schloesser SJ, and I am deeply grateful to them for their patience, their corrections and their encouragement. All mistakes and errors remaining are, of course, entirely my responsibility.

Once again, it has been my pleasure to work with Darton, Longman & Todd towards the publication of this book, and I thank Brendan, Liz, Hannah, Rachel, Helen, Aude and Sandy once again for their cheer, lightness of spirit and sense of both pride and fun in what they do. It is a source of delight for me that my publisher should genuinely be theologically interested and motivated.

The US edition of this book is the first occasion on which I have had the privilege of working with Frank Oveis and his crew at Continuum New York. Frank's enthusiasm for this project and his dynamism in making it work has been a source of great encouragement to me, and I am proud to be included in his list.

Over the last three years my rent has been paid by a friend who wishes to remain anonymous. This gift has given me the space in which to collapse after my trips, to think, to study and to pray, a space much beyond my earning capacity in both size and tranquillity. If there is goodness in this book, then a huge share in it is owed to the generosity of the one who has provided for me the means to make it possible, and I dedicate these pages to my anonymous Maecenas.

James Alison
London, May 2006

PART ONE

monotheism and the indispensability of irrelevance

I would like to honour my compatriot, Julian of Norwich, by attempting to boost something which was dear to her heart: contemplation. I want to do this by taking a long way round to indicate that monotheism without contemplation is dangerous, and to ponder why this should be so. To put it in a nutshell, my claim is that monotheism is a terrible idea, but a wonderful discovery. So I am going to ask you to bear with me as I attempt to fly a series of kites, and see if, when they are all up there, we can make any sense of them.

Here is my first kite. My first kite is a claim that there isn't really any such thing as monotheism. By this I mean that the notion of monotheism is a deeply unstable one, such that it is not at all clear what we mean when we talk about it. Let me explain: normally monotheism is taken to be opposed to polytheism. It is the claim that there is one God alone, as opposed to many gods. Monotheism is different from so-called 'henotheism' which is the claim that while there may be many gods, one should stick to only one of them. In this sense the commandment 'I am the Lord thy God. . .Thou shalt have no other gods before me'[1] is a *heno*theistic commandment, not a monotheistic one. In other words, it presupposes many gods and merely claims that one should stick with this one. In our standard account of the birth of Jewish monotheism, which I will be revisiting later, the key monuments are those passages of Deutero-Isaiah, written after Cyrus' cylinder

---

1. Exod. 20:2, 3; Deut. 5:6, 7 KJV.

promulgated the return from exile in Babylon, which clearly indicate 'I am the Lord, and there is no other'.[2] In other words, there just aren't any other gods, there is only one God.

Well, here is where we hit our first bit of instability. What is meant by the 'one' in mono-theism? Does it mean 'one' as opposed to two, three, or seventy-nine? In which case it is one as a number, and is opposed to other numbers. In that case, since whenever we define something over against something, it is true to say that it is much more like that thing than it is unlike it, 'one' God would be merely a uniquely big, powerful and somewhat lonely member of the series 'gods' all of whose other members have been declared inexistant.

But there is another use of the word 'one', which is not properly speaking a numerical use at all. This is where 'one God' is opposed to 'nothing'. In other words, where 'one' is more like the exclamation 'is!' than it is like a number. The exclamation 'is!' is opposed to 'nothing there!' Now just as the number 'one' is more like the other numbers that it is scrubbing out than it is different from them, so the 'one God' as opposed to 'nothing at all' is more like the 'nothing at all' that it is opposed to than it is to anything else. In other words, following this understanding of the 'mono' in 'monotheism', God is much more like 'nothing at all' than like 'one of the gods'.

And this, of course, is part of the genius of monotheistic Judaism: the realisation that 'one God' is much more like 'no god at all' than like 'one of the gods'. In other words that atheism, which is untrue, offers a much less inadequate picture of God than theism, which is true. For monotheistic Judaism, as for mono-theistic Catholicism, which I take to be universal Judaism, the principal temptation is not atheism, but idolatry.

My second kite which I would like to fly concerns what follows from this: the danger of monotheism. Briefly put, my thesis is, as I indicated, that monotheism is a terrible idea, but a wonderful discovery. Let me explain: You cannot really have an idea about something that is more like nothing at all than it is like anything

---

2. Isa. 45:18d.

that is. I mean, what is it like to have an idea about nothing at all? So when we have an idea about monotheism, our idea tends to latch on to the notion of one as opposed to many, or one opposed to none, rather as if 'none' were simply another number, but a number of a frighteningly negative or absent sort. In other words, inseparable from our notion of 'oneness' is the 'as opposed to' bit. And this is where things get dangerous. Because if there is a God who is not one of the gods, who is not on the same level as anything else at all, then of course it is true to say that there can be no 'as opposed to' in God. Or in other words, there is no rivalry at all between God and anything that is. Which means that whenever in any of our thinking about God we have an 'as opposed to', however residual, that same 'as opposed to' reduces God to some sort of 'god' and that same 'as opposed to' will immediately have sociological consequences.

Let us take a look at a fairly standard sociological description of the big monotheistic religions (and nowadays, as a brief glance at the publishers' advertisements in *The New York Review of Books* will confirm, we are fairly inundated with such descriptions).

I suppose that it is a typical representation able to be found within all three major monotheistic cultures, the Jewish, the Christian and the Islamic, that the One True God has delivered a message: Torah, Torah interpreted by New Testament, or Koran. The message, it too, is one and true, and the written message is guaranteed by the one true and definitive messenger: Moses, Jesus or Mohammed. I don't wish to say that this is the true structure of each of the monotheistic cultures in question, merely that under certain circumstances, adherents of each religious culture can behave as if this were the structure of their 'religion'. While these adherents may at times be thought extreme by other members of the group, it is common for other members of the group to be frightened of suggesting that these adherents are not basically right.

It appears to be true that the same structure can repeat itself within each of those groups thereafter: 'we' are the people who have received the message from the one true God, and live under it, and the way we live under it is to recreate the uniqueness of God by developing a strong sense of what is other than us –

gentiles in the case of Jews, the unbaptised 'world' in the case of Christians, and infidels who aren't members of the Ummah in the case of Muslims. In other words, we become an extension of the 'I' of the one God whose message we have received, and our job is to bring others to obedience from their otherness (often an otherness which is either wicked, or impure, or both), or at the very least to keep high the difference between us and those others and encourage fervour in resisting assimilation to those others when they are more powerful than us.

Now what I would like to claim is that in such an understanding of monotheism, 'God' and his 'messenger' are effectively a function of the group since what they do is guarantee a group's cohesiveness by providing a rallying point, something totemic, around which people can gather and which gives them a strong sense of rightness in being able to interpret the message over against the wicked 'other'. Please notice what this means. It means in fact that there is no real 'other' in the story at all. God and his messenger merely act to reinforce the creation of 'another' over against which 'we' can feel united, blessed by God and so on. And this means that the 'other' is merely a function of 'we', and is in fact a necessary part of the 'we', as its flip side, its dark side. If there were suddenly no 'other' then 'we' would disintegrate, would fall into *anomie*, become meaningless.

A typical way of countering just such an imputation of functional atheism to this sort of monotheism would be to say: 'But the message itself is the sign of a real other, "another Other" if you like, who is not part of the "we", having spoken to us and given us another perspective by which we are right to be building ourselves up in this way: it is what we are commanded to do.' The trouble with this is that it doesn't resist the discovery that interpretation is everything. A message, and a messenger to guarantee it, are simply tokens except in as far as they are kept alive by the group interpreting both the message and the messenger. This means, in other words, that a written message and a guaranteeing messenger are, in themselves, of no worth in maintaining an authentic 'otherness' of voice to the group in question, since it is only as the group interprets them that they have continued life in the group at all.

And that means that it is the group interpretation which is the only place where the presence of the 'other Other' might be found if there were such a presence. But wherever the group interpretation tends to work by creating a 'we' at the expense of, over against, a necessary 'they', we have reason to doubt that anything is present other than the spirit of group building over against another, which is, of course, what is meant by functional atheism. It is where, whatever claims are made about a divinity, the only detectable real 'other' involved is the social other over against which the 'we' is built, and which is in fact merely a function of the 'we'.

In case that was a bit dense, let me offer an example or two of what I mean: One of the strongest ways of maintaining the unity of the one group loyal to its one God is to be able to detect and proclaim ways in which the group is being victimised. Thus, typically leaders in a monotheistic group, or their surrogates and spokespersons, will identify ways in which the wicked 'they' is making life impossible for the true believers, thus rallying people around their interpretation of what makes the group whole and pure. Of course, this need to present the group as victim can be helped by people who are in fact oppressing some members of the group in question. After all, just because I'm paranoid doesn't mean that there aren't people who are out to get me. Nevertheless, it takes a special sort of genius to be able to convince the group of believers that it is themselves *as a group of believers* that are the target of the evil intentions of the other.

In this sense Osama bin Laden was being brilliant as a revivifier of Islam when he managed to convince people that it was *as Muslims* that they were being oppressed and exploited by the wicked west and the United States in particular. By his involvement in the destruction of the Twin Trade Towers in Manhattan, he also managed to provoke a backlash which fed beautifully into his interpretation, thus convincing people, including some of those promoting the backlash from the American side, that this really was a crusade against Islam. It remains to be seen whether the identical tactic being used by some evangelical groups in the States (and even some of their Catholic imitators) when they attack proposed or existing gay rights legislation as being a preparation for persecuting evangelical Christians for their 'Bible-based beliefs', can be equally successful in promoting evangelical unity and fervour through a sense of being victimised. Something similar was at work when certain defenders of the current Catholic ecclesiastical system in the United States portrayed the ongoing scandal concerning systemic clerical ineptitude in dealing with paedophilia as the result of deep atavistic anti-Catholicism, or a Jewish conspiracy to discredit one of the voices that stands up for Palestine, or simply well-orchestrated financial greed, thus attempting to rally round Catholic supporters to the defence of the current ecclesiastical status quo.

What is in common in the case of each of these depictions of a unique group being harassed for its uniquely true beliefs in the midst of a perverted and evil world is that each is monotheistic, and yet that the responses I have described are entirely without faith. I imagine that at the same time as Osama bin Laden offers his metanarrative of an evil 'they' who must be resisted by the good, there are many Muslim believers who hold their heads in shame, for they know that if God really is true, then to exaggerate the strength of the wicked other so as to strengthen the faith of the believer is the worst sort of nihilistic atheism, because it really does suppose that, in practice, it is only by provoking the wicked other to act out his part in the drama that our faith will survive, which means that we don't believe in God, but only in conflict. For if God really is true, then appearances are deceptive, and what look like wicked conspiracies by the wicked other are much exaggerated, because God is much stronger than they.

Likewise, I imagine that there are evangelical Christians who hang their heads in shame when they see their religion being turned into something dependent on a necessary enemy, as though gay people, evil though we may be, could really be such a threat to the order and stability of the Creator of all things, and as though the gospel message really could be reduced to 'thou shalt hate gay people, and having made sure of that, thou shalt love thy neighbour as thyself'. And finally, I imagine that there are not a few Catholic bishops who lowered their heads in shame as they saw confrères and apologists who seemed quite incapable of any sort of systemic self-criticism, and indeed fled from such a painful possibility by orchestrating new attempts to point towards wicked others, within and without.

Well, having attempted to show that monotheism doesn't really exist as a stable reality, and that much of what passes as monotheism in a typical sociological understanding is not really theistic at all, but functionally atheistic, I would like to fly my third kite. This is to begin to explore the positive side of things. Having claimed that monotheism is a terrible idea, I do hope to show that it is a wonderful discovery. But part of this claim, which I will stress continually, is that it is only as a discovery, and in the degree to which it remains a discovery, that monotheism is wonderful. Whenever it shifts status from discovery to idea, then it becomes terrible.

To approach this I would like to revisit the standard account of the emergence of monotheism (moving beyond henotheism) during the period of and immediately after the Babylonian exile. The standard account goes something like this (and I have often used versions of it myself). The Jewish exiles in Babylon were faced with one of two possibilities: either Yahweh and Marduk were competing deities, in which case Marduk was clearly superior, and Yahweh a defeated deity. In that case, it would have made sense to go along with the winning deity and become worshippers of Marduk. Or, on the other hand, Marduk was no deity at all, but was simply a function of Babylonian power and group building, and Yahweh was the only God who was for some reason allowing his people to go through this phase of being conquered and enslaved. But if this latter account were the case, then Yahweh was not in opposition to any god at all, because there are no gods, Yahweh is simply God who brings things into being, and is perfectly capable of using the power and structures of other empires for his own purposes. The literary monument to this breakthrough as it is being made is to be found in Deutero-Isaiah where we get the first uncompromising statements of monotheism as opposed to henotheism.

So far so good. But this account, one which, as I say, I have often used before, in which the Yahwist believers detect the functional atheism of the Babylonian pantheon and are pushed by their own extreme precariousness into making a sort of pole vault into higher ground, a sort of theological *aut Caesar, aut nihil* – this account is open, I think, to the accusation that it is part of the same functionally atheistic, or sociological explanation of the emergence of monotheism. After all, it could be said to be nothing other than a particularly thoroughgoing and complete reaction to Babylonian religion – an example of a particularly triumphant *ressentiment*, as completely triumphant in fact as the completeness of the defeat which led to it. In other words, what I have begun to suspect is that this account is itself far too sociological an account of the emergence of monotheism.

With this in mind I would like to propose something rather different. And this is something rather odd – it is a theological account of the emergence of monotheism. In other words, monotheism as discovery. And this is where, as far as I can see, the typical sociological account of, and discussion about, monotheism falls down. In order to talk about this, let me indicate what I take to be a fairly safe understanding of the chronology of some of the writings in the Hebrew Scriptures.[3] I take it that there was at some stage in the distant past a book called the Book of the Twelve Prophets. This book was composed of twelve fairly short prophetic books, starting with Amos and Hosea, who are the earliest prophets of whom we have written evidence. In an earlier form than we have it, Isaiah of Jerusalem was probably a short book like those we now call the 'minor prophets' and it is probable that the chapters 7–12 of our current Isaiah formed the nucleus of that earlier book. The early Isaiah seems to have prophesied in the period between about 730 and 700 BC, in other words during the time when the northern kingdom, about which Isaiah, a court prophet of the King of Judah, cared little, came to an end.

What is interesting is that this fairly short 'first Isaiah' rather

---

3. The current debates concerning the chronology of the Hebrew Scriptures are too complex to be resumed here. For this particular reading I am reliant on the extraordinary work of Padre Caetano Minette de Tillesse. His *Revista Bíblica Brasileira* published out of Fortaleza, Ceará, Brazil offers the most accessible overview of the ever-shifting world of scholarly criticism of the Hebrew Testament known to me.

than remaining a short book like those of the prophets Amos and Hosea, gradually grew over the next hundred years or so, as it was re-read in the light of changing circumstances so that when Assyria lost out to Babylon, a re-reading could take place in which the prophecies concerning the former kingdom began to apply to the latter. Further change could be introduced during the reign of Josiah (*c.* 640) and later the whole thing could be re-read and expanded in the light of the impending doom from the Babylonian conquest, and the exile (maybe with a deuteronomistic editor at work). Finally, it was the author we call Second Isaiah who was able to do a re-reading adding a whole new section after Cyrus' announcement of the return. And so it was that a few chapters grew and became a much re-worked book of close to thirty-nine chapters, and then a longer book of fifty-five chapters. The last eleven chapters, known as Third Isaiah, were added later still.

So far as I know there is nothing particularly contentious, or new, in this brief description of the editing process. What I would like to bring out is something for which words like 'editing process' become markers which blind by their obviousness. This editing process required people, readers, scribes, a school of Isaiah, call it what you will, to be receiving and understanding something and keeping it alive over a period of something like two hundred years. And that two hundred years includes over one hundred and twenty years before the Babylonian exile.

Furthermore this editing process presupposes people working away at something in which they saw themselves as exercising a continuity such that even the final editor of Second Isaiah saw himself as producing the flower of something which had started much, much earlier. In other words, the great, uncompromising monotheism-over-against-nothing-at-all of Second Isaiah was not understood to be a recent bright spark in reaction to Babylon, but the product of a certain sort of faithfulness over time to a wrestling with something which long preceded the Babylonian exile, and indeed the existence of Babylon as a major power.

Now this is where things start to get interesting, because we are talking, in the case of First Isaiah, of a number of statements which presuppose a certain sort of being addressed and a certain experience which went along with a being addressed such that from this *in nuce* experience the possibility of understanding monotheism-over-against-nothing-at-all was born. Let us look at some of these phrases. The first thing the Lord says to Isaiah that he should tell Ahaz the king is this:

> 'Take heed, be quiet, do not fear, and do not let your heart be faint because of these two smouldering stumps. . .'[4]

And here the prophet goes on to talk about the threat to Jerusalem posed by the alliance between Syria and Ephraim, vassals of Assyria, the two stumps in question. The prophecy ends:

> 'If you will not believe, surely you shall not be established.'[5]

What I would like to bring out about this prophecy is that it is exactly the reverse of the sort of thing that someone interested in promoting monotheism as functional atheism should be about. It supposes that the fundamental experience of God is one of being able to be at peace and unafraid since God is so much stronger than anything else. And it presupposes that what faith in God looks like is a certain sort of being established, made stable, such that 'I' or the group is not moved by the social other at all.

The second prophecy is the famous one about the young maid conceiving and bringing forth a child whose name shall be Immanuel which is familiar to all Christians from our Advent and Christmas readings. Again, the contrast between the realpolitik concerns of Ahaz regarding the defence of his kingdom and the sign offered him could not be greater. By the standards of monotheism as functional atheism, Isaiah's sign is useless. It suggests waiting and watching as something very weak and insignificant is born and grows. A less powerful sign than this could scarcely be imagined, and by the same token, this is a very peculiar pointer to what became the notion of a monotheism over against nothing at all. Because not a competition of powers, rather an indication of a quite different sort of power.

---

4. Isa. 7:4a.
5. Isa. 7:9b.

The third prophecy is, if it were possible, even more stunning in what it presupposes. First there is the prophecy of dismay and disarray for the nations:

> Be broken, you peoples, and be dismayed; give ear all you far countries; gird yourselves and be dismayed; gird yourselves and be dismayed. Take counsel together, but it will come to naught; speak a word, but it will not stand, for God is with us (Immanu-El).[6]

And then there is this, as filling out the picture of the sort of strength of the one speaking. Ganging up together comes to naught, strong promises of leaders will not stand. Instead:

> For the LORD spoke thus to me with his strong hand upon me, and warned me not to walk in the way of this people, saying: 'Do not call conspiracy all that this people call conspiracy, and do not fear what they fear, nor be in dread. But the LORD of hosts, him you shall regard as holy; let him be your fear, and let him be your dread. And he will become a sanctuary, and a stone of offence, and a rock of stumbling to both houses of Israel, a trap and a snare to the inhabitants of Jerusalem. And many shall stumble thereon; they shall fall and be broken; they shall be snared and taken.' Bind up the testimony, seal the teaching among my disciples. I will wait for the LORD, who is hiding his face from the house of Jacob, and I will hope in him.[7]

Immediately, along with this picture of nascent monotheism comes the notion that the sort of person who is faced with such incomparable strength has to learn to pay no attention at all to what people are saying, not to be swayed by what moves them this way and that, and above all not to engage in the sort of group-building activities which flourish with conspiracy theories, in other words, group creations of a wicked other. The God who is wholly Other, genuinely 'another Other', has no part in such activities; indeed, from the point of view of the functional atheists, those for whom

---

6. Isa. 8:9–10.
7. Isa. 8:11–17.

belief is a sort of group-controlled 'Gott mit uns' exercise, the real
God is a stumbling block, a scandal, an offence, something they
won't be able to get over because God works in ways exactly
opposed to their normal understanding of desire.

Isaiah understands that this message will not be palatable, and
had better be confined to disciples who will be able to meditate on
it over time. Let me repeat those lines:

> Bind up the testimony, seal the teaching among my disciples. I
> will wait for the LORD, who is hiding his face from the house of
> Jacob, and I will hope in him.

Here it is quite clear that there is no immediate use to this prophecy. The authentically 'other Other' cannot be understood,
grasped, even listened to now, and the only thing to do with the
prophecy is to prepare a group of disciples who will meditate on
the testimony, which is to say, the witness borne to what the 'other
Other' is like, over time. The 'waiting', the 'hoping', the notion of
the Lord who is 'hiding his face', and the instruction 'not to walk
in the way of this people' all indicate that the 'other Other' cannot
be grasped now, that only time and the alteration of the understanding of the ones listening will enable the nature of the other
Other to become available.

Now, I would like to make two points about this, which flow
from the same perception and which I think to be simply indispensable to any proper understanding of Judeo-Christian monotheism. In this picture of emerging monotheism, the God who is
not one of the gods, in addition to beginning to emerge long before
the Babylonian crisis, emerges *from the onset* as a presence leading to
self-criticism. The stunning words of prophecy are of course a way
of relativising the power of the other nations, but they are simultaneously a source of self-criticism of the 'we' in whose midst they
are pronounced. It is 'we' who are not going to be able to 'get' it
quickly, and thus the prophet and his group have to be prepared for
irrelevance because they are not moved by the same fears and
concerns arising from the events and struggles of this-worldly
power. Hence they are not responding to the same immediate
issues, decisions and choices which are being made about them, nor

seeking advice from the same sources. In other words, time, contemplation and irrelevance were absolutely indispensable to the discovery of monotheism, because it could only be discovered as part of a self-critical process. And being prepared for irrelevance also means being prepared to lose their reputation as the sort of people who might have interesting, useful or important opinions about what is going on. In fact, a severe despoliation of self-importance is going to be a necessary accompaniment to this process of listening to the emerging self-critical voice.

Should anyone be tempted to say, 'Oh yes, well that's just Isaiah', I'd like to point out that even Amos, the first of the prophets whose voice we have, and who was a prophet of the northern kingdom, that is of Israel rather than of Judah, preaching a few years before Isaiah of Jerusalem, works in exactly the same way. The first two chapters of Amos consist of a series of quick prophecies against the nations (Damascus, Gaza, Tyre, Edom, Ammon, Moab and Judah), each starting with the formula: 'Thus says the Lord 'for three transgressions of X and for four I will not revoke the punishment. . .'. But this is the build-up to the real criticism, which is of Israel. Where each of the nations gets a couple of verses of criticism, Israel gets ten, and then, from chapter 3 onwards, the blast is directed entirely at the 'we'. In other words, strictly contrary to the typical sociological understanding of monotheism as an idea, the emergence of Jewish monotheism appears to begin as a voice which is far tougher on the 'we' than on the 'they', and indeed berates the 'we' for paying far too much attention to the 'they'. This is not what Dr Durkheim ordered.

The second point which I would like to develop from this, and the one which is for me the most important of all these points, is this one. In the functionally atheistic picture of monotheism within group sociology the 'we', or even better the 'I', is that of the group, the God is the more or less tokenistic 'he' or the 'it' which backs up the group and gives it the impetus to keep up its group frontiers against the 'they' on which the group is secretly dependent. However, in the picture of emerging Jewish monotheism which I have been attempting to look at, something much stranger seems to be coming about. For in this latter picture, the 'I' or the 'we' is that of God, and the 'other' is the group. In other words, the structure is entirely inverted. The listening group is the 'other' whose 'we' is being discovered as it sits, over time, under the voice of the 'I'.

I would like to make, I suppose, the obvious point about this, but one which we find psychologically very difficult. In the Jewish understanding of monotheism it was the 'I Am' which informed the 'God who is more like nothing at all than like anything that is'. In other words, rather than the birth of Jewish monotheism looking like an intellectual discovery of a logical point, it looked much more like the passive sitting under an 'I Am' coming from nowhere, not in rivalry with anything at all, and undoing the 'over against' of the gods. And this, of course, is exactly what the central Yahwistic text, the self-naming of Yahweh, says.[8] Moses is not ordered to go and say to the people of Israel 'He' has sent me but 'I Am' has sent me. And this for a very good reason, only able to be understood over time: 'He' would merely be a function of my strong-willed 'I'. However, in the Yahwistic picture the 'me' who has been sent is but a highly malleable function of an unutterably strong, and almost unmentionable 'I Am'.

This is the central structure of Jewish and of Christian monotheism, that of an 'I Am' who is not in any sort of rivalry with anything, who is speaking into the midst of a group which is always a 'they' in the first place, and only gradually becomes a 'we' as it is able to let go of being a 'we-over-against-a-they'. Furthermore, this 'I Am' is never a function of the group, but always a voice which can only be heard through self-critical listening. It is, of course, the Christian claim that Jesus is the definitive accentuation of 'I Am', revealing the beneficence which lay behind wanting to address us at all, not out of any necessity, but so as to invite an entirely peripheral reality, the other which is ourselves, to share in the anterior and independent joy and love which is where 'I Am' is speaking from. It is scarcely surprising, alas, that what that

---

8. Exod. 3:14. The burning bush which is not consumed seems to me a magnificent image of the power which is not in rivalry with, and thus not on the same level as, anything that is.

beneficence looked like, in our midst, was the scarcely audible, scarcely visible, victim whom any 'we' is likely to throw out so as to maintain its structure over against a wicked 'they'.

The Catholic and Christian confession of Trinitarian monotheism is the confession that 'I Am' has come amongst us as 'I Am' always on the periphery of our vision, because always in our midst as one who is in the position of the one who is being thrown out, and always coming back as forgiving victim. Thus we are always being kept alive, as we could only be, by our 'we', which is typically blind to our victims, being punctured by the comings of the forgiving victim, the same 'I Am' as Advocate. 'I Am' is teaching us to see ourselves as a 'we' not over against a 'they', but as part of a 'they' which is becoming a 'we' in the degree to which we come to perceive our similarity with our neighbour and thus, from being peripheral objects, come to share in the first person narrative which is Creation out of nothing and over against nothing at all, just delight.

Now I like to think, and I hope that this is not just a fond and foolish imagination, that Julian of Norwich would have agreed with all this, and been happy with it. One of the things which is most remarkable about her work, as Fr John Julian OJN has pointed out in the introduction to his translation[9] of the *Revelations,* is that in a lifespan of over seventy years which included everything from the Black Death, the Hundred Years War, the papal schism, assassinations of a king and an archbishop, the beginnings of Lollard heresy and so on, she makes not a single mention of any of these events. In fact, her life was a constant sitting, as one of the 'they', under the voice which says 'I Am' so as to learn the inner meaning of that 'I Am'. Her revelations are the irrelevant sitting, over time, in the hearing of the unimaginable 'I Am' before whom we are all 'an other' and the learning to listen not to 'walk in the way of this people', to pay no attention to their detection of conspiracies, but instead to listen to the extraordinarily peaceful, powerful meaning

9. *A Lesson of Love: The Revelations of Julian of Norwich*, edited and translated for devotional use by Father John-Julian OJN (London: Darton, Longman and Todd, 1988).

of the love of the one who wants to speak to us, who is entirely without wrath, and because of the serenity of whose power we need be afraid of nothing at all.

I'd like to end by leaving this as a challenge to us. Is the monotheism which we profess an idea or a discovery? If it is an idea, we had better get involved in seeing how we can shore it up by setting up a wicked other, and perhaps the Muslim world would be a good place to start. Furthermore, we'll find that many of them would just love it if we were to play that game, because it will enable them to play the victim card, and so rally their own forces together. If, however, our monotheism is a discovery, then I would suggest that we are in for the long haul as we learn to become irrelevant, learn to find that any strong sense of 'I' or 'we' has to be stripped away from us as we come to find ourselves as the other, invited along with all the other others, including the Muslim others, with whom we will discover our similarity, into becoming a 'we' as we learn a certain passivity to, and a patient bearing of witness to, the 'I Am' not over against anything at all, and giving us no excuse to be over against anything at all. Because that is the only way we will keep the discovery alive as a discovery, a constantly renewing being spoken to, and a being spoken into being, by 'I Am' who is inaudible except in as far as we become habitually self-critical.

And it is only if our love of Christ and our following of him is part of our discovery not of being 'right', or being successful, or being relevant, or able to attract funds, or votes, or bring about democracy, or liberal values, but of being loved into being with all the others whom we might be tempted to think of as our inferiors, being assured that we are liked as we let go of the things we think make us likeable, being assured of a peace which enables us to let go of our addiction to the power of this world and the relevance to which we must cling, it is only these which will enable us, over time, to bear witness to Christ as God. Not the token messenger of a 'he' which shores us up, but the quiet depth of the 'I Am' who shakes us into life.

> I will wait for the Lord, who is hiding his face. . .and I will hope in him.

———◄○►———

worship in a violent world

I am going to talk to you about Worship in a violent world. As though there has ever been any other. There hasn't. It is only because of the introduction into our midst of glimpses of a world, not yet our own, where all is peace that we are able to look at our world and refer to it as 'violent', rather than simply normal. The discovery that might is might, a frightening aberration for which we can take some responsibility, rather than right, a natural part of the order of things which just tends to run away with us, is a hugely complex insight whose consequences we haven't yet worked out.

What I would like to do is to stand back and ask what it is that allows Christians to use a horrid word taken from the world of violence such as 'worship'; what we mean by it when we do use it; and what indeed we do that counts as 'worship'.

In 1215, in the course of condemning some of the opinions of Abbot Joachim of Fiore, the fourth Lateran Council made this striking remark: 'Between Creator and creature no similitude can be expressed without implying a greater dissimilitude'.[1] This remark, sometimes casually referred to as the '*maior dissimilitudo*', is much more important than it seems. It is one of the great bulwarks against idolatry in the western ecclesiastical tradition. It means for instance that when we take the word 'god', a perfectly common pagan word (like *Theos*, derived from *Zeus*) and part of the world of violence which characterises the cult of divinities, what we mean when we apply that word to the Father of our Lord Jesus Christ is much more unlike a 'god' than it is like it. Or if you like, the word 'god' is a deeply misleading starting place with which to

---

1. Denzinger/Schönmetzer 806.

begin to talk about God, but the one we have which is least inadequate.

I would like to suggest that the weight of this observation is not merely that it is a smart philosophical idea concerning how rational animals use language, but that there is behind it a very, very important theological notion concerning what it looks like for this rational animal to be reached by the God who is not an object in our universe, and thus for talking about whom all our language is bound to be, to a great extent, improper.

This notion of the 'greater dissimilarity' presupposes that God likes us so much that he has, over time, made available in our midst a way to disentangle us from the mess we inhabit, before we even knew that it was a mess, and instead has invited us to share with God, at the same level as ourselves, in making something entirely different, together. It is this 'liking us even in the midst of the mess' which is what enables us to talk about a *maior dissimilitudo*, because it means that God takes us *starting from where we are*, with *our* words to do with god, and worship, and sacrifice, and love and enables us to turn them into something quite else, something which is not full of the fear, ambivalence, violence and frenzy which characterise those words in their ordinary usage. What we are enabled to turn them into is something which is itself much more unlike those words than it is like them. However, we find that we are not lying when we say that they are, for instance, true God, true worship, true sacrifice, true love.

Now I suggest that there is a good shorthand term to describe this process whereby someone takes us, starting from where we are, and slowly and gently completely undoes our mindset, starting with the one we find ourselves in, and gives us a completely different mindset such that from the 'new place' it looks as though we are in a completely different space from the old, even though there is in fact a genuine organic continuity between the new and the old. The shorthand term is 'subversion from within' and I would like to suggest to you that to the theological term 'analogy', which is what the *maior dissimilitudo* is about, there corresponds the anthropological process of 'subversion from within'. In other words, it is only if there is a rational way of sitting within the process by which the true meaning of the word can come to be separated from its normal meaning that we can inhabit the *maior dissimilitudo* and thus begin to talk in a way that is other than entirely misleading about the true meaning of 'God', 'worship', 'sacrifice' and so on.

All of that is to enable me to come back to the question of 'Worship in a violent world'. If what I have been saying is true, we can now begin to reframe this question: Worship is a perfectly normal way of being within this violent world, and is part of its violence. The really interesting question is: what does the 'sub-version from within' look like, and how did it happen, by which we come to be able to talk about the True Worship of the True God. And here is the catch: if the True Worship of the True God looks like the worship of a god, or if they look more like each other than unlike, then we have fooled ourselves. We have short-circuited our process of living with the *maior dissimilitudo* and we have failed to allow the ordinary notion to be subverted from within. In short we have been lazy, and settled for more of the same with a different name.

So I will invite you to share with me in this little attempt to inhabit the *maior dissimilitudo*, the strangeness, the unlike-ness, the surprising-ness of what is meant by Christian Worship, in the hopes that this dwelling in strangeness will enable us to understand a little more what we do when we engage in Worship.

For the sake of a convenient peg on which to hang things, I'm going to look at what I call the Nuremberg and the un-Nuremberg. I should perhaps stress that I'm using a Nuremberg rally as an example merely because so many of the different elements of Worship flow together in this one example. We could look instead at the same elements in different places, football matches, celebrity cults, raves, initiation hazings, newspaper sales techniques and so on. My point about a Nuremberg rally is not that it is uniquely awful, but that it is particularly convenient. The liturgical orga-nisers of the Nuremberg rallies knew exactly what they were doing, and did it remarkably well. You bring people together and you unite them in worship. You provide regular, rhythmic music, and marching. You enable them to see lots of people in uniform, people who have already lost a certain individuality and become symbols. You give them songs to sing. You build them up with the reason for their togetherness, a reason based on a common racial heritage. You inflame them with tales of past woe and reminders of past confusion when they were caused to suffer by some shame being imposed upon them, the tail end of which woe is still in their midst. You keep them waiting and the pressure building up. All this gradually serves to take people out of themselves; the normally restrained become passionate, unfriendly neighbours find themselves looking at each other anew in the light of the growing 'Bruderschaft'. Then, after the build-up, the Führer appears, preferably brought in by means of a helicopter or aeroplane which has been seen from beneath by the gradually effervescing crowd and, before long, the apotheosis takes place, and he is in their midst. They are already riveted, the waiting helped prepare that; they are united in fascination with this extraordinary person, to whom they have handed over the task of being the chief liturgist. And he does not disappoint. With a few deft words and gestures he conjures up the mood of those present, pointing to the huge gathering as a sign of a new unity which is overcoming the pains and humiliations of the past, pains and humiliations caused by enemies from afar and, more important, by readily identifiable enemies who are much closer at hand; he need not say more. But none of these will stand in the way of the heroic victory which this new gathering, this huge unanimity portends. A victory which presages a new world order without the presence of those enemies within, one where only the good and the pure such as those who are gathered here, will remain. The Führer is even able to thank God whose providence has allowed him, unworthy servant of the Volk, to expend his life sacrificially on behalf of his people in his daily work of leading them into this new world. By this stage of course, the crowd is delirious, outside themselves, united in love and adoration of their Führer, and of course ready to do whatever he asks of them. On their way home that evening, though they may not notice it, part of the magic of the day will have rubbed off on them. They will look at the Jew from across the road in a different light. He will have lost personality in their eyes, and become a representative of the sort of thing the Führer had suggested to them. They will be that much closer to turning a blind eye to his disappearance, to agreeing that old Mr Silberstein the cobbler is indeed a threat to society. To the divinisation of the one, there corresponds the demonisation of the other, which is the dehumanisation of them all.

And that is what I take Worship to be. It is a dangerous and dehumanising thing.

Now I would like to look at the un-Nuremberg, piece by piece. In the first place who is the 'they' who want us to participate in the un-Nuremberg, and why do they want us to do it? In the case of Nuremberg, it was the party officials, for whom the faithful only had interest in as far as their mobilisation served the purpose of keeping the party officials in power and wealth. The faithful had to be made ready to do things, or acquiesce in things, with which calm and unenthusiastic people might disagree. A quite specific set of desires was being put forward, and the faithful were being inducted into acquiring these as their own. In the case of the un-Nuremberg we have something rather different: the 'they' whose desire the faithful are being inducted into acquiring as their own is God, who has made his desire manifest. God has no desire for us to worship him for his sake; he needs no worship, no adulation, no praise, no glory. No divine ego is flattered, stability maintained, nor is any threatened petulance staved off, by our worship. No, the only people for whom it matters that we worship God is ourselves. It is entirely for our benefit that we are commanded to worship God, because if we don't we will have no protection at all against the other sort of worship. We will allow our hearts to be formed by the desires of the contradictory social other that is around us, and that heart will eventually participate in its own heartbreak and self-destruction. So the insistence on worship, and on prayer, is much more like someone outside the gates of a prison giving us, who think we are living in a mansion, gentle hints as to what it's really like and letting us know how to build the tunnel to get out of the prison, than it is a demand for flattery.

In other words, True Worship is for our own good, no one else's. It is the gradual process by which someone who likes us reaches us while we are in the middle of a Nuremberg rally, and gradually, and slowly gives us our senses, allowing us to stumble out of the rally, and walk away, being amazed at what it is we have been bound up in, and shocked at what we have done, or might have done, as a result of where we were going. Our learning to give glory to God, to render God praise, is our being given to have our imaginations set free from fate, from myth, from ineluctable forces, from historical grudges. It is a stripping away of our imaginations from being bound down by, tied in to, inevitability, submission to power, going along with things. It is the detox of our Nuremberg-ed imagination. Our learning to pray means our being taught how to receive long-lasting, up-building desires, over time, in imitation of the desire of someone who likes us, not the short-term, malleable desires of someone for whom we are a means to an end. It is because we don't know what we desire, and don't have strong enough desire, that we are ordered to pray without ceasing, so that we can have our desire strengthened and made simple rather than contradictory and belittling. In other words, we are being given the sort of desire that will enable us not to be moved by the social other but instead empower us as creators of a quite different social other.

Secondly, and linked to this of course, is a perception of Worship which, unlike the Nuremberg rally, is not linked to a time and a place. The True Worship of the True God is in the first instance the pattern of lives lived over time, lives which are inhabited stories of leaving the world of principalities and powers, and gradually, over time, giving witness to the True God in the midst of the world by living as if death were not, and thus in a way which is unmoved by death and all the cultural forces which lead to death and depend on death. In other words, the True God brings about True Worship not in the first place by organising rallies in order to enthuse us for some new feat. Rather the True God brings about True Worship by inducting us over time into the process of having our desire, and thus our heart, and our way of being with each other, completely reformed. Within this induction over time into the process of the reformation of desire, the True God gives us to become habituated to the process by participating in signs of what it is that we are called to become, which participation is a certain beginning and developing of that becoming.

In other words, in order to help us towards the pattern of lives which are a True Worship of the True God, God gives us to become trained in, disciplined in, the habits of worship which point us to where we are going. Now please notice what this means. It means that any given liturgical action, act of worship, is something to help us on the way, it is not an end in itself. If you like, it is designed to be learned as a discipline to help us inhabit more fully the creative life story, which we are gradually and peacefully receiving, of leaving the world of 'worship', the world of principalities and powers. Unlike the Nuremberg rally, it is not designed to take us outside our ordinary life, but to enable us to dwell more freely and creatively within it, a lifelong therapy for distorted desire.

I would ask you to remember how much a part of the early Christian testimony this is. All the Gospels bear witness to Jesus subverting the Temple from within in one way or another, and making of the gift of his own body and blood, in a ritual which can be celebrated wherever two or three are gathered together, the worship of the New Covenant. All the functions of the Temple, principally faith, prayer and forgiveness, are to be carried out in interdividual relationships between people wherever they are.[2] If we collapse the *maior dissimilitudo* we make Christian Worship a backsliding into Temple worship, but worse. It is only if we remember the *maior dissimilitudo* that our liturgies can be part of our fulfilment of our Lord's prophecy to the Samaritan woman:

> "Woman, believe me, the hour is coming when neither on this mountain nor in Jerusalem will you worship the Father. You worship what you do not know; we worship what we know, for salvation is from the Jews. But the hour is coming, and now is, when the true worshipers will worship the Father in spirit and truth, for such the Father seeks to worship him. God is spirit, and those who worship him must worship in spirit and truth."[3]

2. Mark 11:23–5.
3. John 4:21–4.

It is not for nothing, I think, that in John's Gospel the cleansing of the Temple and the prophecy of its destruction comes right at the beginning of the Gospel. Jesus' discussion of the Eucharistic Bread from heaven, which is how we are inserted into the new temple which is his body, is presented as a meditation on the manna in the desert, the food given for the journey. Any liturgical act is a staging post in a journey, and should point towards the dwelling within that journey. It is an induction into a more fully inhabited, more conscious, and freer creation of that journey, which is itself the bringing about of the Kingdom of God on earth, not a temporary excision from the journey in order to engage in something ecstatic.

In the third place I would like to ask you to consider the difference between the achievement of Nuremberg worship and the lack of achievement in True Worship. In a Nuremberg rally the purpose is to create a sense of togetherness, of new belonging, so as to inspire something to happen in the future. Now, bizarrely, True Worship has none of this at all. It achieves nothing at all, in that sense. And this for a striking reason, which ought in itself to give us pause for thought about how odd a form of worship it is. Christian Worship is predicated on the understanding that there is nothing left to achieve. It has already been achieved, once and for all. The struggle is over; the Kingdom has been inaugurated and obtained. I can't get over how difficult it is for us to pause and sit in this for long enough. We are not building ourselves up for something which is going to happen; we are beginning to be swept up into the rejoicing that is emanating out from something which has already happened.

In order to imagine this more clearly, please go back in your memory to 1989. Now please imagine that you are in Albania. November comes along, and through the ether comes news that many miles to the north, in Berlin, the wall has come down. You know exactly what this means: it means that it's all over, the beast which ran your lives is mortally wounded, has lost its transcendence, is dead. It's all over bar the shouting. It may take some time for the thrashing about of the beast in its death throes to calm down. It may take some time for the effects of that to trickle down through Hungary, Czechoslovakia and Yugoslavia, but fundamentally it's over. You and some friends begin quietly to dance and celebrate in Albania. The very fact that you are dancing and celebrating is itself not only a sign that the beast has lost its transcendence, but is something which is, itself, helping the loss of transcendence, because you can have a party in its face. Something has been undone, somewhere else, and this means that you don't need to undo it yourself, the rejoicing in its being already done is part of what universalises the undoing so that you do find yourself participating in the undoing, but as a recipient who is spreading the effect.

Some people, of course, do not accept that the coming down of the wall means that the beast is dead. They want to say: no, that's a temporary blip, and we're in charge here. So they turn up grunting and shouting and bullying to try and make it look as though nothing has changed. But it has, and even they are losing faith in the old order. Part of the celebration may be learning to help the apparatchiks of the old order discover themselves a place in the new one. Giving them a soft landing: something the old order, built on revenge and triumph over enemies, couldn't possibly understand. While they're around, of course, your celebration will look like, and be made to look like, dancing in the face of the evidence. And that is what True Worship implies: the beginning of the celebration of a new regime even while the old regime hasn't yet grasped the news of its own fall. One of the things which really tickles me, in my own Church, is beginning to celebrate the good news of gay people, just as we are, finding that we really are at the party, and having to be quite gentle with the border guards of the old regime who haven't yet been able to admit that the wall coming down wasn't simply something which happened between Jews and Gentiles long ago, but it just keeps on coming down wherever the apparatchiks try to patch it up and make some people pure and some impure.

I would like to pause here to consider the fundamental place of this 'already having been achieved' in Christian doctrine. The place where this is celebrated is in the, in our day vastly underrated, feast of the Ascension. This is the way in which we describe the fact that it's all over, the Crucified and Risen Lamb is already in heaven. His marriage supper has already started. Heaven is now irreversibly and eternally intertwined with human life stories, in a movement ever expanding outwards from the altar of the Lamb. There's nothing we can do about it! It's already happened. We can be like the apparatchiks of the old regime if we want, trying to pretend that nothing has happened, but if so, we will find ourselves less and less convinced of our own battening down of the hatches, and we will be bemused at finding other people tolerating our sacred duty without minding too much, because they are already on the way somewhere else, and know that somewhere else is ineluctably coming here.

My fourth point develops straight from this. In the Nuremberg model, the central apotheosis has to be produced by careful orchestration, a deliberate build-up of fascination and mimetic intensity in the worshipping crowd, so that in their eyes the Führer really does acquire an aura and a divinity. In the case of True Worship, however, following on from what I said about the achievement having been already achieved, there is no apotheosis to be produced, no whipping up of emotions in order that we glimpse the crucified and risen Lamb. Exactly the reverse. Part of the effect of the achievement having already been achieved, is that the crucified and risen Lamb *is just there*. This seems to me to be a central part of True Worship. True Worship presupposes that the crucified and risen Lord is *just there*. In the address he gave during his enthronement as Archbishop of Canterbury, Rowan Williams described a moment when he was on a retreat in an Orthodox monastery, and was taken to a small chapel and shown a not particularly distinguished icon, and as he looked at it, it was suddenly alive to him as the crucified and risen Jesus who was *just there*. So we can relax, because we know he's just there. And relaxing is exactly the reverse of a mimetic build-up of fascination.

Now unless we sit in this bit of the *maior dissimilitudo* we will be inclined to think that we must do a liturgy right so as to make something happen, and then he will be there. But the reverse is true. Because he is just there, our liturgy is an ordered and relaxed way of habitually making ourselves present, as worshipping group, to the one who is just there, already surrounded by festal angels and our predecessors in the faith. If you like, it is an orchestrated detox of our mimetic fascination with each other which is the only way we are going to be able to glimpse the other Other who is just there, and who has been inviting us, all along, to his party.

My fifth point concerns the build-up to unanimity and the victim. In the Nuremberg rally, the build-up involves a mythical story in which the people gathered together are themselves presented as the victims. It is they who have suffered terribly. They are told a story about themselves in which they have been having a hard time, but the saviour figure will himself take them forward into the new Reich. The miserable enemies within, who have luckily, thanks to the Führer, been detected, will be eliminated, and so the long-suffering Volk will enter the promised land. Now it is unfair of me to go on using the German language, when I could be using Serbian, or English, or any other, because the story is invariably the same. 'We the victim', being led by our glorious hegemon to triumph over our enemies and acquire what is rightly ours. But in the True Worship, there is something very different, because in the True Worship there is no attempt to build up the unanimity of those who feel themselves victimised, no propagation of a comforting myth. On the contrary, those who are gathering are only doing so in the degree to which they come out of comforting unanimities, and learn to recognise and reject the myths that have sustained those unanimities for the lies which they are. And it is the hegemon who is gathering them together who is the victim, not the group that is gathering. The group of those gathering is having all their fake unanimities, their fake belongings, their myths, uncovered, peeled away, by their drawing close to the one at whose expense their unanimity existed. The interpreter who is telling their story to them is the one who is exposing them to their own collusion in a myth, and is doing so not out of confrontation, or hate, or revenge, but out of forgiveness.

The one true victim in the Christian story is there, the one who occupied the place of shame and disgrace because he liked those who needed to create such a space, so great was their fear of death. He liked them so much that he left a memorial supper for them so that after he had been killed, and after the resurrection had revealed to his fore-chosen witnesses that the victim was given back to them as their forgiveness, they could remember that even before he had died, he had deliberately set up his own interpretation of what he was doing beforehand, and they could remember that he had been pleased to occupy that space for them. That means that for those who allow themselves to be forgiven there is neither fear of death nor place of shame any longer, and they can walk in the same path as he, without fear.

I want to stress this point, the point concerning the remembrance of the victim, because it is exactly the reverse of the memory of 'how we were victimised'. The memory of the victim, which is only possible for us because the victim is forgiving, is the condition of the possibility for True Worship. The repetition, the rehearsal of the memory of being victimised, is always mythical, always a lie, and always part of a worship which is a manipulation into more self-destructive desire.[4] Constantly to be brought up face to face with the forgiving victim is constantly to be encouraged into not being frightened of telling the truth, of having the myths stripped away. Because it is a reminder of how we are victimisers, when we thought we were being good and holy and just, and how we need no longer be. In other words, the presence of the forgiving victim is forever producing that deflation of us out of myth and into truth. There is no true worship except in the presence of the true victim, because it is only from the victim that the voice which can undo the lies will come.

But this again means, as my sixth point, something very odd about the sort of group unanimity which is being produced in group worship. In the Nuremberg model, unity is absolutely of the essence of the worship, and it is a unity whipped up by the loss of individual life stories so as to acquire a collective persona, fuelled by a myth of victimage, being pointed towards a new future, and having shown to it the piffling obstacle it must kill in order to keep

---

4. And of course this is something which is especially delicate for people who really have been victimised: if they repeat and rehearse their memory of themselves as victims they condemn themselves to remaining prisoner of those who victimised them.

its unity. But in the True Worship, there is no such unity, no such unanimity. On the contrary, since everyone in the new gathering is undergoing a personal story of how they left such rallies, each one is entirely different. And yet, each story comes, over time, to bear a remarkable resemblance to the story of one who 'for the joy that was set before him endured the cross, despising the shame'.[5] Yet it is different in every historical detail. It is in fact a different creative act in every single particular, it is that person's own story, and yet can be seen to be a respectful and flexible multiplication of the same story. And this of course means that our liturgical celebrations are all automatically skewed from the start as regards any attempt to produce unanimity, a feeling of togetherness, a shared group narrative.

In any given celebration of Holy Mass neither the celebrant nor the participants have any idea of where in their journey, where in their story of having their robes washed in the blood of the Lamb, are any other given members of the assembly, all of whom differ in age, generation, sex, marital status, employment status, health, background, class and so on ad infinitum. And there is, and should be, no attempt at all to affect the subjectivity of those involved, to whip them into any sort of uniformity of feeling. The one who *is there*, the forgiving victim himself, is drawing towards himself all those who are there, starting exactly where they are, through the forgiveness, the prayers, the Scriptures, the opening of the Scriptures so that they are given a sudden sense of some shift in their perception. And then the forgiving victim entrusts himself to them, handing himself over so that they can become him, and he them, over time. In doing this the forgiving victim is engaging in a huge creation of a quite new sort of respectful unity entirely bereft of any need to produce uniformity, shared feeling or any of the excitement that goes along with such things.

When people tell me that they find Mass boring, I want to say to them: it's supposed to be boring, or at least seriously under-whelming. It's a long-term education in becoming un-excited, since only that will enable us to dwell in a quiet bliss which doesn't

5. Heb. 12:2.

abstract from our present or our surroundings or our neighbour, but which increases our attention, our presence and our appreciation for what is around us. The build-up to a sacrifice is exciting, the dwelling in gratitude that the sacrifice has already happened, and that we've been forgiven for and through it is, in terms of excitement, a long drawn-out let-down.

My seventh and penultimate point, though I suppose we could go on and on, is a different point about the group-building exercise in the Nuremberg rally. One of the things in Nuremberg-style worship is what I referred to in my initial description as 'Bruderschaft'. This is the sense in which, as they gradually become worked up in their enthusiasm, so those involved in the crowd begin to discover a special sort of love for those who are there along with them, a deep camaraderie, a sense of being one with, and delighted to be with, these others who, but a few hours previously, were entirely unknown to them, and, in a few hours' time, will be just as unknown once again. Part of worship is a sense that love enables you to leave behind the tedious banalities of the particular, the petty irritations, the timidities, the quirks, and instead find yourself together, and in communion, with these people whom an outside viewer would describe as strangers, but you, at the time, would swear that you were united by a special and mystical bond. And that ecstasy, that *ek-stasis*, can be quite overpowering, and indeed quite addictive.

Now I want to say that, from the perspective of True Worship, this is all completely ersatz. True Worship leads to a slow, patient discovery of being able to like people in their bizarre particularities, and see the beauty in those things, not abstract from them. Just as true friendship requires time and stretching and self-examination, and trust building, and vulnerability and time wasted doing nothing in particular. This is part of the sense that we don't need to hide from each other if we are all being forgiven together by the forgiving victim, and that un-hiding, that discovery, happens very slowly. Worship requires the suppression of the particular because it requires all those involved to share in a lie which will lead to a new form of unity creating a new sacrifice by casting someone out. All those involved in the unity are automatically, by the mere fact of being involved, abstracting from their particular stories and sharing in a lie, a cause that is beyond them. The love, the friendship, the real brotherhood which comes with and through True Worship, is a certain sort of being able gradually to bask in particular beauties discovered without any cause beyond themselves.

My final point in my attempt to sit in the *maior dissimilitudo* before I finish with a story which will, I hope, illustrate what I think Worship in a world of violence looks like, is as follows. Typically within worship as the world knows it, Nuremberg-style worship, we have a sense of being caught up in something bigger than us, which envelops us, is comfortingly ritualistic, whose outcome we know. It is part of a creation, or recreation, of an order which we know. It is part of a sense of everything being OK. There should be nothing too unfamiliar about it, nothing particularly new, no great discoveries about the world. It should not threaten us with hazard, except the comfortingly controlled hazard of the choosing of the victim. There should be nothing too risky or open-ended about it. No good liturgist, Führer or Hierophant would let the liturgy follow uncharted paths.

And often enough, by failing to sit in the *maior dissimilitudo*, we manage to reduce the events of Holy Week to a comforting expression of some eternal return. I would like to suggest that True Worship was inaugurated in the events of Holy Week as a wholly uncomforting, wholly contingent, wholly creative, wholly open-ended, wholly vulnerable and risky act of human imagination, taking symbols and forms and recasting them in a quite new and unique way, offering through them a way out of a sacrificial world of death and violence, and opening something up in a way which I can only describe as 'with jagged edges'. It is the strange combination of the contingent, the creative, the brave, the unimagined, the revealing, the not yet clear or tied up which is quite outside all the normal forms of comforting and regular worship, and it is this 'jagged edge' quality which is one of the things which it is most difficult to imagine and to continue to make alive. But I associate this with the bringing about of the New Creation, something which we don't yet know what it will look like, and something we are

invited to have a go at making up along with the one who inaugurated it. It is this jagged edge of creative imagination in the midst
of contingency which seems to me to be one of the indispensable
qualities of True Worship, and one of the most difficult to learn
and to perform.

So I'd like to close with a story which I think illustrates the
elements of what I think True Worship in a violent world looks
like, and is about. It is a story which I have gleaned from Chris
Hedges' book *War is a force that gives us meaning*,[6] a book, which, I
should say, has been particularly instructive to me as I thought
through this subject. Hedges, a war correspondent who covered
the Bosnian war extensively, tells of meeting the Soraks, a Bosnian
Serb couple in a largely Muslim enclave. The couple had been
largely indifferent to the nationalist propaganda of the Bosnian Serb
leadership. But when the Serbs started to bomb their town,
Goražde, the Muslim leadership in the town became hostile to
them, and eventually the Soraks lost their two sons to Muslim
forces. One of their sons was a few months shy of becoming a
father. In the city under siege, conditions got worse and worse, and
in the midst of this Rosa Sorak's widowed daughter-in-law gave
birth to a baby girl. With the food shortages, the elderly and infants
were dying in droves, and after a short time, the baby, given only
tea to drink, began to fade. Meanwhile, on the eastern edge of
Goražde, Fadil Fejzić, an illiterate Muslim farmer, kept his cow,
milking her by night so as to avoid Serbian snipers. On the fifth day
of the baby having only tea, just before dawn, Fejzić appeared at
the door with half a litre of milk for the baby. He refused money.
He came back with milk every day for 442 days, until the daughter-
in-law and granddaughter left for Serbia. During this time he never
said anything. Other families in the street started to insult him,
telling him to give his milk to Muslims and let the *četnik* (the
pejorative term for Serbs) die. But he did not relent.

Later the Soraks moved, and lost touch with Fejzić. But Hedges
went and sought him out. The cow had been slaughtered for meat

---

6. New York: Public Affairs, 2002, pp. 50–3.

before the end of the siege, and Fejzić had fallen on hard times. But, as Hedges says:

> When I told him I had seen the Soraks, his eyes brightened. 'And the baby?' he asked. 'How is she?'[7]

This for me is the sign of True Worship: not only the complete lack of concern about his reputation with his own group; not only the refusal to believe the lies about the despised other whose fault it all was; not only the daily trudging, for fourteen and a half months, through the dawn with milk before the snipers could see well enough to shoot. But the brightening of the eyes at the contemplation of the baby in whose jagged-edged creation he had found himself playing a part.

This attempt of mine to dwell with you in the *maior dissimilitudo* leaves me with a certain fear. It is the fear that True Worship in a violent world is going on all around us, particularly unnoticed by those of us who have a strong interest in Worship and liturgy, and are thus particularly likely to succumb to the attractiveness of the *similitudo* and to be blinded to that of which it is supposed to be a sign. I ask you to pray with me that our deliberations and our liturgies be part of our being inducted, even if it be kicking and screaming, into finding our role in the jagged edge of creation and the brightening of the eyes.

7. *ibid.*, p. 53.

———◄○►———

an atonement update

I tried, over three chapters[1] of *On Being Liked,* to set out some bases for thinking through what it means to say that Jesus died to save us. That was, and is, very much an ongoing project. Since writing those chapters I have been greatly helped by the work of Margaret Barker, especially *The Great High Priest*[2] and her study of the book of Revelation *The Revelation of Jesus Christ,*[3] in helping me take this further. Barker's insights seem to me to combine extraordinarily well with the New Testament detective work of scholars like J. Duncan M. Derrett[4] and the anthropology of desire which René Girard has made luminous for us[5] to offer the possibility of a richer and deeper understanding of the atonement, and one which will, I hope, not only help to overcome divisions within Christianity as to how Jesus' death is to be understood, but also give a far more positive account of the Jewishness of that saving death than we are used to.

So, I'd like to give you a kind of progress report on where I think this understanding is going, by trying to defend a thesis with you. My thesis is that Christianity is a priestly religion which

---

1. *On being liked* (London: DLT, 2003) chapters 2, 3 & 4.
2. *The Great High Priest: The Temple Roots of Christian Liturgy* (London: Continuum, 2004).
3. *The Revelation of Jesus Christ* (Edinburgh: T&T Clark, 2000).
4. Derrett's *Law in the New Testament* (London: DLT, 1970) is classic, and his several volumes of *Studies in the New Testament* (Leiden: Brill) are jewels for those lucky enough to have access to them.
5. In more works than I can mention here. M. Kirwan's *Discovering Girard* (London: DLT, 2004) is, by Girard's own avowal, the best introduction to his thought.

understands that it is God's overcoming of our violence by substituting himself for the victim of our typical sacrifices that opens
up our being able to enjoy the fullness of creation as if death were
not.

The first thing that I ought to do, therefore, is to rehearse for
you my brief account of what is traditionally called the substitutionary theory of atonement. This is what we are up against. It is a
certain crystallisation of texts threaded together in a way that has
kept us captive, and my interest is in how we are going to move
from this two-dimensional account to a three-dimensional account
and see that in reality all the creative lines in the story flow in an
entirely different direction. So, here's the standard story, which, in
one version or other, I'm sure you've all heard before:

God created the universe, including humanity, and it was good.
Then somehow or other humankind fell. This fall was a sin against
God's infinite goodness and mercy and justice. So there was a
problem. Humans could not off our own bat restore the order
which had been disordered, let alone make up for having dishon-
oured God's infinite goodness. No finite making up could make up
for an offence with infinite ramifications. God would have been
perfectly within his rights to have destroyed the whole of
humanity. But God was merciful as well as being just, so he
pondered what to do to sort out the mess. Could he simply have let
the matter lie in his infinite mercy? Well, maybe he would have
liked to, but he was beholden to his infinite justice as well. Only an
infinite payment would do; something that humans couldn't come
up with; but God could. And yet the payment had to be from the
human side, or else it wouldn't be a real payment for the outrage
to be appeased. So God came up with the idea of sending his Son
into the world as a human, so that his Son could pay the price as a
human, which, since he was also God, would be infinite and thus
would effect the necessary satisfaction. Thus the whole sorry saga
could be brought to a convenient close. Those humans who agreed
to cover over their sins by holding on to, or being covered by, the
precious blood of the Saviour whom the Father has sacrificed to
himself would be saved from their sins and given the Holy Spirit by
which they would be able to behave according to the original order

of creation. In this way, when they died, they at least would be able to inherit heaven, which had been the original plan all along, before the fall had mucked everything up.

Now, rather than make mockery of this storyline, I want to suggest that the trouble with it is that it is far too little conservative. I want to put forward a much more conservative account. And the first way I want to be conservative is to suggest that the principal problem with this conventional account is that it is a *theory*, while atonement, in the first place, was a *liturgy*.

That doesn't sound like too much of a contrast in our world because we tend to have an impoverished notion of liturgy. And we do not realise how much our dwelling in theory complicates our lives. However, in fact treating atonement as a theory means that it is an idea that can be *grasped* – and once it is grasped, you have 'got' it – whereas a liturgy is something that *happens to and at you*. I want to go back and recover a little bit of what the liturgy of atonement was about; because when we understand that we begin to get a sense of what this language of 'atonement' and 'salvation' is about.

Let's remember that we're talking about a very ancient Jewish liturgy about which we only know from fragmentary reconstructions of what might have gone on in the First Temple. For this liturgy the high priest would go into the Holy of Holies. Before the high priest went into the Holy of Holies he would sacrifice a bull or a calf in expiation for his own sins. He would then go into the Holy of Holies, having chosen by lot one of two lambs or goats – a goat which was the Lord, the other goat was to be Azazel (the 'devil'). He would take the first with him into the Holy of Holies and sacrifice it; and with its blood he would sprinkle the Mercy Seat (the throne above which were the Cherubim), the Ark and so on.

Only the high priest was allowed to enter the Holy Place. Now the interesting thing is that after expiating his own sins with the bull, he would then don a brilliant white robe, which was the robe of an angel. From that point he would cease to be a human being and would become the angel, one of whose names was 'the Son of God'. And he would be able to put on 'the Name', meaning 'the name which could not be pronounced', the Name of the Lord, represented by its four letters, YHWH. With the Name contained in the phylacteries either on his forehead or wrapped around his arms, he would be able to go into the Holy of Holies. He was to be Yahweh-for-the-day, an angelic emanation of God most high. (Remember the phrase, 'Blessed is he who comes in the name of the Lord'? This is a reference to the rite of atonement, the coming of the high priest – one of the many references to the rite of atonement we get in the New Testament – and of which we are largely ignorant!)

So, the high priest becomes an angelic emanation of YHWH; and one of the angel's titles is 'the son of God'. He sacrifices the goat that is 'the Lord', and sprinkles his blood about the place. The purpose of this was to remove all the impurities that had accrued in what was meant to be a microcosm of creation, because the Holy of Holies, in the understanding of the Temple, was the place where the Creator dwelt, beyond and outside creation. The idea was that creation started from the Temple Veil outwards, while the Holy Place was beyond time, matter and space. The rite of atonement was about the Lord himself, the Creator, emerging from the Holy of Holies so as to set the people free from their impurities and sins and transgression. In other words, the whole rite was exactly the reverse of what we typically imagine a priestly rite to be about. We tend to have an 'Aztec imagination' as regarding the sacrificial system. The hallmark of the sacrificial system is that its priest sacrifices something so as to placate some deity.

The Jewish priestly rite was already an enormous advance beyond that world. They understood perfectly well that it was pagan rites that sacrificed victims in order to keep creation going. And one of the ways in which they had advanced beyond that, even before the fall of the Temple and the exile to Babylon, was the understanding that it was actually *God* who was doing the work, it was *God* who was coming out wanting to restore creation, out of his love for his people. And so it is YHWH who emerges from the Holy of Holies dressed in white in order to forgive the people their sins and, more importantly, in order to *allow creation to flow*.

The notion is that humans are inclined to muck up creation; and it is God emerging from the place that symbolises that which is before creation began, 'the place of the Creator'. The Holy of Holies was the place that symbolised 'before the first day' – which, of course, meant before time, before creation was brought into being.

The priest emerged from that and came through the Temple Veil. This was made of very rich material, representing the material world, that which was created. At this point the high priest would don a robe made of the same material as the Veil, to demonstrate that what he was acting out was God coming forth and entering into the world of creation so as to make atonement, to undo the way humans had snarled up that creation. And at that point, having emerged, he would then sprinkle the rest of the temple with the blood that was the Lord's blood.

Now, here's the interesting point: for the Temple understanding the high priest at this stage *was* acting 'in the person of Yahweh', and it was *the Lord's* blood that was being sprinkled. This was a divine movement to set people free. It was not – as we often imagine – a priest satisfying a divinity. The reason why the priest had to engage in a prior expiation was because he was about to become a sign of something quite else: acting outwards. The movement is not inwards towards the Holy of Holies; the movement is outwards from the Holy of Holies.

So the priest would then come through the Veil – meaning the Lord entering into the world, the created world – and sprinkle all the rest of the Temple, hence setting it free. After which, as the person who was bearing the sins that had been accumulated, he would place them on the head of what we call 'the scapegoat', Azazel, which would then be driven outside the town, to the edge of a cliff and cast down, where it would be killed, so that the people's sins would be taken away.

That was, from what we can gather, the atonement rite. But here's the fascinating thing: the Jewish understanding was way ahead of the 'Aztec' version we attribute to it. Even at that time it was understood that it was not about humans trying desperately to satisfy God, but God taking the initiative of breaking through towards us. In other words, atonement was something of which we were the *beneficiaries*. That is the first point I want to make when emphasising that we are talking about a liturgy rather than a theory. We are talking about something that we undergo over time as part of a benign divine initiative towards us.

This puts many things in a slightly different perspective from what we are used to. It means, for instance, that the picture of God in the theory that we have that demands that God's anger be satisfied, is a pagan notion. In the Jewish understanding it was instead something that God was offering to us. Now here's the crunch with this: the early Christians who wrote the New Testament understood very clearly that Jesus was *the* authentic high priest, who was restoring *the* eternal covenant that had been established long before; who was coming out from the Holy Place so as to offer himself as an expiation for us, as a concrete living out and demonstration of God's love for us; and that Jesus was acting this out quite deliberately.

There are a number of places where we get hints of this language. One of them is in Jesus acting out the role of Melchizedek. For example, the announcement of the Jubilee, which Jesus preaches in the synagogue in Nazareth,[6] was the way in which the high priest Melchizedek would come back and work for the liberation, the 'atonement' or 'redemption', of the people. In fact, what Jesus says and does in Luke is to fulfil the Melchizedek agenda, which includes going up to Jerusalem and being killed.

There are different ways in the other Gospels in which this is depicted. The classic example is in St John's Gospel, chapter 17. Jesus' last speech to his disciples before the Passion is a speech based on the high priest's atonement prayer. And Jesus then goes off to act out the role of the high priest who is making available the new temple in his body (which, of course, John had given us a hint about in the beginning of his Gospel).

One of the ways in which this is told in St John's Gospel is that Jesus is crucified on Thursday, not on Friday. So on Thursday afternoon he is going outside the city walls to be killed at exactly the same time – three in the afternoon – when the priests in the Temple were killing the lambs for the Passover feast. So, while

6. Luke 4:16ff.

they were killing the lambs, the real Lamb, the one who was identified as 'the Lamb of God', was going to the place of execution to be killed. But – bizarrely – he was going dressed in a 'seamless robe', a *priest's robe*: hence the importance of his robe being 'seamless', and lots having to be cast for it rather than it being torn.[7] So the high priest was going – *the Lord* was going – to 'the Temple' where he would be 'the Lamb', for, as we are told, when they look on him after he has died they see that not a bone of his body was broken, alluding to the Passover lamb.

The identification is complete. And of course, Jesus' cry on the cross in John's Gospel is 'It is finished', 'It is completed': meaning the atonement, and therefore the inauguration of creation, is completed. In John's Gospel the 'I shall go to my Father' is always synonymous with 'I shall go to my death, in which I shall be lifted up, and that is how I will glorify my Father.' All of these things we know; but usually we do not see them in the context of Jesus being the authentic high priest doing the high priestly thing.

You can tell that that was how it was read because in John's Gospel immediately after this, at the resurrection, we are transferred to the garden. We are back to the 'first day' and we are in 'the garden'. Peter and John come to look, then Mary Magdalene comes in. What does she see? Two angels! And where are the angels sitting? One at the head and one at the foot of a space that is open because the stone has been rolled away. What is this space? This is the Holy of Holies. This is the mercy seat, with the Cherubim present.[8] The Holy of Holies is now open, because creation is able to flow completely freely. No more tangling up of creation. The Holy of Holies has been opened up. The high priest has gone in who did not need to sacrifice a bull for his own sins because he didn't have any. Then he was able to come out of the place of creation and into the whole world.

---

7. That Christian tradition has never entirely lost sight of this can be seen by looking at Giotto's Scrovegni Chapel Crucifixion (1303–6), where the robe being handed over is very clearly priestly.
8. For a particularly beautiful reading of this see Rowan Williams' 'Between the Cherubim: the empty tomb and the empty throne' in *On Christian Theology* (Oxford: Blackwell, 2000), pp. 183–96.

And remember that in the epistle to the Hebrews, as in much of the Pauline literature, and in John's Gospel, Jesus was the Word of God who was with creation from the beginning – 'all things were created through him'. This is the high priestly language of the One who is coming from God to offer atonement so as to open up creation. That is what is being fulfilled. And you get a sense of a realisation in John's Gospel that this is what has been acted out: Jesus' fulfilling of the liturgy of the atonement. So far so good! This is an explanation that allows us to see Jesus' 'subversion from within' of the ancient liturgy of atonement – which was also practised in the Second Temple period.[9]

In the Second Temple there was no longer a mercy seat. There was no longer anything inside the Holy of Holies. The priestly mysteries had been lost. And this was one of the reasons that there was excitement that here was a priest who was going to fulfil the promises and restore the priestly mysteries. But of course 'restored' in a skewed, 'off stage' way – i.e. the real high priest was engaged in *being* the sacrifice, 'the victim', the priest, the altar and the temple on the city rubbish heap, at the same time as the corrupt city guys – which is how the ordinary Jews saw them at the time – were going through the motions in the corrupt Second Temple, which was not of such great concern to the people. They didn't think it was the real thing. Many of Jesus' contemporaries would have regarded the Temple which they knew and the priesthood which ran it as, if you'll excuse the imagery, the diet-Pepsi version of a long-lost real Coke.

From our point of view these are all aspects of atonement. What Jesus was doing was fulfilling a set of prophecies concerning a liturgical happening, which is to us largely mysterious. The reason I wanted to tell you about it is that it is very important for our understanding when we see that this is not simply an abolition of something that was bad, but someone fulfilling something that was considered good but not good enough. Do you see the difference?

---

9. Sirach 50 gives us a wonderful Second Temple account of the high priest Simeon performing this liturgy with many of the ancient elements clearly recognisable.

That means that our tendency to read the whole world of priest-hood and sacrifice as an 'unfortunate Semitic leftover' is really very wrong. The Jewish priestly thing – apart from being responsible for some of the most extraordinary texts that we have in what survives in the Hebrew Scriptures – was also *the pattern* which enabled the relationship between creation and salvation to be held together. And that is the pattern of the Catholic faith, as I want to explore a little bit more: it is the notion of God making available for us the chance to participate in the fullness of creation by God becoming a sacrifice for us in our midst.

We are all – quite rightly – allergic to liturgy by itself. We are absolutely right because that is one of the things that the New Testament is insistent on. The genius of Jesus lay, among other things, in bringing together the liturgical and the ethical, which is why atonement matters to us. Because what Jesus did was not really, as it were, to fulfil a series of prophecies regarding a somewhat bizarre ancient rite that involved lots of blood and barbeque. What Jesus did – and this is the fascinating thing – was to make an extraordinary *anthropological* breakthrough. And this is where atonement is 'substitutionary'.

Here I want to make a little aside: normally, in the *'theory'* based approach to substitutionary atonement, we understand the sub-stitution to work as follows: God was angry with humanity; Jesus says, 'Here am I'; God needed to loose a lightning rod, so Jesus said, 'You can loose it on me', thus substituting himself for us. Boom: lightning rod gets struck: sacrifice is carried out: God is happy: 'I got my blood-lust out of the way!'

The New Testament points to an entirely different way of conceiving this: what Jesus was doing was *substituting himself for a series of substitutions*. The human sacrificial system typically works in the following way: the most primitive forms of sacrifice are *human* sacrifices. After people begin to become aware of what they are doing this gets transferred to *animal* sacrifices. After all it's easier to sacrifice animals because they don't fight back so much; whereas if you have to run a sacrificial system that requires you to keep getting victims, usually you have to run a war machine in order to provide enough victims to keep the system going; or you have to keep pet *pharmakons* around the place[10] – convenient half-insider half-outsiders, who live in splendour, and have a thoroughly good time, until a time of crisis when you need people to sacrifice, and then you sacrifice them. But this is an ugly thing, and people are, after all, human; and so animals began to be sacrificed instead. And in some cultures from animals you move on to more symbolic forms of sacrifice, like bread and wine. You can find almost any cultural variation on the theme of sacrificial substitution.

The interesting thing is that Jesus takes exactly the inverse route; and he explains to us that he is going in the inverse route. 'The night before he was betrayed. . .' what did he do? He said, 'Instead of the bread and the wine, this is the lamb, and the lamb is a human being.' In other words he substituted a human being back into the *centre* of the sacrificial system *as the priest*, thus showing what the sacrificial system was really about, and so bringing it to an end. He was the Great High Priest giving portions of himself as lamb to his fellow priests, just as the high priest in office would distribute portions of the sacrificed lamb to the other priests.

So you do have a genuine substitution that is quite proper within the Christian living out of atonement. All sacrificial systems are substitutionary; but what we have with Jesus is an exact inversion of the sacrificial system: him going backwards and occupying the space so as to make it clear that this is simply *murder*. And it *needn't be*. That is what we begin to get in St John's Gospel: a realisation that what Jesus was doing was actually *revealing* the mendacious principle of the world. The way human structure is kept going is by us killing each other, convincing ourselves of our right and duty to do it, and therefore building ourselves up over and against our victims. What Jesus understands himself as doing in St John's Gospel is revealing the way that mechanism works. And by revealing it, depriving it of all power by making it clear that it is a lie: 'your father was a liar and a murderer from the beginning'. That is how the 'prince' – or *principle* – of this world works.

So what we get in St John's Gospel is a clear understanding that

---

10. Some ancient Greek cities kept just such made-to-measure future victims in supply against the day when their sacrifice would be 'necessary'.

the undoing of victimage is not simply a liturgical matter, it's not simply a liturgical fulfilment. Jesus is substituting himself at the centre of what the liturgical tradition was both remembering and covering up, namely *human sacrifice*, therefore making it possible for us to begin to live without sacrifice. And that includes not just liturgical sacrifice, but more importantly the human mechanism of sacrificing other people so that we can keep ourselves going. In other words, what Jesus was beginning to make possible was for us to begin to live as if death were not, and therefore for us not to have to protect ourselves over against it by making sure we tread on other people. Do you see how he is putting together the ethical and the liturgical into the same space so that this is a space of dense anthropological revelation? When Jesus brings together the liturgical and the ethical understanding of victimhood, thus showing us what we typically do and how we need no longer do it, God is showing us something about *ourselves*.

Now, this was quite clearly seen at the time, as is evident from references in St John's Gospel to Jesus understanding this mechanism as that of 'the prince of this world'. But there are also some give-aways in St Paul that are very revealing.

Here is a story from 2 Samuel,[11] that takes us straight back into the world of expiation, propitiation and atonement, in the anthropological sphere, not the liturgical sphere. Remember, the two are linked, but they haven't yet been linked clearly:

> Now there was a famine in the days of David for three years, year after year; and David sought the face of the LORD. And the LORD said, "There is bloodguilt on Saul and on his house, because he put the Gibeonites to death." So the king called the Gibeonites. Now the Gibeonites were not of the people of Israel, but of the remnant of the Amorites; although the people of Israel had sworn to spare them, Saul had sought to slay them in his zeal for the people of Israel and Judah. And David said to the Gibeonites, "What shall I do for you? And how shall I make expiation, that you may bless the heritage of the LORD?" The

---

11. 2 Sam. 21:1–9.

Gibeonites said to him, "It is not a matter of silver or gold between us and Saul or his house; neither is it for us to put any man to death in Israel." And he said, "What do you say that I shall do for you?" They said to the king, "The man who consumed us and planned to destroy us, so that we should have no place in all the territory of Israel, let seven of his sons be given to us, so that we may hang them up before the LORD at Gibeon on the mountain of the LORD." And the king said, "I will give them." But the king spared Mephibosheth, the son of Saul's son Jonathan, because of the oath of the LORD which was between them, between David and Jonathan the son of Saul. The king took the two sons of Rizpah the daughter of Aiah, whom she bore to Saul, Armoni and Mephibosheth; and the five sons of Merab the daughter of Saul, whom she bore to Adriel the son of Barzillai the Meholathite; and he gave them into the hands of the Gibeonites, and they hanged them on the mountain before the LORD, and the seven of them perished together. They were put to death in the first days of harvest, at the beginning of barley harvest.

After a short time the famine and the drought went way. A lovely story! The interesting thing about it is that it makes clear something we often forget: how expiation worked. Here King David is expiating something, offering propitiation to the Gibeonites. In other words, the Gibeonites have a right to demand vengeance, they are owed something, and David is offering it to them. St Paul seems to know about this story since he says in Romans: 'What then shall we say to this? If God is for us, who is against us? He who did not *spare his own Son* but gave him up for us all, will he not also give us all things with him?'[12] Do you see what St Paul is pointing to here? St Paul is saying that God, unlike King David, did not seek someone else as a stand-in sacrifice to placate us, but gave his own son (which, for a monotheist like St Paul, means himself) to be the expiation, putting forth the propitiation.

In the Samuel text, who is propitiating whom? King David is

---

12. Rom. 8:31–2, my emphasis.

propitiating the Gibeonites by means of Saul's sons. God is propitiating *us*. In other words, who is the angry divinity in the story? *We are*. That is the purpose of the atonement. *We* are the angry divinity. *We* are the ones inclined to dwell in wrath and think we need vengeance in order to survive. God was occupying the space of *our* victim so as to show us that we need never do this again. This turns on its head the Aztec understanding of the atonement. In fact it turns on its head what has passed as our penal substitutionary theory of atonement, which always presupposes that it is *us* satisfying God, that *God* needs satisfying, that there is *vengeance* in God. Whereas it is quite clear from the New Testament that what was really exciting to Paul was that it was obvious from Jesus' self-giving, and the 'out-pouring of Jesus' blood', that this was the revelation of who God was: God was entirely without vengeance, entirely without substitutionary tricks; and that he was giving himself entirely without ambivalence and ambiguity for *us*, towards *us*, in order to set *us* 'free from our sins' – 'our sins' being our way of being bound up with each other in death, vengeance, violence and what is commonly· called 'wrath'.

Now, what is particularly difficult for us, and why I want to remind us that this is a liturgy rather than a theory, is that the way we live this out as Christians is to remember that the one true sacrifice – that is to say, the place where God gave himself for us in our midst as our victim – has been done. It's over! The whole of the sacrificial system has been brought to an end. The Holy of Holies has been opened for good.

The way in which we depict this in our theological imagination is through the doctrine of the Ascension. Remember what happens at the beginning of the Acts of the Apostles. Jesus is with the apostles on a hillside outside Jerusalem, and then he is taken up into heaven. He blesses them on the way – i.e. we have the high priest. They stand looking up; and there are a couple of angels – who are, of course, our old friends the cherubim in the Holy of Holies, which has now become everywhere – saying, 'Why are you standing there looking up to heaven? Go and wait to be empowered from on high.' What we have here is Jesus going to 'sit at the right hand of the Father': the place of the priest – the Word, the Creator – the sacrifice having been fulfilled. We live under *that*. And the way we live under it liturgically is by our participation in the Eucharist.

The purpose of the Eucharist is not us trying to make Jesus come down here but our obeying Jesus' instruction to invoke him, to do this in memory of him, so that we find ourselves transported into participating in the 'heavenly banquet', the place where the Lamb is standing as one slaughtered, as in the vision described by the book of Revelation. This is a Holy of Holies vision; this is a vision of the Holy of Holies now open and flowing everywhere. It is the one true sacrifice that has been done. That does not mean to say 'over and done with'. It means that the victorious Lamb is there; his blood is flowing out; the victim, the *forgiving* victim, is present. And we have access to participate in that atonement, which has been achieved through it being made available to us in our Eucharist. What the Eucharist is for us is the high priest emerging out of the Holy of Holies, giving us his body and blood, as our way into being a living priesthood and a living temple in the world.

If that picture is true, then it seems that what our Eucharistic life is supposed to be about is that we are a people who are being turned into the new temple by receiving the body and blood of the self-giving victim, who is already victorious. We are being turned into the new temple that is able to participate in the life of God who is coming out to us here and now. That is what the doctrine of transubstantiation is about. It means: this is not merely our memorial supper; this is, in fact, the heavenly banquet where someone else is the protagonist and we are called out of ourselves into it. We are being called 'through the Veil', into the participation. We are given the signs; which is why the body and blood are not something that hide the divinity but make it manifest. They are signs reaching out to us of what God is actually doing for us.

Now, all that is happening in heaven. That is the purpose of the doctrine of the Ascension: the Holy of Holies fulfilled, and us beginning to receive all that flows from it.

This has ethical consequences. And these are tremendously important for our understanding, because, if you have a *theory* of atonement – something grasped – you have something that people can 'get right', and then be on the inside of the good guys. 'We're the people who are covered by the blood; we're the ones who are OK, the ones who are good; and then there are those others who aren't.' In other words, rather than *undergoing* atonement, we're people who grasp onto the *idea* of the atonement. But the whole purpose of the Christian understanding is that we shouldn't identify too soon with the good guys. On the contrary, we are people who are constantly undergoing 'I AM' – that is to say, God – coming towards us as one who is offering forgiveness as our victim. And we are learning how to look at each other as people who are saying, 'Oh! So that's what I've been involved in.' Which means that *we* are the 'other' in this package; that *we* are the 'other' who are being turned into a 'we', in the degree to which we find our similarity with our brother and sister on either side of us. This, rather than: we are the people who, because we've grasped the theory have become part of 'I AM', and therefore the 'other' is some 'they'. If you are *undergoing* atonement it means that you are constantly in the process of being approached by someone who is forgiving you. That, it seems to me, is the challenge for us in terms of imagination when it comes to imagining and re-imagining atonement.

The difficult thing for us is to sit in the process of being approached by someone. Because we are used to theory we want someone to say, 'This is what it is. Get the theory right. Now put it into practice.' This imagines that we are part of a stable universe that we can control. But if the real centre of our universe is an 'I AM' coming towards us as our victim who is forgiving us then we are *not* in a stable place. We are in that place of being de-stabilised, because we are being approached by someone who is entirely outside our structures of vengeance and order.

Imagine what it is like to be approached by your forgiving victim. It is actually very difficult indeed to spend time thinking about our being approached by our forgiving victim! What is it like to actually undergo being forgiven? We tend to try to resolve this by saying, 'Oh, it's not being forgiven that matters. It's *forgiving*: I must forgive!' So we work ourselves up into a moral stupor, straining ourselves to 'forgive the bastard!' This then becomes very, very complicated. But in fact the Christian understanding is quite the reverse: it's because we are undergoing being forgiven that we can forgive; and we need to forgive in order to *continue* undergoing *being* forgiven. But remember: it's because we are approached by our victim, that we start to be undone. Or in Paul's language: 'even though you were dead in your sins he has made you alive together in Christ.' Someone was approaching you even when you didn't realise there was a problem, so that you begin to discover, 'Oh! So that's what I've been involved in.'

This is vital for us: it means that in this picture 'sin', rather than being a block that has to be dealt with, is discovered in its being forgiven. The definition of sin becomes: *that which can be forgiven.*

And the process of being forgiven looks like the breaking of heart, or 'contrition' (from the Latin *cor triturare*). What forgiveness looks like in the life of the person is 'breaking of heart'; and the purpose of being forgiven – the reason why the forgiving victim has emerged from the Holy of Holies offering himself as a substitute for all our ways of pushing away being forgiven, trying to keep order – the reason he has done that is because we are too small; we live in a snarled-up version of creation, and hold on to that snarled-up version of creation because we are frightened of death. What Jesus was doing was opening up the Creator's vision, which knows not death, so that we can live as though death were not. In other words, we're being given a bigger heart. That is what being forgiven is all about. It's not, 'I need to sort out this moral problem you have.' It's, 'Unless I come towards you, and enable you to undergo a breaking of heart, you're going to live in too small a universe, you're not going to enjoy yourselves and be free. How the hell do I get through to you? Well, the only way is by coming amongst you as your victim. That's the only place in which you can be undone. That's the place you're so frightened of being that you'll do anything to get away from it. So if I can occupy that space, and return to you and say, "Yes, you did this thing to me. But don't worry! I'm not here to accuse you. I'm here to play with you! To make a bigger space for you. And for you to take part in making that bigger space with me."' And of course the way Jesus acted this out before his death was setting up the last supper, in which he would give himself to us so that we would become him.

This is a risky project. That is the point! That is why I want to bring together the notion of creation and atonement, recovering the priestly dynamic. This is the risky project of God saying, 'We don't know how this is going to end. But I want you to be co-participants with me on the inside of this creative project. And that means I'm running a risk of this going places I haven't thought of because I want to become one of you as you, so that you can become me as me.' We get this in John's Gospel: 'You will do even greater things.'[13] And we think, 'Oh Jesus is just being modest about his miracles.' No, he is being perfectly straightforward anthropologically. To the degree in which, by receiving this sacrifice, we learn to step out of a world which sacrifices, tries to run things protectively over and against 'them', to that extent we will find ourselves – as we *have* found ourselves! – doing greater things than he could even begin to imagine. That's what the opening up of creation does.

The opening up of creation works in our midst through the Spirit who is the advocate, the defence counsellor, who therefore rejects the accusatory tendency. While we accuse, while we live in a conspiracy theory, we never learn what *is*, so we never learn to take responsibility for it. We never learn to inhabit creation with fullness.

Do you see that there is a huge movement in the atonement? The movement is from creation to us becoming participants in creation by our being enabled to live as if death were not. This is the *priestly* pattern of atonement; and it is the priestly pattern that Jesus had the genius to combine with the ethical, bringing together the ancient liturgical formula, the prophecies, the hopes of fulfilment of the anointed one, the true high priest who would come and create a new temple, the true shepherd of the sheep who would come to create a new temple – fulfilling those, and revealing what it meant in anthropological and ethical terms: the overcoming of our tendency to sacrifice each other so as to survive. That is the world, which thanks to him, we inhabit.

Now, do you see why I said that I wanted to give you a much

13. John 14:12.

more conservative account than the atonement theory allows? What we are given is a sign of something that has happened and been given to us. What is *difficult* for us is *not* grasping the theory, but starting to try and *imagine* the love that is behind that. Why on earth should someone bother to do that for us? That's St Paul's issue. 'What then shall we say to this? If God is for us, who is against us? He who did not spare his own Son but gave him up for us all, will he not also give us all things with him?'[14] St Paul is struggling to find language about the divine generosity. That is the really difficult thing for us to imagine. We can imagine retaliation, we can imagine protection; but we find it awfully difficult to imagine someone we despised, and were awfully glad not to be like – whom we would rather cast out so as to keep ourselves going – we find it awfully difficult to imagine that person generously irrupting into our midst so as to set us free to enable something quite new to open up for us. But being empowered to imagine all that generosity is what atonement is all about; and that is what we are asked to live liturgically as Christians.

14. Rom. 8:31–2.

transubstantiation: a tour of zion

> Walk about Zion, go round about her, number her towers,
> consider well her ramparts, go through her citadels; that you
> may tell the next generation that this is God, our God for ever
> and ever. He will be our guide for ever. (Ps. 48:12–14)

The best analogy I know for Transubstantiation – the conversion,
during the Mass, of the substance of bread and wine into the body
and blood of Christ – is the phenomenon of 'Magic Eye' images.
These are glossy, colourful, two-dimensional pictures of what
appear to be a series of wavy lines or patterns. For the viewer to
get the 'magic' effect, they should gaze upon the picture for some
time, allowing the eyes to relax. At first there is a moment of
dizziness as the stereoscopic functions of the brain kick in, trying to
make sense of the two-dimensional surface, then, sometimes
helped by the viewer moving the picture towards, or away from,
the eyes, suddenly a three-dimensional image is apparent. It has no
necessary relationship at all to the content of the wavy lines or
patterns. Indeed the wavy patterns simply yield and become the
contours of, for instance, three dolphins leaping out of the water.

Once the eyes have picked up the 3-D image, they stay fairly
easily relaxed in their resting on the image, and it is possible for the
viewer to move the eyes around, and look at different elements of
the 3-D world which is opening up before them. The eyes no longer
have to be fixed on one single spot.

Of course, there is no magic trick here at all. The 3-D image is
embedded in the wavy-lined pattern by an artist, and there is nothing subjective about what can be seen. It is not that some people
looking at a 'Magic Eye' picture see dolphins, and others a

Wensleydale cheese. Nor do the eyes need to be strained in order to see the image. The stereoscopic functioning of the brain will pick up what is there if given half a chance by the viewer, which may mean that the viewer must learn to un-strain their gaze.

This is, it seems to me, what is meant by Transubstantiation. We come into a church building, with a group of people like ourselves, and in a quiet and relaxed and ordered way we start to give thanks, our gathering led by a priest. Giving thanks allows the gaze to relax. After all, the giving thanks, which is the most active thing we do in the Mass, and the basis for its proper name – Eucharist – is directly dependent on our confidence that Our Lord has given himself for us, once and for all, to be a perfect living sacrifice, that this is now done, and he is ascended to where he is triumphant, as a lamb slaughtered, on an altar in heaven, surrounded by a festal chorus of angels and of those who have gone before us in the faith. Giving thanks is our mode of presence to the reality which is going on constantly in heaven, and goes on even if we don't know about it.

The idea behind the Eucharist seems to be this: that as we relax into our thanksgiving, so the apparent pattern which we are seeing, and taking part in – words of Scripture, prayers, priest, gestures and symbols of bread and wine – becomes the contour of something else, something 3-D, and we find ourselves actually participating in the heavenly liturgy which we know to be *just there*, but cannot usually see.

Typically in the prayers, the Spirit is invoked, and Jesus' words are repeated in the first person, and what we find is that rather than this being something we are doing, we are in the presence of someone doing something *to us*. The 3-D picture kicks in. Not dolphins, but a Great High Priest, who is also a slaughtered Lamb, coming out of the veil-less Holy of Holies, and giving us his body and sprinkling us with his blood.

This is what is central to 'transubstantiation' – the shift from the perception that it is we who are doing something, to the realisation that someone is doing something to, and for us, so that it is the crucified and risen Jesus who is the 3-D protagonist of the Eucharist, rather than the 2-D object of it.

Of course, this whole process is significantly focused on the presiding presbyter and on the bread and wine, because in the course of the thanksgiving, the Great High Priest takes advantage of the sign of the presbyter reciting words in the first person, to show himself coming forth from the Holy of Holies where he has offered his own blood as that of a Lamb, so that the bread and the wine actually become the living signs of that self-giving.

Consider the way in which, in the 'Magic Eye' illustration, what had seemed to be a relatively independent picture (the wavy lines) suddenly became not a picture at all, but merely the contours of the 3-D image that emerged as your eyes became focused. Once you have seen the 3-D picture emerge you understand that there are not two separate pictures present simultaneously, one picture consisting of wavy lines, and another consisting of 3-D dolphins.

Rather you see that the wavy lines are not a picture at all, but are only there as the contours which make possible the presence of the 3-D dolphins. And to someone who objected, 'Even if there are those 3-D dolphins, it is still basically a picture of wavy lines', you would say, 'I'm afraid you haven't yet got it. The moment you glimpse the 3-D thing, you will understand that those wavy lines are not a picture, they are merely the contours which make possible a 3-D picture.'

This I take it, is the reason why the Church has insisted that what takes place at the Eucharist is **Trans**substantiation and not **Con**-substantiation. Once the elements have been made alive to the reality of which they have become the living sign, their 'breadness' and 'wineness' are nothing but the contours of that reality, and not a 'thing' in themselves at all.

We shouldn't imagine that, after the consecration, Jesus is somehow present *hidden* under the appearance of bread and wine, as though those appearances were somehow an obstacle to our seeing him. The logic of that would be that if we could somehow peel back the visible obstacle, we might catch a glimpse of Jesus underneath it all. This would be the same as someone teaching you to look at a 'Magic Eye' picture by saying, 'The 3-D object is there, hidden under all those wavy lines, so you've really got to strain your sight until you can catch it.' The exact opposite is the case:

since the 3-D reality is there, and the whole purpose of the picture is that it wants to make itself visible to you as 3-D and this is the easiest way for it to do that, it is in fact as you relax your sight that it is able to manifest itself to you.

So in the Eucharist, it is because we can approach the reality in a relaxed way, confident that Jesus wants to make himself known to us, that we can trust that the bread and the wine, rather than being the obstacles to the act of communication, actually become the glowing reality of that act of communication. Jesus' showing forth his self-giving is not something hidden by the elements of bread and wine; the elements of bread and wine are the manifestation of what that self-giving looks like and is.

With the 'Magic Eye' picture we can be confident that once we 'get' the 3-D image, we know we won't lose it, or can easily get it again, so we can allow our eyes to travel over the page, looking round the corners and up at the 3-D angles, seeing if we can catch a glimpse of some other detail of the 3-D image. Just so, in the Eucharist, as we become confident in our trained relaxation that the whole occasion will become an opportunity for the crucified and risen Jesus to show himself and share himself with us, so also we needn't be frightened of looking around, getting to know the ramparts and towers of the city of Zion to which we have been invited.

This is one of the reasons why the Mass is so inexhaustible. It becomes possible to dwell, through the open Holy of Holies, on the different angles by which Our Lord chose to show his love for us. There is the 'angle' of the Great High Priest, the one who was girt about with the Name of the Lord when he went into the Holy of Holies; that is, he was the Lord himself coming forth into creation in order to unsnarl the ways in which our transgressions have snarled it up. This is the way in which Our Lord is a 'Victim' in the traditional sacrificial sense, indeed how he fulfilled that sense perfectly, since at last he was Priest not as a stand-in for the Lord, but was the Lord himself. So his self-giving was the one true sacrifice.

But he is also 'victim' in the modern, ethical sense, an entirely innocent person who was killed so as to assuage the wrath of people who needed a victim in order to keep their system going. And it was because he voluntarily chose to occupy this space of being a 'victim' in the modern sense that he brought to an end sacrifice. Indeed it is perfectly possible to say that his giving himself up to death wasn't a sacrifice at all in the traditional sense of the word, but rather, by showing that at the root of what we call 'sacrifice' there is a simple, mendacious mechanism of murder, that is, by revealing that there is nothing holy at all in all our mechanisms for creating victims, he brought the world of sacrifice to an end.

The one true sacrifice, and not a sacrifice at all – different angles of the same emerging 3-D image of the ramparts of Zion. One of the delights of the Eucharist, being able to spend time in the courts of the Lord, gazing upon his Holy Place, is that there is no hurry, no strain needed as we allow ourselves to be made aware of the extraordinary deliberate intelligence which brought together those two senses of 'victim', and did so as part of a benevolence, of a longing for us to be free, and to be happy, and to be involved in a daring act of creation. Such benevolence, such loving, cannot be seen in itself, except through signs made regularly and trustably alive.

'deliver us from evil'

When we begin a discussion about evil, I think it important to start with a distinction which I hope is obvious: the distinction between *theodicy* and *theology*. The former is the philosophical discussion concerning the possibility, or otherwise, of justifying the ways of God to men; the latter is a discipline whose ground of possibility is God speaking, and which is therefore at least supposed to partake of the dynamic of the One speaking. With the former discussion, human discourse, and its logical possibilities, is not only the place of the discussion but also its ultimate arbiter. In the latter discussion human discourse, and its logical possibilities, is always tentative since even as they take place they are being undone from within and recreated by something outside their frame of reference. Whether these two discussions, at least in their modern forms, are compatible, I'm not sure. What I am sure of is that I am trying to be a Catholic theologian, and therefore come to this discussion from within a specific tradition of discourse which takes as its starting point, both logical and experiential, the form of undergoing at the hands of God which we call 'creation'.

I would like to offer what I hope will turn out to be a straightforward presentation of what one might call the old-fashioned or traditional view typical of Christian theology. Namely that what we call evil is a non-thing, something which is properly speaking uncaused and inexplicable, incomprehensibly parasitic on reality. I am not only going to attempt to present this, but will also try and defend it, since it is the theological approach to this matter which I believe to be true, and I think that the psychological consequences flowing from it, and the psychological consequences of ignoring it are very weighty indeed.

What has traditionally been called the 'privation of being' approach to evil nowadays sounds such a weird position that I would like to take some time to try and set forth for you something of the bigger picture within which such a way of looking at things has its sense.

This means attempting to explain the understanding of God and of creation which underlies the whole sense of the discussion. In the first place, about whom or what are we talking when we talk about God and creation? I am talking within the tradition of discourse which goes back to the Hebrew prophets of several hundred years before Christ, and some of whose monuments we see in the texts referred to as the Hebrew Scriptures.

Briefly, for this tradition, a hugely decisive rupture was made at some stage between the seventh and the fifth century BC between the notion of God who was one of the gods, just a bigger and more powerful one, and the notion of God who is much more like nothing at all than like one of the gods. The rupture with normal forms of thinking which is implied in this is far greater than I can suggest here, since with it there comes the realisation that God is not a large creature within the universe, but the universe is something which is at all thanks to God. To put it crudely: God is not something that 'is' in any normal sense, God is the living 'oomph' behind the 'isness' of everything that is, including us, for whom God is not an object of our consciousness, nor could be an object of which we could be conscious, but is the condition of possibility of our being, and being conscious at all.

Along with this rupture there developed the extraordinary notion that God is good, faithful, trustworthy, that there are no gods. So everything which seems mysterious and conspiratorial and dangerous about the lives in which we find ourselves is not to be attributed to strange wheeler-dealings among divinities, or to malignant fates and curses. Instead we can rely on the goodness, the regularity and the order of which we are part as signs helping us towards flourishing and growth. In other words, where the 'gods' dwell, there is a tendency to keeping alive a seriously 'religious' universe; where God emerges, so the tendency towards what we would call secularism emerges. After all, the notion of the Creator and the goodness of all that is tends to limpidity, regularity and visibility of cause, and tends away from purely arbitrary, capricious and conspiratorial views of reality.

And along with this there developed a tendency constantly to move in the direction of ever less ambiguity and ambivalence in the divinity, such that other gods became: first a council of lesser gods, then angelic hosts, until finally you get our now traditional picture of the devil as a fallen angel – in other words, something good in itself which turned bad for reasons which are completely incomprehensible since coming from nothing at all and leading to nothing at all, creative of nothing at all, and purely parasitic on reality. But in no way a rival divinity or a source of alternative creative power.

Another feature of this movement, the discovery of the one God who is not one of the gods at all, is that this Creator is actually attempting to involve us on the inside of God's creative project so that we are not merely passive recipients of something, but are undergoing being made active participants in something whose final form is not yet determined. Not only, if you like, do we find ourselves the clay which the potter is working, but mysteriously we find that we are becoming cells of the skin of the potter's thumbs. And with this goes the awareness that we are often enough involved in the project in such a way as to tend to snarl it up rather than contributing to it. So every year, on the Day of Atonement, the Creator's emanation, the high priest, would come out of the Holy Place, the place where the Creator dwelt outside creation, and come through the Temple Veil into creation bringing the Lord's purifying blood to unsnarl, disentangle, our ensnarlment of the project. In other words, creation is not something which happened in the past, it is an ongoing project in which God is involving us now by loosing our ensnarlments.

Now please notice what this means: it means that there was already, in the period of the First Temple, something of a need to begin to work out what it is in humans which is inclined to snarl up creation. The lists of sins have varied from generation to generation, but over those same generations there was a gradual anthropologising tendency to understand that the real issue was one of desire. So even in the ten commandments, the real issue is seen as being one of desire, with the dynamic of the previous nine commandments being wrapped up in the final précis:

> 'Thou shalt not desire the house of thy neighbour; thou shalt not desire the wife of thy neighbour, nor his male or female slave, nor his ox or ass, nor anything that belongs to him.'[1]

By the time of the rabbis, the distinction was regularly made between two sorts of desire – the good impulse and the bad impulse,[2] with the one being recommended and the other treated against, especially by reading, studying and observing Torah. Even if these impulses were still seen as something 'within the ego' rather than received and essentially other-related, the possibility was certainly present in Torah of an understanding of desire as binding us in rivalry, thus pitting us against our fellow humans in more or less lethal ways. It is fratricide, not parricide, which causes most grief to the authors of the sacred texts.

As I understand it, it is within this frame of reference that a new understanding emerged through a significant group of heirs of the fairly heterogeneous Hebrew tradition from before the destruction of the Temple in 70 AD. This understanding was, and is, that God, in fulfilment of widespread prophecies, has become his own High Priest, has come into the world, has accomplished the definitive sacrifice, in which he was also the victim, putting to an end the world of sacrifice, because finally allowing creation to flow free, unensnaring us for ever from our involvement in futility. This futility was seen to be linked to the human tendency to create 'good' and 'order' mendaciously by allowing what we would now call 'scapegoating' to turn into murders, and then calling these murders 'sacrifices'. Our growing inability to hide from ourselves for long what it is that we are doing when we scapegoat, is the space from within which our whole pattern of desire can be made new and transformed. This perspective on what is, is what we call Christianity.

Christianity introduces a slight, but important, modification in

---

1. Exod. 20:17.
2. *Yetzer ha-tov* and *yetzer ha-ra*.

the understanding of desire which had been available before. This slight, but important, modification in the understanding of desire has, since the time of St Augustine, gone by the name of 'the doctrine of original sin'. Very briefly put, this doctrine posits that, in the light of Jesus' resurrection from the dead, it became possible to look back and see that all humans, ever since there has been a humanity (and the codeword for this was 'since Adam'), have been involved, by the mere fact of being born and socialised into human culture, in a culture run by death, vengefulness and its scapegoating and sacrificial outcomes. We are thus all born into a culture in which desire is distorted against itself and frustrated. This culture seemed to all of us simply to be what is normal. But in fact it is not. In fact we are brought into being so as to share, by means of human desire, in the life of God, which is so far removed from death that for God human death is not the opposite of life, nor its enemy. Rather it is the form of biological finitude proper to the gift of being the sort of creature which we are, one of the contours of creatureliness, which is the condition of possibility of our coming to enjoy God.

Thus the doctrine of original sin is a highly sophisticated quali–fication of human desire. Far from being an abstract denigration of what it is that humans are, it is the claim that we are all created good, and that there is no such thing as an intrinsically evil desire. All desire is severely distorted, and yet all is capable of being undistorted over time, of being brought to share, starting from where it is, in the life of God. Furthermore, it is also the case that none of us can be the judges in any definitive sense of anyone else, since none of us, not even the holiest of saints, is outside the social construction of meaning produced by distorted desire, and so none of us is able to look at anyone else in a way that does not partake of the imagination which dominates us, an imagination run by rivalry, resistance to change, the longing for security, and by the need to protect ourselves against death by seeking our survival at the expense of others.

The doctrine has its sense because with the foundation of the Church, an amplification of the people of Israel, God is bringing into being a visible sign of a completely different imagination, one which is not based on death and its fear, or the distortion of desire into various forms of conflict, and which enables all humans to dwell together with each other as enriching each other and enabling each other to share God's life and God's goodness, starting now.

So we might talk about two sorts of imagination alive in humanity, one, the apparently normal one, in which we are run by death and given meaning starting from death, in which the search for meaning is always over against some other, and in which we lure each other on, and which is inevitably futile – haunted by vanity; then the other sort of imagination which has been made available by the installing in our midst of the first fruits of a counter-lure: the possibility that our imaginations and our desire can be made alive to meaning and goodness in a way which does not lead us into conflict and rivalry.

The doctrine of original sin merely makes the obvious point: it is what seems to us to be a counter-lure, the lure made available by God, that is the real and original lure, the lure of the Creator which calls into being what is and what cannot be frustrated; what seems to us to be the 'normal' lure is in fact the counter-lure, leading to futility. Furthermore the depth of our involvement in the culture of original sin is shown by the degree to which we are ignorant that it is not really 'normal' at all, but a pale and misleading simulacrum of what is.

I offer you a silly image. Imagine that you are a wallflower, only you don't know that. As far as you are concerned you are just a flower facing south looking for the sun, and so are unaware that there is a wall behind you. With all the wonderful energy and capability of growth which is part of what you are, you rapidly head off across the ground, spreading further and further, and thinking you are getting closer to the sun – you aren't of course, but you don't know that. Everything about your growth is good, but you are in fact getting the wrong sort of nutrients from the ground, digging little shoots into it, and feeding yourself in a way which is less than optimal, and sometimes severely unhelpful. Now imagine that from behind you, and thus invisibly to you, there appear a pair of gloved hands which gently start to pull you up, detaching your little shoots somewhat painfully from the earth, and reattaching them to a wall which was behind you and you either didn't know about, or vaguely did, but thought that growing upwards was both hard work, and not so obviously in the direction of the sun, which seemed to come from the south.

At first the shift is painful, but after a bit you begin to get the idea: what you are in fact is a wallflower, not a ground-spreader as you had thought, and furthermore, as you become adjusted to the idea, you find that the nutrients in the wall are just the right sort for you, and that the wall holds you in just the right sort of way, and not only that, but you realise that actually your very clinging onto and integration into the wall is making the wall a different and a better wall. The glance down from your new becoming at what you had thought was normal, and now realise is not, that glance is the doctrine of original sin.

Well, if you will allow me to carry on in this vein, I would like to draw some inferences from this picture. It all sounds very complicated, but I suggest that rather than the doctrine of original sin being a complicated series of ideas, it is something much more like part of the necessary fine-tuning to our perception of what undergoing creation looks like. That is to say, it is an attempt to indicate what sort of thing, both immensely strong and immensely fragile, the adventure which we are involved in, and which we call creation, is.

We find ourselves being taken out of the realm of one lure, a lure which is not even a real lure, but a concatenation of relatively superficial fake lures, into the realm of the true lure which is bringing us into being. Which means to say, we are not discussing anything from a position of neutral objectivity standing outside anything with an overall view of it. We are in the middle of a dynamism which is heading somewhere much bigger than we are, and we discover to our amazement that we have been short-changing ourselves and each other about what it is that we thought we were, and where we are heading. This means that we also begin to be aware *as part of this dynamic* that there is risk, adventure and also the possibility of, as it were, falling off the wild ride.

We also learn that one of the ways of falling off the ride is precisely to identify too exactly what it is that we are leaving behind, and therefore what we can call evil. We are tremendously susceptible to returning to our former lure, and becoming fixated on tendentious and symptomatic signs of 'something going wrong' as things which really *are* in themselves, are significant, give us meaning, make us good *by contrast, over against them*. To do this is to refuse to undergo being given meaning, significance, life, at the hands of the only lure which really can do so, and to grasp at ersatz meaning instead. To settle for instant but fake meaning instead of deferred meaning, and being over time.[3]

It is for this reason that the Christian tradition recommends such parsimony of language and indeed of *interest* in the question of evil. Our own use of words like 'evil' represents a real temptation to an entirely fake sort of fascination which is capable of taking us over and turning us into something much less than we are. For us the really creative challenge is the discovery of, and the becoming fascinated by and entranced with, the *good*. And what the fascination and entrancement with the good will always look like will be a shift in our pattern of desire and imagination. It is a decisive shift such that we are able to perceive our own likeness in what seems 'evil' around about us, not fear it, nor fear being lured by it, but become able to be merciful and gentle with it as part of helping it and ourselves to un-attach and be re-attached. In short, behind what appears to some to be the indifference to evil of the one who is being reformed by and towards the interesting good, there begins to emerge the only quality and perspective which is strong enough to be immune to fascination by evil, which is that pity which comes from a stretched equality of heart.

It is because of this that Hannah Arendt's notion of the banality of evil rests so easily within the traditional Augustinian framework.[4] Her conception de-demonises evil, thus making us more aware of the lessons we can learn from our likeness. It is also

---

3. For a good example of someone who understands the dangers in the addiction to junk meaning, see Chris Hedges' book *War is a Force that Gives Us Meaning* (New York: Public Affairs, 2002).

4. cf. John Milbank's magnificent treatment of this theme in *Being Reconciled* (London: Routledge, 2003), chapters 1 and 2.

because of this that the imagination of the good is very often the refusal to name, the refusal to label, to categorise, and instead patiently to study, to relativise, to see what might work. This is the way in which, like Cinderella in Ann Ulanov's marvellous reading,[5] we can become capable of sorting through things and thus find ourselves discovering what really is. What is the real sign of belief in the Creator? Taking a paedophile and pronouncing him a monster, run by incomprehensible and evil desires? Or insisting, against all the evidence, that we have here someone who in principle is one of us, who is like us, and whose very distortions of desire will eventually yield to understanding and some form of therapy of benefit to us all as humans?

It also means that the real challenge for us is alertness and vigilance lest we be overcome by the inertia and easiness of things going on as they seem to go. Which is why the recognition of evil is always in our case a self-critical process of learning, lest we be ensnared by something too small. A recognition of a certain sort of awakening, and a certain sort of breaking of heart as I become aware of what I had allowed myself to become, and what I find that I am being hauled painfully into being bigger than. This is why, in the scheme of things which I am attempting to rehearse for you, repentance is so important.

Repentance is not the need to bow the will before some authority, much less a religious authority. Rather it is the gift of the ordinary access to being created which is proper to us good creatures whose goodness has inexplicably got involved in being something less than we are, a gift whose shape is a certain breaking of heart.

I would like to end with a very brief allusion to something which I think may be helpful here to anyone who is interested in the relationship between psychology and the understanding of evil which I have been trying to set out. This is the work of French psychiatrist and Professor of Psychopathology at the Sorbonne, Jean-Michel Oughourlian. In particular I would like to highlight

---

5. Ann and Barry Ulanov, *Cinderella and Her Sisters: the envied and the envying* (Philadelphia: Westminster, 1983).

some key observations concerning psychological time in his work *The Puppet of Desire: the psychology of hysteria, possession and hypnosis.*[6] Oughourlian compares and contrasts the movement of desire in physical time and the movement of desire in psychological time and shows how they are related.

In physical time, a desire or set of desires in a social other, a model either individual or social, inspires and creates a desire in the fledgling human, and this desire in turn produces in a given human body the very malleable construct known as the self. In other words, in physical time, the 'self' is the symptom of desire which is itself received according to, by imitation of, the desire of another. This objective flow of physical time however has, from the point of view of the 'self', no psychological significance.

For all of us, the movement of time which has psychological significance is that by which the self, the symptom of the whole process, develops as a result of memory and forgetfulness of what brought it into being, which includes all the forms of reaction and separation and individuation by which we claim to be original and unique. In other words there is what seems to be a necessary form of 'non-recognition' of what really happened, which can be exacerbated into a serious form of self-deception, within the way in which the self is brought into being.

I bring this to your attention, because it seems to me that here we have something very close indeed to what has traditionally always been meant by the distinction between 'creation' and 'original sin' in the theological tradition from within which I am speaking. I recognise a great affinity with Oughourlian's recommendation of understanding better the way the memory attempts to appropriate as its own what can only be its own as received and I suspect that there may here be a genuinely therapeutic way of both caring for, and sitting loose to, such ensnarlments as tempt us to reify those moved by them as 'evil'.

---

6. University of Stanford Press, 1991, pp. 237–9.

Select Bibliography (apart from texts cited in footnotes):

Burrell, D., *Faith and Freedom: an interfaith perspective* (Oxford: Blackwell, 2004), esp. Chapter 4, 'Maimonides, Aquinas, and Gersonides on Providence and Evil (with a bow to Dorothy Sayers)'

Girard, R., *Things Hidden since the Foundation of the World* (Stanford: Stanford University Press, 1987)

Phillips, D. Z., *The Problem of Evil and the Problem of God* (London: SCM Press, 2004)

'so, they've set little lions on me?'[1]
priesthood and penitent
messianism

the shape of don quijote's madness

Don Quijote, in case our romantic imagination should make us forget what Cervantes never forgets, is quite mad.[2] His madness consists in imitating someone who never existed, in doing things which that person, Amadís de Gaule, and others like him, never did. So complete is the imitation that Don Quijote sees things through the eyes of this non-existent person; his desire and his self are formed by the literary hallucination of Amadís' supposed desires and set of values. However, Don Quijote's imitation is not entirely that proper to the victim of a dupe. There is a certain element of deliberate wilfulness in his madness, a desire to outdo Roland, Amadís and the whole host of the heroes of chivalry. When Sancho Panza points out to his master that whereas these others typically go mad, or become enraged, by real events happening to them, nothing has happened to him to cause him to

---

1. '¿Leoncitos a mí?' *Don Quijote* II, 17.

2. I am dependent for my reading of *Don Quijote* on the opening of René Girard's seminal *Deceit, Desire and the Novel* as well as on the more recent (and no less superb) *'Monda y desnuda': la humilde historia de Don Quijote* by Cesáreo Bandera, especially his chapter 7, 'La penitencia de Don Quijote y el episodio de los leones'. This latter book is forthcoming in English as *The Humble Story of Don Quixote: Reflections on the Birth of the Modern Novel* (Washington: Catholic University of America Press) at the end of 2006.

behave in this way, Don Quijote replies in words of astounding lucidity:

> "That's exactly the point, and the splendour of my undertaking. What merit is there in a knight errant going mad for a just cause? The real art is to go crazy for no reason at all. . ."[3]

Cervantes is well aware that Don Quijote's madness is the cause of significant social disturbance, and he does not rejoice in it. Rather he shows how people become infected by that madness and gradually become madder even than the knight, precisely by their tolerating and playing with him, taking advantage of him in order to add meaning to their lives. There is one character in the book who is not affected by all this madness, and this is Don Diego de Miranda, the knight of the green cloak. He is both the most boring character in the book, a model of Christian virtue and peacefulness, and the only character who does not seek to take advantage of Don Quijote in any way, but rather to care for him and respect him as far as possible without going along with his craziness. If ever the phrase 'love the sinner but hate the sin' was properly applied, it was by Don Diego. His appearance is, as it were, that of a unique ambassador from a foreign country quite unperturbed by the events in La Mancha.

Don Quijote and Don Diego come together at an interesting point in Part II of the book. In Part I there has been an incident regarding a barber's basin which the barber had temporarily worn on his head to protect himself from a sudden rainstorm as he crosses the plain. Don Quijote sees the shiny object, but since he sees objects through the eyes of Amadís, he does not see a barber's basin, he sees Mambrino's helmet, the helmet of a great figure of knightly lore. That is to say, because of the hallucination of a madman, the object acquires a meaning and a value that in fact has nothing to do with it, and of course it is necessary for Don Quijote to liberate this chivalric relic from the unworthy barber who is

---

3. 'Ahí está el punto. . .y esa es la fineza de mi negocio; que volverse loco un caballero andante con causa, ni grado ni gracias: el toque está en desatinar sin ocasión. . .', *Don Quijote* I.25.

manifestly unsuitable to be its guardian, which he does, thus depriving the honest barber of one of the tools of his trade.

Now in Part II, Sancho Panza has gone to collect some milk or curds from local herdsmen. Summoned by his master as some carts flying royal colours draw up, and having nowhere else to put the curds, Sancho puts them in his master's helmet. When, of course, Don Quijote puts on his helmet, the pressed curds start to run down his face, and Don Quijote's first reaction is that his brain must be melting thanks to some wicked enchantment. When he takes off the helmet, he finds the compressed curds, and immediately, and quite sanely, blames his treacherous and impudent squire. Sancho, no fool he, defends himself by attempting to blame the presence of the curds on wizards whose spells must have affected him too, as an employee of Don Quijote. What is curious here is that faced with Sancho's attempt to save his skin by using the same logic by which Don Quijote inspires himself to do mad things, Don Quijote gives a surprisingly cynical answer: 'All things may be', as though he doesn't really believe it, but has to go along with his own discourse coming from Sancho, even though Sancho can't quite enchant the curds in his helmet as Amadís had enchanted the barber's basin. Don Quijote then turns to the matter at hand, which is the arrival of some lions.

The lions are in caged carts and are being taken to the King of Spain as a gift from the General of Oran in North Africa. They are very big, and very real. They are not domestic cats which have been transmogrified into lions by Don Quijote's fervid imagination. Everyone else knows this except Don Quijote, whose madness is such that he cannot imagine that a lion could ever be just that, a lion, a dangerous beast worthy of respect and in this case a present for someone else. No, if there are lions present, then they have been sent against him. Hence his paranoid reaction, 'So, they've set little lions on me?' The lions are quite specifically not little, but the biggest that have been seen in Spain heretofore, but Don Quijote belittles them as part of belittling those who have set them upon him. He then commands the lion keepers to open the cage door of the male lion so that he may fight it. Sancho, the knight of the green cloak, and the lion keepers do their best to dissuade him, and when all else fails, sensibly enough they run away and hide. By threatening him with his lance, Don Quijote forces one lion keeper to open the door of the cage. At this point there occurs one of the great literary miracles of the western canon. The lion does nothing at all. It turns itself round in the cage, stretches out, licks its face with a huge tongue, looks outside the cage with eyes ablaze, where Don Quijote is waiting for it. Then it turns its back on him and shows him its backside, settling down immovably.

Don Quijote cannot persuade the lion keeper to annoy it by beating it so as to make it come out and get him. And so it stays there. Eventually the lion keeper manages to shut the door, and Don Quijote has to be consoled by all and sundry that his bravery is not in doubt, and that even though the enchanters have managed to trick him out of the adventure, his exertion and spirit could not be taken from him.

Astoundingly Cervantes has shown us the limits of Don Quijote's madness by showing us something which is not capable of being infected by it. An inanimate object, like a basin, since it cannot speak for itself, is entirely dependent on the game of human value giving, which is to say, of human desire, for acquiring its worth and meaning. Humans, like the other characters in the novel, can speak for themselves and prove, time and time again, to be completely liable to infection by Don Quijote's madness, starting by reacting against it, or taking advantage of it, and ending up by multiplying the social disturbance it causes. Not so the lion. The lion is neither inanimate nor a human. The lion is just a lion. It might have attacked, it might not have. It didn't. However, one thing is clear: it is entirely innocent of and indifferent to the crazy world of meaning into which Don Quijote wants to draw it. It might be physically prodded into action, or starved into action, or attacked. But it is absolutely immune to the world of mimetic desire, self-fulfilling obstacles and hidden forces of inimical enchantment which run Don Quijote. It can't play games with Don Quijote. It is just a lion, and quite splendid enough and worthy enough of respect as that.

And the principal witness to this is Don Diego de Miranda, the only character in the novel who is entirely free from the need to acquire meaning by gossip, fascination with others, cruelty, mockery and so forth. It is to his house that they will now quietly repair. Cervantes is taking us down the road which will, many chapters hence, lead to Don Quijote's deathbed conversion, the moment when the great knight is able to give a penitent account of all the terrible things he has done and in which he has involved people of greater innocence than himself, and to thank God for his mercy in giving him at last the clarity of mind to repent of having allowed himself to be led astray by the abominable tales of chivalry, all of which are the purest nonsense. With this, the first and, according to many, the greatest of novels ends. Its author had, almost certainly without knowing it,[4] opened up one of the richest possible veins for truth telling available to humans, that of telling the truth by means of fictionalised penitent autobiography.

lead us not into temptation

I suppose that the part of the Lord's Prayer which most closely comments on all this is the phrase 'lead us not into temptation', and it is strictly a comment on the same set of realities as *Don Quijote* sets outs, the same pattern of desire. For there are, it seems to me, two principal reasons why we are urged to pray 'lead us not into temptation' (which means discover ourselves within an unfolding pattern of desire flowing from 'lead us not into temptation'), and these two reasons flow into one. The first is that we are being told to refuse an imagination of God as one who might lead us into temptation. If we consider that the one to whom we are praying, whom we are inviting to possess us with his desire, is capricious, and might play about with us, then how will we be sufficiently relaxed to allow that possession? How would we be able to tell if God might not say after any particular incident in our lives, especially one requiring some exertion, 'just testing!' thus reducing the value of the incident to naught. What would be the

---

4. Cervantes was convinced that his greatest work was *Los trabajos de Persiles y Segismundo*, now almost unknown to all but specialists in Golden Age Spanish literature.

difference between God and the crowd of onlookers, characters and participants in the story, all of whom know perfectly well that Don Quijote is mad, and yet all of whom are led by him into temptation, and go along with leading him into temptation, thus compounding madness among all of them? There is no caprice in God, and yet part of being human is that we are surrounded by, formed by, and led on by, caprice, which is why we have to learn how to pray 'lead us not into temptation'.

The second reason follows from this. It is not only that we might have an imagination of God as involved in caprice in the way in which the world of enchanters and those who are out to get us may be; but even worse, we actually want to be led into temptation, so as to *be*, so as to have an identity. How tiring and tedious is the business of being brought into being patiently without excitement! How much more exciting to grasp at ersatz meaning and a quick-fix identity over against some convenient other who can give me a sense of being by becoming an obstacle so that I can become a hero or a victim and thus have a story. I suspect that we are taught to pray 'lead us not into temptation' because the need to turn windmills into giants is so strong, and because not all 'little lions' will be so obliging as to turn round and show us their backsides. When faced with the question 'Who am I? And what am I for?' it is much easier to grasp at a quick answer provided by an unnecessary but glamorous challenge than to allow myself to be brought quietly into being, trusting that I will be given to be someone, that that being will be of worth, and that I don't have to do anything special in order to be given that being.

The second reason and the first flow together because, of course, it is by learning to trust that I am being given to be by someone who is trustable, not out to get me, but has my real interests at heart, that I can dare to undergo reality rather than seek to score cheap points against it in a way which undervalues both its givenness as real and the being which I thereby receive.

professional hypocrites

I would like to take this in the direction of some thoughts on clergy life. And the strange way in which we find ourselves living an intersection between two patterns of desire. The first is that of the penitent autobiography as set out by Cervantes, and which we are living in the first place simply as Christians, that is as disciples, those who are learning to imitate and follow one who refused all the 'being' offered him by temptation so as to receive the fullness of being God's Son in giving himself up to death so as to set us free from the mirages which obscure the reality of the creation in which we are invited to participate. Unlike Amadís de Gaule, the one whom we imitate was not glorious or successful, but was happy to be counted among the transgressors, to be considered a wrong-doer, to occupy the place of shame which we all of us try our very best to avoid occupying.

This penitent autobiography is one of apparent loss. One of its first rules of grammar is, 'For you have died, and your life is hid with Christ in God.'[5] How do we write the autobiography of a dead person? Usually the only way is by letting go of the false bits of autobiography which depended on being over against another, whether individual or social, in order to be someone. And that means allowing ourselves to become someone along with, as part of, and gratefully dependent on others whose meaning we do not control. In other words, we wait for grace to bring us to our senses, to our right minds, by refusing all sorts of lures and temptations into easy meaning, and we are only able to do this by living as if death were not. That is, by treating death, and all the ways in which it runs, frightens, compels, hurries, threatens, shames us, as something which is not out to get us and has no power over us. It also means refusing to make our own or any other person's death 'meaningful' in a way which flatters us, helps us to round off stories. We leave it to the Deathless One to hold us in being through death and as dead so that it is God, not anyone we

---

5. Col. 3:3.

can manipulate, who gives us the final shape of our meaning and being, the final sense of our story.

Well, so far so good. But few of us are contemplative monks. Many of us are more or less active clergy. And we face the strange disjunction, in addition to being disciples undergoing being brought to life through a penitent autobiography, of being professional hypocrites, creating and maintaining a series of signs which all too often seem to point not towards the deathless one and his effervescent and non-reactive meaning, but towards cheap meaning, rivalry and odious comparison.

This is not something which we do merely by accident, but it seems that we can't avoid it. Let us take Cromwell's great phrase: 'I beseech you, in the bowels of Christ, think it possible you may be mistaken'.[6] It is difficult to get a more accurate statement of the message of the crucified one than that. It seems to me to come close to Paul's wonderful statement, 'So we are ambassadors for Christ, God making his appeal through us. We beseech you on behalf of Christ, be reconciled to God.'[7] And of course, Cromwell, by the very act of saying this, was opening himself up to the charge that the moment he held power and sway, he would be shown to be a hypocrite, himself incapable of that imagining that he might be mistaken which he was so right to urge on others. Just as we clergy are left open to the same charge.

The difficulty seems to be that we all sense that the bowels of Christ, Christ speaking viscerally, comes from a place which is not ours to control, and which is non-negotiable. It comes from one occupying a place of shame and death not so as to criticise but so as to forgive, indeed so as to make it possible for us to think it possible that we may be mistaken by showing the fragility and contingency of our certainty and the suffering inflicted by it. But we also know that we very rarely get to occupy that place, and if we do, it is only very temporarily; and yet we all too easily find ourselves able to use the words and gestures which flow from that

---

6. Written in a letter to the Synod of the Church of Scotland in August 1650.
7. 2 Cor. 5:20.

place and turn them into a story which flatters us and turns us into improbable merchants of goodness.

Nevertheless, how otherwise are we to be 'ambassadors for Christ, God making his appeal through us'? We face the tension between being people who are agreeing to lose meaning so as to be given a meaning that is not ours, and people who are constantly engaged in the creation of a meaning which we would like to think is that of an embassy for Christ, and yet, time and time again, we discover ourselves liars and purveyors of false certainty, false boundaries, conditional belonging and thus of cheap meaning.

It is not only a matter of observing that all our ecclesiastical institutions produce in us forms of behaviour, of belonging, of fascination and of excitement which are the direct reverse of what we are preaching, precisely because they encourage us to keep our noses clean, to avoid giving scandal, the appearance of impropriety and so on. We are tempted to notice that and so to suggest that we should be free of institutions. However, there is no such thing as being free of institutions. Humans are incurably institutional, and we wouldn't be functional without institutions. It is the institutions which give us the words, and the beginnings of a sense of what they mean, if only by frustrating our sense that 'we know it all already' by making us undertake long studies in theology during which we may have the fortune to discover that what we thought we knew already was a journey into an unknown and wonderful land.

The ideal ambassador for Christ would be one who could put words to the experience of undergoing the place of shame and invite others to inhabit that space by showing that it is possible to inhabit it non-toxically, which is why a genuine penitent is such an attractive figure, and such a peaceful one, and why non-penitent peacefulness is somehow so threatening. But such a person becomes a sign, an ambassador, because they have so obviously become a citizen of another land that they cannot but point towards the land of which they have become a citizen. But this means that they have already found themselves swept into and beyond death in a certain sort of undergoing, and we call them saints, the most obvious ones being martyrs, those martyrs who didn't seek out what happened to them in any way at all, but who allowed it to happen when it must, confident that this was relatively incidental to the story that they were being given to inhabit.

However, none of us can bring about such undergoing. Of its nature, it can only happen to us. Freely, and at the hands of someone else over whom we have no control. Doesn't this sometimes create an impossible position in our lives as clergy? We are required to be professionally exemplary in ways which satisfy ordinary social senses of basic goodness, and yet we are aware that the real exemplariness of which we are supposed to be signs is given improbably and unexpectedly, that the sort of undergoing which turns an ordinary bishop into a Monseñor Romero, or an ordinary priest into a Maximilian Kolbe or a Padre Pio comes along all too infrequently, and we would rather not be there when it did. Or rather, it would be extraordinary if we were there, because if history is anything to go by, most of us would have run away by adapting to the situation and choosing to regard the exemplary one as scandalous, and a counter example until some time after their death.

half-heartedness, contempt and low self-esteem

I hope that I am not speaking for myself alone when I say that this strange disjunction between being officially designated ambassadors of Christ, those who are charged to say, in season and out, 'I beseech you, consider that you may be mistaken' and those who are only occasionally capable of saying it in a way that is not a form of hypocrisy, has the effect of producing a certain professional malaise.

It is rather as though, instead of being an ambassador for Christ, which is intrinsic to the vocation of every Christian, I have got saddled with, and settled for, being an immigration official for Christ, a rather more lowly post in his kingdom's diplomatic service. The ambassadors go in and out of the fold, just as Our Lord said they would, at peace and not troubled by the violence and conflict in this world, a world in which they often seem to travel incognito and unrecognised, and able, whenever they want, to go in to the very centre of the other world and be made radiant by it. We immigration officials, however, are thoroughly recognisable. Nothing incognito about us. Our uniforms and twirly moustaches give us away instantly as the representatives of the Kingdom of Ruritania on earth. Ruritania of course has no uniforms, so we wear uniforms like all other nations' immigration officials, but ours are more gloriously operatic, so as to suggest the otherness of the kingdom of which we are the border guards. Other nations' immigration officials have moustaches as well, but none so twirly as ours, our way of indicating that there is a lighthearted and comic element to the kingdom, access to whose borders we like to think we control.

And yet, merely by living on the border, we are more than usually susceptible to envy of what we see in the land which abuts onto ours. And we are more likely than other inhabitants of our land to be mistaken for citizens of that world, precisely because we find it so difficult to leave our frontier posts, to forget that defending the frontier is not really our business, and to move more deeply into the land whose ambassadors we once aspired to be. Instead we live cheek by jowl with the other land and don't notice quite how much of it rubs onto us.

Along with this goes, at least in my experience, a sort of half-heartedness. It is as though I live paralysed half on one side of the border and half on the other. The half of me that lives on the side of the border of the country whose ambassador I'm supposed to be knows that it will win, and that the reason I am in its diplomatic service is that it has in fact won, and that the other country is in fact in the process of collapsing from within, of its own futility, violence and self-destructive meaninglessness. It also knows that that other country feigns not to know this, but secretly does, which adds to its pathos and its anger.

But the half of me that lives on the other side of the border, for professional reasons of course, just finds the lures of that other country so darned attractive. Its temporary meaning glitters so, the value it offers seems so great, its melodies and songs pull me in so easily. Even though I know perfectly well that they are so much illusion and fakery. Even worse, I know that God has no love for the half-hearted, and yet I seem to be addicted to being half-hearted. It is as though I know perfectly well that in the eyes of the world anyone who is to be an ambassador for Christ must be an off-scouring of the world, must be as one who is not, and I have signed up for that. And yet, the eyes with which I look at myself for having done that are those of the very same world I am supposed to have left behind. I hold myself in contempt for not being something that is 'wise, that is powerful and of noble birth'[8] – that is, I really mind being a failure in the eyes of the world. And that of course means that the values which form my self-regard are those from the other side of the border. I receive myself according to the regard from the wrong side of the border.

The trouble with contempt is that it is, of course, not a value proper to the kingdom of which I am an official. Unlike most of the silly things to do with sex which we tend to obsess about, I suppose because they are so close to shame, and thus so inclined to make us vulnerable, contempt is really rather seriously not a value which is of the kingdom, implying as it does a loneliness, a superiority and a sealing off from others which has no place in the kingdom of which I am an employee. So contempt, intractable and almost uncon-fessable, close cousin of heartlessness, must be hidden behind a façade of courtesy and graciousness.

And of course, as the anthropology of the kingdom in whose employ I live teaches, I cannot love my neighbour other than I love myself. If I have a secret contempt for myself, that will certainly, however hard I try to fool myself, come out as a contempt for my fellow customs officials. I will try to scratch meaning out of my dealings with them, derive prestige from my little triumphs over them, heroism from being mistreated by them, and I will seek dependence of reputation, and thus of being, from their approval. The trouble is that if enough of us are such half-hearted people, and we are all scrabbling for reputation, and none of us has approval to give, then the battle for prestige will be like a scrum attempting to squeeze blood from a rugby-ball-shaped stone. We will all hurt ourselves on it, and no one will get any blood out of it, because there is none there. Isn't it curious how the degree of bitchiness

8. cf. 1 Cor. 1:26.

increases exponentially in inverse proportion to the value of the rewards available to those in a particular employment?

I once worked in the completely non-transcendental world of launching and distributing a free newspaper paid for entirely by selling advertising. A wholly circular means of wealth production. Yet the levels of bitchiness in the job were low, because the financial rewards and differentials were real, and there was plenty to go around, and plenty of success to admire and to emulate. However, in more transcendental forms of employment, the lower the reward differentials and the signs of success, the higher the degree of bitchiness, as though there were that much less prestige to go round, and therefore one needs to fight all the harder to get a piece of it.

Doesn't this make the clergy the ultimate low self-esteem occupation, even lower than academics and charity workers? And is this not a continuous source of conflict? We know we ought to have the highest self-esteem of any employment group. After all we have been summoned to be servants of the Most High. We know that we are dispensers of the graces and favours of the ultimate victorious kingdom. We know that we are to be given meaning by the source of all meaning, no mere non-transcendental 9–5 job. And yet we neither value each other as if this were really true, and thus, inevitably nor do we value ourselves, nor expect to be valued. Half-heartedness, contempt and low self-esteem feed on themselves in a vicious circle. I am fearful of being more auto-biographical than this, but am I alone in knowing this pattern of desire from within?

'consider your call'

Wouldn't it be splendid to have a good positive response to this, with which to wrap up my attempt to open up our discussion! Yet I hope that you would recognise that such a positive answer would come from a desire to make things look good, and would in itself be something of a betrayal of what I've been attempting to point to. And Yes, I do have that desire, and Yes, I am suspicious of it. When Paul is reminding the Corinthians that before their baptism they were no great eminences, it was because they seem to have been so puffed up, so swollen by an apparently new 'good' identity that they were falling straight into rivalry and comparison, identity politics and sectarian group creation. And I suspect that our inversion of that into half-heartedness, contempt and low self-esteem is simply the reverse side of the same reality, an impatience with being given being, with allowing ourselves to be turned into children of God.

Paul's response is not merely to deflate them, though he does that constantly, as he does with most of his correspondents, but rather to point them towards something richer than what they have. So I suggest that we read the phrase 'Consider your call'⁹ not merely as a request to examine how faithful they are being to what they should be doing, but rather to open their minds to the one calling them, and dwell in the significance given by that. I think rather the same thing happens in Luke's Gospel when the seventy returned from their mission with joy,

> saying, Lord, even the devils are subject unto us through thy name. And he said unto them, I beheld Satan as lightning fall from heaven. Behold, I give unto you power to tread on serpents and scorpions, and over all the power of the enemy: and nothing shall by any means hurt you. Notwithstanding in this rejoice not, that the spirits are subject unto you; but rather rejoice, because your names are written in heaven.¹⁰

I think that 'but rather rejoice, because your names are written in heaven' and 'consider your call' mean the same thing: they are getting us to turn our imaginations towards the one who calls or who writes our names rather than to what we achieve. In other words, we are pointed towards a constant tension between our grabbing a bit of new identity and running with it, often using it for coinage in an economy for which it was not made, and the arduousness over time of discovering ourselves on the inside of the One

9. loc. cit.
10. Luke 10:17–20 (KJV).

who gives us reputation, esteem, glory and so on, and allowing that One to call us further into his kingdom.

What indeed does it say that I was called? Not about me, but about the one calling? What does it say of his spaciousness, his power, his gentleness, the security which he offers, that it becomes possible not to have to construct a story which makes clear sense, not because of a paucity of meaning, but because of an excess. What delicacy is able to pick an individual human being as such and make that one special without putting anyone else down? What does it mean that a reputation and even a boasting, a dwelling in my story with delight should not be over against anyone else's, need exclude no one else, need have no frontiers, need provoke no one? What abundance of creativity is there constructing a story of 'me discovered in us' which is even more miraculous than what Miguel de Cervantes did with his madman as he retired him from fake meaning? An Author even greater than he is, after all, writing me in.

And what does this say about the light-heartedness with which our Ruritanian frontier posts can be treated by us as something like a huge joke, one in which we are involved with all our hearts as we apparently ape the glories and sacralities of the other kingdom so as to subvert it from within, and do so knowingly. I sometimes refer to this as navigating wrath, and that is what it is, but there is something more of a skip, and maybe, if the Vatican can be dissuaded from taking too seriously its own policies concerning getting rid of the gays, more of a sashay, to it than that. The curious thing is that our frontier posts, with all the temptations we undergo to make them part of the coinage of the realm whose economy they are supposed to be subverting, can, as we discover ourselves given the heart which alone can give this task both its gravity and its lightness, be a real part of the embassy of mercy.

If we continue to stand in the place of those who are undergoing loss of meaning and apparent integrity and worth and being given a meaning and an integrity and a worth which is not dependent on us at all, we may find that we can help people who are scandalised by the way in which the coming Kingdom disrespects the solemnity and deathly awe of so much fake meaning, and the way we will help overcome these conflicts is by being an extension of the sheer unexpected good fortune, improbability, daring and fun which will be sinews of the new story, and we its unworthy symptoms. And maybe we will even find ourselves being given whole-heartedness on the way.

CHAPTER SEVEN

———◄O►———

reconciliation in the wink of a hippo

One of the greatest moments that I know in all cinema is the ballet set to the music of Ponchielli's 'Dance of the Hours' in Walt Disney's 1940 film *Fantasia*. I ask you to remember the scene. Ostriches wake up and stretch, they dance about, and after a bit, and shortly before being blown away, they start to circle towards a divan in the centre of a classical garden. On this divan there reclines a simply delicious hippopotamus, complete with pink tutu, which she modestly brushes into place whenever her abundant curves dislodge it. She too awakens, and begins to dance. But before long there is a change of tone: raffishly sinister crocodiles emerge from behind various columns, and the dance acquires a darker hue. The movements begin to suggest the feel of a hunt, and a tragic dénouement is hinted at. Before long, and to no apparent purpose, elephants have joined in, and the animators, whose feat in suggesting at the same time both the immense weight and the balletic lightness and gracefulness of their heroine is surely one of the pinnacles of their art, have the hippo rushing from one side of the gardens to the other, with enemies on all sides.

It is in the midst of this desperate flight that the great moment of glory occurs: as she hurtles tragically between opposing enemies, our two-ton sylph suddenly breaks into a skip, turns to the camera and gives a little wink; but not for long. Soon she is back to her heavy duty 'let me out of here' routine, and eventually the music leads to its proper conclusion, and a return to sleep. But, Oh! That moment of glory! It is as if Maria Callas, about to be put on the pyre at the end of *Norma,* had suddenly sung a few notes from

Hello, Dolly! before returning to Bellini's master-score, or a child performing in the *Oresteia* had lifted up her mask and given a stage whisper to her mum to let her know that it was all OK really, and she shouldn't worry.

Well, I hope you will forgive me such campery, or perhaps I had better say: enjoy the campery while you can, for you are listening to what may turn out, if the raffish crocodiles of my Church get their way with their pink tutu-ed brethren, to be a member of the last ever generation of gay Catholic priests (fat chance!). But this is the easiest way-in I could find to point to where I want to take you. Faced with the various extremely painful and distressing circum-stances in our lives and our world where reconciliation is needed, we run, I think, the great danger of falling into the trap of ser-iousness, and even worse, into talking morals. I would like at least to begin by hinting at a path to which I may very well not be able to keep: the delicate tightrope walk of the debonair, devil-may-care quality whose presence can aerate suffering and allow heartfelt concern to become both richer and more bearable. On one side of this tightrope there lurks the mire of seriousness, and on the other the froth of a frivolity which is only a mask for despair.

So, I would like to see if I can do something to undercut the apparent heaviness of reconciliation. You see, my fear is that the necessary seriousness of our ethical and political searches may lead us to miss out on the extraordinary sensation of being in luck, of having fallen, despite ourselves, on our feet in the midst of a piece of ridiculously good fortune. In other words, I want to suggest that every attempt to search for reconciliation starting from philoso-phical and political strategies will fall short of the mark if not undertaken from within that sensation of sheer luck, of having been found, of enjoying an adventure where you are safe and swimming spaciously, a sensation of which we experience glimmers every now and then, and to which we rightly apply words like 'gratui-tous', for this is what it is like to undergo grace.

I would like to start by inviting you to dwell with me in a couple of scenes by which I hope to make clear what I mean by this sense of spaciousness and good luck. The first scene is the Presentation in the Temple which we celebrate liturgically on 2 February, and of which we have an account in St Luke's Gospel.[1] I invite you to join me in the Temple. Let us imagine that we are there,[2] ordinary inhabitants of Jerusalem, hanging around for evening prayer, or to meet friends, or whatever. It is just an ordinary day, not a major feast. The Temple is a big and imposing building with its series of courts; there are a variety of sacrifices going on at altars up in front of us, priests doing their stuff with impressive seriousness, other priest-like figures scurrying hither and thither looking as though they know what they are doing, temple guards standing on quite relaxed duty at the various entrances and exits. There are money-changing tables, booths for selling the various animals for sacrifice and, inevitably, a fair smattering of adolescent boys running here and there as messengers, carriers, pick-pockets and so forth.

There is smoke, there is incense, and there are the smells and the background sounds of cattle, sheep and caged birds. In different places, there are people involved in prayer, by themselves, or in groups, some attending the sacrifices, others apparently making deals with the Almighty with much bobbing and bowing. Over all this, there presides the Holy of Holies. The Veil is in place, and all that is going on is going on with some, but not too much, reference to the apparently indifferent gaze of the One who dwells there.

Someone tugs your sleeve, and points to a small gathering which is happening just out of the corner of your eye. Nothing special. A couple with a baby come in for the rite of Purification. And who's that coming up now? Oh, that's old man Simeon – older than Methuselah! He looks so old that he might very well be the High Priest Simeon himself from three hundred years ago – one of the last decent high priests in Jerusalem. In fact he probably is a real descendant of his. Funny to think that someone like him would be high priest today if it hadn't been for the various bits of skuldug-gery by which the current bunch had co-opted, bought and stolen

---

1. Luke 2:22–40.
2. I have found the writings of Margaret Barker, and especially her *Temple Theology: an introduction* (London: SPCK, 2004) and *The Great High Priest: The Temple Roots of Christian Liturgy* (London: Continuum/T&T Clark, 2003) to be especially helpful in allowing me to imagine that I am there.

their hold on office. Anyhow, the couple have got someone proper to do their rite for them. Old Simeon will take the thing seriously.

Now watch out, crazy Anna has spotted them and is rushing up! Didn't anyone warn them? She's older than God and has been around the Temple since before time began. Actually, she's a survivor from one of those tribes which went into the desert generations ago and didn't go along with the whole return from Babylon and second Temple project. She thinks that if she stays here day and night, fasting and praying, then God will bring the first Temple back, Ark, Mercy Seat, Fire, Wisdom and all. She makes it clear that she considers the current priestly families to be little more than pretenders – well, she isn't unique in thinking that, but she has the courage of her convictions, since she actually stays in the Temple to try to make it holy. Good luck to her, and to all whom she pesters!

Ah, now the Evening Sacrifice is about to start up, let's turn towards the Holy Place, the dwelling of the Most High, and get on with it. Curious though that as the couple are leaving with their child, both Simeon and Anna, normally a mixture of the cranky, the zealous and the infuriating, look suddenly peaceful, as though something had happened to them. Oh well, funny things go on in the Temple! Maybe they got given a bigger than usual tip for their services. Let's press forward and join in the chanting which is starting up: 'I will gaze on the Lord in the Sanctuary to see his strength and his glory'.

Well, of course this is not the version of the story we hear in St Luke's Gospel, and celebrate on 2 February. My version is the majority report – what a normal passer-by would have noticed that day. We celebrate the minority report: for Luke, anything else that was going on in the Temple on that date was quite irrelevant. We get no mention of it, so we have to supply with our imagination. What we remember is that on that day, Malachi 3:1–4 was fulfilled. God suddenly came into his Temple. But he was almost off-stage, along with the Ark and the Seat of Wisdom which had borne him, and was noticed only by a couple of eccentrics who had been hoping for him in quite specific ways as fitting in with their expectations for how God would show himself to his people, to

Jerusalem and to the Temple; expectations which were regarded as indecent pieces of folk-culture by the people who ran the show in the Temple. In other words, the shape of the arrival of God on the scene, the God to whose worship the Temple was dedicated, was that of a tiny off-stage interruption, scarcely to be noticed. Not even enough for us to talk about, the Temple authorities having been blindsided by God, since they remained unaware of what had happened. Only much later would it become clear how completely blindsided they had been.

Now let us shift our scene completely, though you will notice that its structure remains intact. We are in the late eighteenth or early nineteenth century, at a ball given in a magnificent colonial house. There is a splendid orchestra, highly dignified dancing going on, and all the chatter and gossip proper to such a party. All heads turn as new guests arrive. Who is talking to whom? Who is dancing with whom? Who is on whose dance card? What deals will be quietly sorted out in background chats between cigars? Whose future will be decided, whose fall decreed? Liveried retainers stand on more or less decorative guard at various places. Children play chaotically in their own world, blissfully unconscious of consequence in the midst of all this activity. There are servants everywhere, carrying trays, opening and closing doors, re-filling and collecting glasses. A torrent of gossip also flows between servants and kitchen. Gossip about the hosts and guests, and gossip about the other servants. All have their affairs, their quarrels, their hopes, their ambitions, their jockeying for place, their resentments and their loves.

As you are caught up in all this, you notice a little scene developing near one of the splendid French windows which lead to the lawn outside. There is a small group gathered around someone who is wearing a livery similar to that of those who are on duty, and who seems to have burst through the windows into the ball-room. The orchestra tails off as attention turns to this interruption. Some of the other retainers seem to be undecided as to whether they shouldn't be escorting their apparent colleague firmly outside, and some of the other guests seem to be half-listening to what the intruder is trying to say. They look a little puzzled. But what catches the attention, at least for a moment, is the range of expressions on the face of the intruder. He seems to be undergoing a series of very strong, and apparently contradictory emotions almost simultaneously. He looks shocked, as though he's coming in bearing news of some terrible happening which has just occurred, or is on its way. He also looks strangely elated, as though whatever has happened might also have been curiously good. There is something pleading, beseeching about his eyes as though he wants not only to warn people of what is coming, but inviting them to come and see for themselves. And yet there is something oddly peaceful about him, even in the midst of all this exaltation, as though whatever has happened has left him with a sense that he isn't part of the group that is gathering around him, some pulling him, some trying to work out what he's saying. It's as though part of him is already somewhere else.

After a bit, order seems to reassert itself, and as the intruder is led away – still gesticulating and explaining something – those who had been closest to the scene drift away, some shrugging their shoulders and obviously keen to get on with the party, others talking among themselves with quizzical looks. The orchestra starts up again, before long the ball is back in full swing, and the incident has scarcely registered. A far greater commotion occurs as the city's leading diva finally appears at the head of the principal staircase, the details of her gown for tonight having been the great secret of the season.

Once again, I am giving you the majority report, but only so as to help create the proper context for the minority report as it begins to become available from the few who interacted with the man who was escorted out, and who remained quizzical after listening to him. The man was, of course, St Paul, and I'm going to try to recreate with you some sense of what he was attempting to communicate as he stood by the French windows. Mostly I'll be attempting to reconstruct what he was on about from what he says in 2 Corinthians 5,[3] since it is there that he talks most frequently

---

3. I provide the text in Appendix I, p. 231.

about reconciliation, but I'll bring in material from elsewhere in his writings as well.

First of all Paul is trying to get across that Something Has Happened. Something huge. So much so that he's in what is most comparable to a state of shock. A good illustration of this is Steve Martin in the film *Leap of Faith*. Martin plays a touring charlatan preacher who is a consummate master of working his audience, raking in cash from people of simple faith, and producing well-staged fake miracles. Then suddenly, out of nowhere, in the middle of one of the staged revival meetings, a genuinely crippled boy genuinely begins to walk. In other words, in the midst of all the fakery, and able to be recognised only by those like the preacher, who knew that the show was all fake, suddenly the Real Thing happens. The film ends as a shocked Steve Martin hitches a lift on a truck and gets out of town, presumably on his way to a complete rethink of his life.

Something like this is behind all of Paul's preaching. It's not that he'd been a charlatan before. But he had been the machine man, the system man, the man who knew how it all had to be, how to make it perfect. This involved living with an attitude of perpetual war against those who threatened the system of goodness – what we call 'zeal for the Law'. And in the midst of this there suddenly happened the Real Thing. That is to say that the Rock, Yahweh, about whom he had talked, whose Law he had obeyed, to whom he had prayed and for whom he had preached, organised and persecuted, was suddenly present to him in a way which completely inverted everything he had known.[4] As for most of us, God was for him an 'it', a 'he' about whom he knew, an object within our human way of knowing things. But suddenly, God was an 'it' or a

---

4. The Rock of Israel, present in Genesis 49:24 and a multitude of Psalms, had 'happened' to Paul in such a way that he was able to say:

> I want you to know, brethren, that our fathers were all under the cloud, and all passed through the sea, and all were baptized into Moses in the cloud and in the sea, and all ate the same supernatural food and all drank the same supernatural drink. For they drank from the supernatural Rock which followed them, and the Rock was Christ. (1 Cor. 10:1–4)

'he' no longer, but was 'I am' coming towards him out of nowhere.

This 'I am' coming towards him out of nowhere is the classic shape of the self-revelation of Yahweh. In other words Paul was undergoing a theophany of the sort that experts in the sacred texts, such as he was, could recognise as being that of the Lord. One of the features of such theophanies was that they could not be conjured up by anyone, but happened to whom they would happen. And when they happened, they changed everything, and yet left everything unchanged. Because unlike the gods, Yahweh was not in rivalry with anything at all. Yahweh was involved in the creation of all things, and was thus not on the same level as them in any way at all. One of the telltale signs of Yahweh was that part of the experience of undergoing 'I am' coming towards a human is that thereafter the human becomes aware of the universe tilted on a new axis. Hence the strange term 'Rock'. The centre of stability, of gravity, shifts from the world formed by the desires and struggles of humans, which is only an apparent centre of stability and gravity, and rests on something entirely outside the human world of perception and desire. What appears to be the most ethereal and least solid part of the universe comes to be the real centre of solidity and rooted-ness in being. Part of the authentic nature of the experience of undergoing Yahweh is this Copernican revolution out of human and cultural foundations and security into receiving a centre and a non-grasped-after solidity that was entirely outside of human control and from which all comes to be.

However, in Paul's case there is more to it than this; for 'I am' did not just appear to him as 'I am' but appeared with more specific historical content than that. 'I am' came to him as 'Jesus, whom you are persecuting'. This was Paul's Steve Martin moment. The Real Thing, with a concrete historical name and narrative presence, happened 'at' him, waylaid him out of nowhere and interrupted him as he persecuted those who followed this man's way. Later on Paul would talk about how he used to regard Christ from a human point of view[5] but did so no longer. He means something rather

---

5. 2 Cor. 5:16.

more than, 'I used to think about him as just another human, but now I see him as a great spiritual leader touched by God.' He means, 'I used to see him as a failed false messiah who had led people astray, and then Yahweh revealed himself to me as Jesus, the rock of ages present in this dead man who is not dead. In other words, Jesus wasn't simply one of us, a religious searcher of sorts from this side of the Veil; Jesus is Yahweh, coming through the Veil, where he is anchored in the real permanence in whose gaze we are all peripheral and passing.'

So, Paul has been shocked by the Real Thing having happened to him, this Yahwistic self-disclosure, but he knows that this is no merely individual experience. In fact, he had never known Jesus during Jesus' life and ministry. Paul had to go off and spend time learning what had in fact happened, not merely to himself, but publicly, long before he had even got to hear about it. What had happened in fact between the time of the couple leaving the Temple in my first scene, and Paul irrupting into the Aristocratic Ball in the second. And what he learned was that something like an extraordinary invasion and successful conquest of the world had taken place. And that this had a quite specific shape and contours.

Yahweh had come among us in the person of Jesus of Nazareth. He had gone about doing signs and wonders, and had eventually been put to death by the leaders of the people. But his being put to death was not merely the usual scenario of a 'necessary' piece of capital punishment. Nor even the usual lynch-mob death of questionable legality. It looked like that; it could be described like that; but very shortly after his being put to death a group of disciples started showing signs of themselves having undergone a Yahwistic theophany in which the dead man Jesus had shown himself to them as alive in a way which made him no less the dead man they had known – the classic 'everything is changed yet nothing is changed'. They quickly began to be able to piece together what he had really been about, up to and including his death. He had in fact been fulfilling all the prophecies of old about Yahweh coming to be with his people by coming among them as the Great High Priest who performed the definitive sacrifice, coming out of the Holy Place as the self-giving Lamb whose blood was shed for them. Only he had done all this not in the Temple itself, using animal substitutes, but had come through the Veil as he revealed himself in his dying on the cross, such that his tomb, with the stone rolled away, where there was no body, was the now frontier-less Holy of Holies, because the Creator had come out into the world so as to reconcile it with himself and make it forever a sharer in the Creator's inner life.

Paul's shock is not merely that of stunned recognition, as a new narrative sense is made of all the Scriptures which he knew backwards. His shock is the growing sense that what this does is reveal Yahweh as having done something not merely Jewish – though the Jewish tradition had given all the details that made the story begin to be imaginable in human terms – but human. This human being has given himself up to be killed by us, finding himself in a role in a typical scenario of the very worst kind of our human behaviour, where we most violently and stupidly blind ourselves to who we are and what we are doing; but he has entered in not as a puppet master, but as the victim, one who understood in advance what was to happen, and explained it to his disciples. They, of course, when push came to shove, had fled and undergone the contagion of the crowd like everyone else except a few women.

What Paul has fixed on – some would say fixated – is what this concrete human acting out by this human being delates, gives away, reveals, about the power which made the acting out possible. To be killed takes no power at all – in fact it is the very symbol and meaning of powerlessness. However, to be able to occupy the place of powerlessness, shame and death publicly, within a given developing human narrative tradition, but taking, and living out, that narrative tradition in a direction it had never fully imagined; and to do so deliberately, and as a creative act, this takes more power than any that a human can imagine. And this is because it is a power that works at the human level, and yet is not in rivalry with, and not run by, death.

Furthermore, this power is not impersonal, mechanical, but personal. Anyone who has ever taken part, however minimally, in a lynch mob, or a culture which depends on such mechanisms of unanimity against a victim to keep itself going – which is to say, everyone – now has access to our victim coming towards us in the midst of our violence enabling us to see what we have done to him or her. What the victim is saying is, 'Yes, yes, I know that you thought that you had to do this sort of thing to me in order to get ahead, to survive, to be someone; and guess what, because I knew that these are the only rules of the game you know how to play, I occupied the place of shame for you so as to show you that even where you are at your worst and most fearful, I like you and I want to play with you a different game. Now where shall we take it?' In short, there is no ambivalence, no caprice and no 'out-to-get-you' in the power that enabled Jesus to live into his death in the way he did. It is pure, un-ambivalent 'I am for you starting where you are'.

Those who have begun to glimpse what has happened in the death of Jesus thus start to be able to undergo, as a normal part of their life, the Yahweh experience, the Presence, but a newly content-filled Yahweh experience coming towards them, honed to remove any possible question as to the sheer unadulterated loving kindness for them and gentleness towards them of the power which moves the sun and stars. As they begin to grasp that what they had thought of as the normal rules of the game of human survival and togetherness, are in fact something peripheral to reality in which they had got bogged down out of fear and failed imagination; and as they begin to grasp that the one who stepped into their periphery did so not so as to punish them, but out of an astonishing gentleness and love for them, so they begin to have their lives re-centred on an 'elsewhere' not run by anything in this world. They begin to find that the rock to which they are anchored is before them and mysteriously guiding them into a far, far bigger space than they had been able to imagine previously. In short, in Paul's language, they have started to become a new creation.

This stunning shock has consequences. It completely relativises all anthropological structures and ways of being together which depend on identity derived over against each other, on comparison, on rivalry and ultimately on death. That is to say, it completely relativises all our squabbles, fights, triumphs, glories and empires, revealing them as so much vanity, so much froth. This is because it reveals not only that all those things are founded on lies and murder, which they are, but also that there is a huge new empire being slowly, quietly and gently brought into being, unnoticed by all who are engaged in the squabbles of comparative meaning and death-bound glory. This empire is real, definitive, and is being established whether we like it or not, whether we notice it or not.

The sign of it being established is what Paul refers to as Christ's victory procession.[6] He uses the image of a Roman military 'triumph', where the victor would lead a procession of captives into the city after a great victory. However, Paul fuses this with the image of the offering up of a sacrifice of sweet aroma to God, so that Christ, the one and only true sacrifice, having occupied the place of shame and thus de-toxified it, is able to lead us, his captives, as so many other sweet-smelling sacrifices. We living sacrifices are able peacefully to occupy the same space of shame and death spaciously because we are already beginning to participate in a creation not run by the same parameters at all. For those who are part of the world of death, this looks like so many losers on their way out of existence, but for those who are being taken into the new creation, this is the fragrance of life opening out into new flourishing.

Now begin to imagine Paul breaking through the French windows of the colonial house where the ball is being held, he who had once been a liveried retainer in the world of order and meaning which helps keep societies going, and you may start to get a sense of why he has the stunned, shocked look on his face. He has seen the equivalent of a tsunami which has in fact already surrounded the house and, unbeknownst to those within it, is carrying it away; and he's rushing in to try and get across to those who are at the ball that they've got to get real – the real thing has happened, it's big, it's here, and it's won. For God's sake, make your peace with it, or you'll be swept away by so much power and energy, not because anyone wants to sweep you away, but merely because what is real is being brought into being, and the only way to be is to allow yourself to become part of it.

And of course, Paul is aware that once your true centre of

6. 2 Cor. 2:14–16.

meaning, life, desire and heart is in this new creation, then it possesses you so that you become its ambassador, a representative of its power, in the midst of this failing world. But finding yourself the ambassador of this huge power which has made itself known in a human victim, the only way to represent that power is to beseech others to be reconciled, while yourself living the sort of life of one who is being carried off – hence the plaintive sound of God, the Creator of all things, interrupting our social scene in the voice and garb of someone easily to be dismissed. And being drowned out by the orchestra and the party, but still refusing to play the part of the hostess or the dressed-up diva, or someone who might be noticed. But constantly coming and beseeching us to get with the pro- gramme, to actually allow ourselves to be created, to be reconciled to God.

So, at last we have come to the place of reconciliation in all this. I hope you can see why I took the scenic route rather than plunging straight in. I wanted to make it clear that for us the first and root meaning of reconciliation is not an ethical demand. In the under- standing of the Christian faith, it is first of all something which has triumphantly happened in a sphere more real than ours, and which is tilting our universe on a new axis, whether or not we understand it. This means that what we think of as real, as stable and as ordered is not so, and what is real and true and ordered and stable is not what is behind us, but what we can become as we learn to undergo being set free from our imprisonment in what we might call 'social order lived defensively'.

The traditional way in which Christian theology has talked about this has been by means of the doctrine of original sin. This doctrine is a way of describing reality such that we become aware that our starting place is not in fact what we really are, but an enclosure into a defensive social order centred on death so that we are all marked by an aversion to being called into being. We are formed in a serious futility and vanity such that we seek protection, identity and life in things that are not safe, and do not do us any good. What Paul was belly-aching about was that the real, creation, the life of God, is much, much bigger, more spacious, safer, freer and more delightful than anything we could imagine; and he begs us to leave our self-fulfilling enclosure, our self-enclosing fulfilment, and come and take part in the power that brings into being, causes to be, and knows no vanity, no futility, no violence, no deception. The only way into this is to allow ourselves to be recognised by the victim whom we have killed; and begin to see how much love and desperation to get through to us was made present in allowing himself to be killed so that we could get the message that yes, we are like that, and it is *this* bunch of murderers, persecutors, traitors, cowards, liars and thieves that we are, who are being welcomed into the new creation and given a heart to match.

If you like, we are being shown that we start off from a skewed reality, that what we call normality is in fact out of kilter, and true reality is much more alive than anything we know; so much so that we need training and new hearts and new eyes to be able to glimpse it along with that gift of being able to relax into spaciousness and being held by a power greater and more trustable than our own, which we call the gift of faith.

Well, this I hope gives us a slightly different perspective on how we might come to be involved in and practise reconciliation. Because it means that our starting place is not, in the case of any of us, that of good people who are going to do something good. Our starting place is that of people who are undergoing being forgiven, undergoing being seduced out of an aristocratic ball, often enough kicking and screaming, only half wanting to leave, knowing that the reality we are leaving is futile, but not yet gifted with the heart and eyes of the diamond-bright aliveness that is coming to be.

And this means that there is no beginning of reconciliation amongst us that is not the first inklings of a learning of an entirely new way of being together, by people who are accomplices in war and who are undergoing being forgiven as their necessary induction into the real. Forgiveness is not something which is in the first instance a moral imperative. Forgiveness is the shape of being inducted into the real in the case of all of us human creatures who, basically good, find ourselves inextricably caught up in an addiction to being less than ourselves.

Let me give a counter example to make what I'm aiming at clearer.

There's an obvious sense in which, in the world we call normal, to get committed to reconciliation is a waste of time, an absurdity. Because what we all normally want is to win. What is typical in our world is that reconciliation does indeed have a certain role, the role of Plan B. Plan A is simple: crush the bastards and get what we want, wiping the board if possible. The only place which others have in this vision is the place of the defeated, gazing up at us with envy and hatred. And those gazes will be radiant jewels set into our crowns of victory. However, should it be the case that for some reason or other there is not such an imbalance of forces that we can win straight off, perhaps it might be better for us to compromise and to look, for now, for a convenient reconciliation with some of the forces in play, forging an alliance with them, and suspending some elements of what we want, understanding that the ally will do the same, so that together we can attack and triumph over the others. This is Plan B, considered better than Plan C, which is simply to be defeated, and we don't even contemplate going there.

However, those of us who take part in Plan B know very well that the temporary ally is just that – temporary. We know full well that our allies have their own interests and their aims, and that they haven't changed them, merely contracted them, as a tiger does its claws, and that the moment that there is a shift in the balance of powers, everything will have to be renegotiated. And we, and they, also suspect that the target of our joint attack is not necessarily the preferred target of either of us, but merely the most convenient one. But better them than us.

So it seems as though, in the normal world, reconciliation is the losers' game, and you only go there if you have to. I think it very important that we don't lose sight of the fact that the first emotion, the first desire which we typically have in this field, is wanting to win. And winning typically means that there will be losers, and the whole terminology of reconciliation typically starts from losers, because if they could win, they wouldn't be looking for reconciliation. The reason why I'm so keen on not losing this from sight is that if we insist on reconciliation without having worked through its connotations of being the losers' gambit, with all that that means for our desire and our self-esteem, then it is quite possible that we will end up falling into the sanctimonious hypocrisy of wanting to paint with gold leaf something made of clay or some even baser material. Even worse, we will compensate for that sensation of castrated insufficiency with a huge energy of moral seriousness. As if that could satisfy us anywhere near as well as a beautiful and resounding victory.

Now, what I'd like to explore is the abyss between this normal sense of the word reconciliation, with all its connotation of second best and making a virtue out of a necessity, and the sense which I began to try and sketch out for you earlier, the one coming from the shocked intruder beseeching the guests at the ball. For the key to all this is how we traverse the route between the normal sense and the Pauline sense. In other words: what does it look like, what shape does it have in our lives, that we, aristocrats, servants, musicians and hangers-on in general at the Colonial Ball, find ourselves invited to be on the inside of something much, much bigger, but only if we are able to begin to understand the invitation which is being made to us, and which comes from someone whose status is not so much in doubt, as downright contemptible?

And here I think we have begun to comprehend something absolutely essential in St Paul's understanding of the Holy Spirit, the power which comes from the One who was able peacefully to occupy the place of shame, of annihilation and of death as if they were things of little import. One who, being the rock, was not beguiled by the spirits, the winds of meaning and of desire, of imitation and of approval which make us all avoid that place like the plague. That is to say, the Holy Spirit is the power which is capable of moving us from within, without displacing us as people – so that everything changes and nothing has changed – keeping us in being and in existence without depending in any way on the world of significance and meaning which comes from our typical social movement.

And this Holy Spirit, being the shared-out unflappable 'rockitude' of the heart and mind of God, is characterised by making available an extraordinary spaciousness in the midst of turbulence. This is because it comes neither from fear, nor from necessity, nor from togetherness, nor from contagion, nor from hate, nor from

vengeance, nor from survival, nor from any other of the struc-
turing forces of our society. And so it enables the person who is
moved by it and recreated by it to begin to swim spaciously in the
midst of violence without that violence infecting them.

A good example would be the martyrdom of Maximilian Kolbe.
He went to his death in a concentration camp, offering to die in
place of a father with children. For fifteen days he occupied the
space of death with such panache that once he had died there was,
according to the survivors, a noticeable change in the ambience of
the camp. The permanence and stability of a power far greater than
that which the guards wielded day and night against their prisoners
had given itself away. The hippo had winked. In the face of that
power, the guards were simply impotent, its having 'happened'
making it impossible for them to dominate and subjugate effectively the hearts and imaginations of their prisoners.

No one reaches such spaciousness in a day. Certainly Maximilian
Kolbe was not born with this capacity to be an ambassador of this
other power, a bridgehead of a different and indestructible Reich.
What I find interesting, and I hope you do too, is the process by
which someone with a strong investment in the world of meaning,
of approval, of being honoured by a system which depends on
winning comes to be an ambassador from another world. That is to
say, the process of conversion understood as a process of the restruc-
turing from within of desire.

I wonder whether I am the only one for whom this process is
something rather like finding yourself dragged through a bush
backwards while you try desperately to run in the other direction.
There is a fatal moment in this process which is the moment when
one is half on one side of the bush and half on the other. Certain
that the Victory is that of the coming kingdom, but also aware
that many, if not all, my desires and values are formed by what
this kingdom offers, its meaning, approval and glories. And with
this there comes something like a gnawing depression, a half-
heartedness which says, 'Fatally the coming kingdom is going to
win, it's not worth fighting against it, but my heart isn't really in its
victory, so I'd better try to make a virtue out of a necessity.'

The problem is that this attitude of the divided heart, which seeks to make a virtue out of a necessity, is just another disguise donned by the resentment which Nietzsche so justly criticised, and it will tend to propagate a version of reconciliation as something to be resented, as the loser's option. What interests me is discovering how the Holy Spirit which makes it possible to occupy the place of shame also makes it possible to discover the delight of being undeceived, the amazing good fortune of finding oneself caught up in the flow of the real, the unmerited luck of finding oneself on the inside of a huge project whose final parameters are way out of sight.

Here I think we are getting close to what is central: if reconciliation is a matter of morals, to achieve which I just have got to be damn heroic, and which is going to be bloody painful, it doesn't much matter if my heart is set on the outcome: the important thing is to be heroic. But then I'm always going to be left with the sensation of second best, of the silver medal, of the lump of clay decked out with gold leaf. What I want to suggest is something different. The Holy Spirit is not, in the first place, a force driving us towards an ethic of 'going against the grain'. It is the Creator Spirit. And Jesus' occupation of the place of shame, of loss, of death and of annihilation wasn't, in the first place, to offer us an example of how to behave heroically. Rather it was the Creator-of-all-things' way of opening up for us the possibility of entering into the full meaning, weight and flow of creation.

That is to say, and this is what is curious: that spaciousness owes its grandeur not to its being an extra cushion of resources so that we can carry out and achieve something heroic here. Rather it is luring and carrying us towards something much richer and more fun, which isn't here yet, and in whose light the fights and definitions and approvals of here are only pieces of small-mindedness from which it is greatly to our advantage that we become unbound so as more richly to be able to enjoy what is coming upon us.

With this, the search for reconciliation becomes something enflamed by other fires. Something rather like a deep unconcern about myself is born, and a desire to be reconciled with the other because I know that both he and I will be much more, and will be able to enjoy ourselves much more if we are reconciled. That is to say, triumph for me passes through his being made whole and not his diminishment. Along with this there goes the sensation of how undeserved it is that we are even beginning to want to participate in this triumph, of how extraordinarily lucky I am to have found myself caught up in this adventure, and because of that, of how lightweight, and almost frivolous it is.

Now, to reach this point we are invited to undergo a rather strange shift of perspective, becoming aware of a generosity which wants to distract me from my self-absorption in too small an identity, always defended over against some other person or group; a generosity which lures me into receiving an identity which cannot be mine except in as far as it is the other who gives it to me. In other words, I start to discover that the other is not the obstacle in the way of my coming to be, but is what makes that coming-to-be possible. And because of this, reconciliation isn't a second prize, once I've accepted that I'm not going to be what I wanted. Rather it is the only way of coming to be, and even of wanting to become, something much greater than I could imagine.

This generosity, the same generosity which occupied the place of shame so that we should learn not to flee that place, begins to incite in us the strange sensation that a victory of mine over someone would be, in fact, a defeat for me. Because I wouldn't have achieved or savoured all the possibilities which would be opened out for me by the flourishing of the other, and which would take me to a much richer flourishing myself. That is to say, I would be discovering for myself that 'reconciliation' rather than being a merely moral imperative is instead the way in which being created happens in us, taking for granted our sad starting condition of selling ourselves short and remaining stuck with identities forged over against each other, and for that reason fated to a short circuit of mutual reduction to negativity.

This is what is surprising: that we have no access to being created which doesn't pass through our allowing ourselves to be reconciled. And being created is adventure, delight and irresponsibility, since we aren't in charge; it is lightness of spirit, undeserved security, luck and fortune. And along with this, as we allow ourselves to be stretched into this spaciousness, there comes a greatness of heart, a magnanimity that is playful, because trusting, since we have discovered, rather despite ourselves, that there is no greater victory than the mutual enrichment of those who are not frightened of losing themselves in the other, but who know that on the flourishing of the other depends their own capacity to be and to enjoy what they really are on their way to being, with all their heart.

For many of you, thinking through issues of reconciliation will lead you into places of much greater bravery, drama and dignity than anything which I can plausibly represent to you. I merely beg you not to forget the graced spaciousness of tumbling into the luck of finding ourselves secure on the inside of the vertiginous adventure of creation, and discovering that an unashamed quest for reconciliation passes through our reception of an enflamed heart.

PART II

'but the bible says ...'?
a catholic reading of romans 1

Few Catholics are likely to interrupt a theological discussion with the phrase: 'But the Bible says. . .' And this is not so much the result of the famed stereotype concerning Catholic ignorance of the Scriptures but because in a Catholic discussion, it is unlikely that an appeal to authority would take the form of an appeal to the Bible. It is more probable that an appeal to authority would take the form 'But the Holy Father says . . .' or 'But it's in the Catechism'. So why bother people by attempting a Catholic reading of Romans 1?

What has pushed me in the direction of offering this reading is really two things: in the first place, I was brought up Evangelical Protestant, and this text, Romans 1, was really a text of terror for me, a text in some way associated with a deep emotional and spiritual annihilation, something inflicting paralysis. So, finding myself ever freer of that terror, it seems proper to try and offer a road map to others who, whatever their ecclesial belonging, may suffer from the same binding of conscience that a certain received reading of this text has seemed to impose. But there is a second reason, no less important to my mind: owing to arguments surrounding episcopal appointments in the Anglican Church on both sides of the Atlantic, a huge amount of press has been generated in which it has been repeated ad nauseam that 'The Bible is quite clear. . .' about this or that. Furthermore we are told time and again that those who think either that gay people should be allowed to marry, or that being gay should be no bar to episcopal consecration, are in some way repudiating an obvious written sacred injunction. The impression that 'the Bible is quite clear' has passed largely unchallenged in the media, which has found it easiest to present the argument as being between conservative people who take the Bible seriously (and are thus against gay people) and liberal people who don't (and thus aren't against gay people).

Well, what is being treated to public travesty here is the Bible. Indeed it seems to me that, if anything, the truth is closer to being exactly the other way round: you need a very modern liberal reading of the Bible in order to make it a weapon against gay people, and those who refuse to do this are, by and large, much more traditional in their biblical reading habits. But this sounds so counterintuitive in our world that I'd like to take time to show that there is at least one perfectly respectable Catholic way to read this text which enables us to see it in a quite different light.

Before actually looking at the text I'd like to make two points as a build up. If any of us is faced with the following verse from Romans 1, it seems to have an obvious and clear meaning:

> For this reason God gave them up to dishonourable passions. Their women exchanged natural relations for unnatural . . .[1]

A quick show of hands in any English-speaking country nowadays would probably agree to the following statement: 'This quite clearly refers to lesbianism. That is the obvious meaning of the words. To deny that this refers to lesbianism is the sort of thing that you would expect from a clever-clogs biblical exegete with an ideological axe to grind.' Well, all I'd like to say at this point is that we have several commentaries on these words dating from the centuries between the writing of this text and the preaching of St John Chrysostom at the end of the fourth century. None of them read the passage as referring to lesbianism. Both St Augustine and Clement of Alexandria interpreted it straightforwardly as meaning women having anal intercourse with members of the other sex. Chrysostom was in fact the first Church Father of whom we have record to read the passage as having anything to do with lesbianism.

Now, my first point is this: irrespective of who is closer to the

---

1. Rom. 1:26.

mark as to what St Paul was referring to, one thing is irrefutable: what modern readers claim to be 'the obvious meaning of the text' was not obvious to St Augustine, who has for many centuries enjoyed the status of being a particularly authoritative reader of Scripture. Therefore there can be no claim that there has been an uninterrupted witness to the text being read as having to do with lesbianism. There hasn't. It has been perfectly normal for long stretches of time to read this passage in the Catholic Church without seeing St Paul as saying anything to do with lesbianism. This means that no Catholic is under any obligation to read this passage as having something to do with lesbianism. Furthermore, it is a perfectly respectable position for a Catholic to take that there is no reference to lesbianism in Holy Scripture, given that the only candidate for a reference is one whose 'obvious meaning' was taken, for several hundred years, to be something quite else.

This point is a negative one. It clearly demonstrates that there is *no obligation* on a Catholic to agree that what St Paul is saying is obvious, or to read those words as referring to lesbianism.

My second point is slightly more positive. According to the official teaching body of the Catholic Church, Catholic readers of the Scripture have *a positive duty* to avoid certain sorts of what the authorities call 'actualization' of the texts, by which they mean reading ancient texts as referring in a straightforward way to modern realities. I will read you what they say, and please remember that this is rather more than an opinion. This is the official teaching of the Pontifical Biblical Commission, at the very least an authorised Catholic source of guidance for how to read the Scriptures, in their 1993 Document *The Interpretation of the Bible in the Church*:

> Clearly to be rejected also is every attempt at actualization set in a direction contrary to evangelical justice and charity, such as, for example, the use of the Bible to justify racial segregation, anti-Semitism or sexism whether on the part of men or of women. Particular attention is necessary . . . to avoid absolutely any actualization of certain texts of the New Testament which

could provoke or reinforce unfavourable attitudes to the Jewish people. . .[2]

The list which the Commission gives is deliberately not exhaustive, but it has the advantage of taking on vastly the most important of any possible improper actualization, which is that related to the translation of the words οἱ Ἰουδαῖοι , especially where they are used in St John's Gospel. I ask you to consider quite clearly what this instruction means. It means that anyone who translates the words οἱ Ἰουδαῖοι literally as 'the Jews' and interprets this to refer to the whole Jewish people, now or at any time in the past, is translating it and interpreting it less accurately, and certainly less in communion with the Church, than someone who translates it less literally as something like 'the Jewish authorities', or 'the local authorities' who were of course, like almost everyone in St John's Gospel, Jewish.

Given how vitally important the Jewish people and the relation between the Jewish people and the Church has been in the development of Christian doctrine, if we are urged to avoid *absolutely any actualization* of the text, then the following statement must, a fortiori, be at the very least perfectly reasonable, if not actually highly recommended, as a guide to a properly Catholic reading of a passage dealing with something rather less important. Here it is: given the possibility of a restricted ancient meaning in a text which does not transfer readily into modern categories, or the possibility of one which leaps straight and expansively into modern categories and has had effects contrary to charity on the modern people so categorized, one should prefer the ancient reading to the actualized one.

So far two minor introductory points: there is no obligation on Catholics to read Romans 1 as referring to what modern readers claim is its obvious meaning; and indeed, given the possibility of an ancient limited meaning, or a more expansive modern one potentially harmful to a modern category of people, a Catholic reading should prefer the ancient limited meaning.

---

2. *The Interpretation of the Bible in the Church* IV.3.

Now to a reading of the text. I am going to go over it with you twice. Once in the standard version which you will find in almost any modern biblical translation – actually I'll be using the Revised Standard Version. And once in exactly the same version, and in fact in exactly the same translation, so with exactly the same words, but this time I'll be taking out the bits which are not by St Paul. Before you say: 'Aha! – that's his trick – he's got some complicated reason why St Paul couldn't have said such and such, so he's going to claim that some bit he doesn't like isn't really by St Paul', I would like to rush to assure you. I am going to remove *no word at all* from the text. But I'm going to remove all the numbers. That is, the verse and chapter numbers. These are the bits that are not by St Paul. They were a mediaeval addition; first the division into chapters and later the subdivision by verses. They are supposed to be, and are, a simple help to finding your way in the text, just as a book cataloguing system is supposed to help you find your way round a library rather than point out which books are important and to be read. Of course Paul didn't write his Epistle to the Romans in chapters and verses. He wrote, or dictated, it, in scarcely punctuated continuous Greek prose. What you will see is quite how much the introduction of numbers has done to freeze a certain sort of reading into place as though the numbers had the authority to do that, and quite how differently the passage reads if the numbers are removed.

You will notice also a difference of tone in the reading. The first time I will read it in the portentous tones of Ayatollah Paul, who has just stepped down, Charlton Heston-like, from Mount Sinai, with a burning zeal to dictate the univocal word of the Lord concerning iniquity. Without my knowing those long words, like Ayatollah, or portentous, and without having seen the Charlton Heston movie, this was the reading which was obvious to me in my early teens, the one which read itself through my eyes, and it may well be one that has been obvious to you. I hope to suggest that the tone which we bring to the text when we read or hear it is at least as important as the words on the page for creating the meaning that seems obvious. The second time we will go through it in the bathetic tones of Rabbi Paul, heir to a rich tradition of ironic and quizzical readings. And lest you be worried that, in referring to him as Rabbi, I am in some way trying to undercut his apostolic authority, which is somehow upheld if he is read in the tones of an Ayatollah, I would like to make clear that the word 'Rabbi' here refers, in my understanding, to his style and rhetoric and in no way undermines his authority: he was Apostle precisely as someone who was extremely well educated in the rabbinical tradition of interpretation. I hope that this second reading will, after I have given it to you, be obvious to you, as it now is to me.

So here goes with Romans 1:14 to the end from the RSV:

> [14] I am under obligation both to Greeks and to barbarians, both to the wise and to the foolish: [15] so I am eager to preach the gospel to you also who are in Rome. [16] For I am not ashamed of the gospel: it is the power of God for salvation to every one who has faith, to the Jew first and also to the Greek. [17] For in it the righteousness of God is revealed through faith for faith; as it is written, "He who through faith is righteous shall live." [18] For the wrath of God is revealed from heaven against all ungodliness and wickedness of men who by their wickedness suppress the truth. [19] For what can be known about God is plain to them, because God has shown it to them. [20] Ever since the creation of the world his invisible nature, namely, his eternal power and deity, has been clearly perceived in the things that have been made. So they are without excuse; [21] for although they knew God they did not honour him as God or give thanks to him, but they became futile in their thinking and their senseless minds were darkened. [22] Claiming to be wise, they became fools, [23] and exchanged the glory of the immortal God for images resembling mortal man or birds or animals or reptiles. [24] Therefore God gave them up in the lusts of their hearts to impurity, to the dishonouring of their bodies among themselves, [25] because they exchanged the truth about God for a lie and worshiped and served the creature rather than the Creator, who is blessed for ever! Amen. [26] For this reason God gave them up to dishonourable passions. Their women exchanged natural relations for unnatural, [27] and the men likewise gave up natural relations with

women and were consumed with passion for one another, men committing shameless acts with men and receiving in their own persons the due penalty for their error. [28] And since they did not see fit to acknowledge God, God gave them up to a base mind and to improper conduct. [29] They were filled with all manner of wickedness, evil, covetousness, malice. Full of envy, murder, strife, deceit, malignity, they are gossips, [30] slanderers, haters of God, insolent, haughty, boastful, inventors of evil, disobedient to parents, [31] foolish, faithless, heartless, ruthless. [32] Though they know God's decree that those who do such things deserve to die, they not only do them but approve those who practice them.

Sound familiar?

Well, now for the second go. First some background details. As far as we can tell, Paul wrote this letter in Corinth. It appears to be written to two groups of Christians who constituted the Church at Rome – the group of Jewish believers in Christ, and the group of Gentile believers in Christ. There appear to have been some problems with rivalry between these two groups, with the Jewish Christians thinking themselves superior to the baptised Gentiles, and the Gentiles thinking themselves superior to the baptised Jews. Paul first of all speaks to the Jewish Christians explaining to them that even though all the treasures of revelation had come through the Jewish people, they are in fact not superior to the Gentiles, but in just the same need as the Gentiles of the redemption which has been effected by Jesus. Then he turns to the Gentiles to explain to them how they are not superior to the Jews by never having had the Law, but are likewise dependent on Christ's redemption. The point of this is to bring out that all humans are dependent on Christ's salvation: all have sinned, and all need grace, without exception. As far as I am aware this basic framework for the reading of the Epistle to the Romans is pacifically accepted by the majority of scholars of all stripes. Nothing particularly controversial here.

Given that, my starting point for reading Romans 1 isn't in Romans 1 at all. It is in fact what we know as Romans 2:1 and you didn't hear it in the passage I just read. It reads as follows:

> Therefore you have no excuse, O man, whoever you are, when you judge another; for in passing judgment upon him you condemn yourself, because you, the judge, are doing the very same things.

Now, I suggest to you that it is extremely odd to start a new argument, or a new chapter, with the word 'Therefore'. Normally, a sentence beginning 'Therefore' is an indication that the conclusion to the preceding argument is about to be given. That is, the whole point of what went before is about to be made clear. Let us suppose that we had no reliable manuscript for the beginning of St Paul's letter to the Romans, but merely knew that a short chunk was missing, and the manuscript we have begins with what we call 2:1. Well, you can bet your bottom dollar that all attempts to reconstruct the missing passage would work on the sure presumption that whatever it was about, it was leading in some way to an indication that no one should be able to judge anyone else. Given the thrust of what we call Chapters 2 and 3, arguing against Jewish superiority over Gentiles in the Church, exegetes are very likely to posit that whatever the missing passage said, it is very likely to have contained an argument building up to the conclusion that whatever apparent signs of superiority were enjoyed by Jewish believers in Christ, they were in fact fundamentally in the same boat as the Gentiles as regards everything that actually mattered.

Well, you will be amazed to hear that the great, and almost certainly German, Biblical Palaeontologist, Herr Doktor James Alison, by dint of extraordinarily adroit, and indeed almost Nobel Prize-worthy, use of computer buttons in operating his Hermeneutika Bible Works Scripture software, has managed to discover and reproduce the missing chunk which leads up to what we call Romans 2:1, and it does, perfectly, conform to what those clever exegetes said it would contain, basing their deduction on the first verse available to them, the verse forbidding judging anyone else. Let me read to you how the rabbinic writer Paul builds up to his point:

> I am under obligation both to Greeks and to barbarians, both to the wise and to the foolish: so I am eager to preach the gospel to

you also who are in Rome. For I am not ashamed of the gospel: it is the power of God for salvation to every one who has faith, to the Jew first and also to the Greek. For in it the righteousness of God is revealed through faith for faith; as it is written, "He who through faith is righteous shall live."

Here Paul sets out quite clearly what he wants to do, justifying his mission to some potential Jewish listeners who may not be so happy with Paul's emphasis on the Gentiles. So he moves on to speaking in terms with which any educated religious Jew living in the Diaspora would be familiar. He is almost quoting from, and certainly taking as known, the book which appears in Catholic Bibles as the Book of Wisdom, or the Wisdom of Solomon. Part of this is a straightforward Jewish treatise against all the iniquities of pagan idol worship. Moses had his preachers in every city, expounding Jewish monotheism and attracting people from the Gentile cults, and this was just the sort of thing those preachers said. I have appended the relevant verses from chapters 13 and 14 of the Book of Wisdom for you to see this for yourselves.[3] Those verses and St Paul's are extremely similar in their analysis of idolatry.

> For the wrath of God is revealed from heaven against all ungodliness and wickedness of men who by their wickedness suppress the truth. For what can be known about God is plain to them, because God has shown it to them. Ever since the creation of the world his invisible nature, namely, his eternal power and deity, has been clearly perceived in the things that have been made. So they are without excuse; for although they knew God they did not honour him as God or give thanks to him, but they became futile in their thinking and their senseless minds were darkened. Claiming to be wise, they became fools, and exchanged the glory of the immortal God for images resembling mortal man or birds or animals or reptiles.

OK. So here we have a standard piece of Jewish polemic about

---

3. See Appendix II, p. 233.

pagans in general: the sort of thing they do is 'exchange' (a word we also get in Wisdom) – something like 'travesty' – the glory of God for images. All Paul's readers and listeners would know exactly to what he was referring. Ancient cities were full of temples and shrines with images of gods, goddesses, cats, jackals, crocodiles, serpents, Isis, Osiris, Anubis, Mithras and so on.

> Therefore God gave them up in the lusts of their hearts to impurity, to the dishonouring of their bodies among themselves, because they exchanged the truth about God for a lie and worshiped and served the creature rather than the Creator, who is blessed for ever! Amen.

Here, as in the Book of Wisdom, which sets out to explain the link between idolatry, the source of all evil, and the evil of which it is the source, it is *because* pagan people became involved in the idolatrous cults that *then* they were led to get involved in passions which did them no honour. You can tell Paul is on something of a riff here, playing to his audience, his listeners, because he interrupts his own argument to make an exclamation after mentioning the Creator:

> who is blessed for ever! Amen.

This is the sort of exclamation where, in a Pentecostal church, we would expect voices to emerge from the listeners saying 'Hallelujah' or 'Right on, Brother!' It is part of a rhetoric of convincing people that he is on their side, that he is one of them, that they can count on him. And of course, it is for a very deliberate purpose as we will see. Paul moves on:

> For this reason God gave them up to dishonourable passions. Their women exchanged natural relations for unnatural, and the men likewise gave up natural relations with women and were consumed with passion for one another, men committing shameless acts with men and receiving in their own persons the due penalty for their error.

These are exactly the sort of things that went on in and around pagan temples throughout the Mediterranean world in Paul's time, as at the time of the writer of the Book of Wisdom, which goes into rather more detail than Paul does.[4] These would include women dressing up as satyrs with large phalloi so that they could be the penetrators rather than the penetratees with their partners (and it was this travestying or exchanging of role, going against 'farmyard logic', rather than the gender of the partner which seems to have been what was regarded as going against type here). This is what Clement of Alexandria had to say on the subject:

> For that reason, births are infrequent among hyenas, because they sow their seed contrary to nature . . . Such godless people 'God has given over,' the Apostle says, 'to shameful lusts. For the women change their natural use to that which is against nature . . .' Yet nature has not allowed even the most sensual beasts to sexually misuse the passage made for excrement . . . Blurring the natural order, men play the part of women, and women play the part of men, contrary to nature . . . No passage is closed against evil lusts; and their sexuality is a public institution – they are roommates with indulgence.[5]

We have, you will not be surprised to hear, even more evidence from antiquity about the sort of things that the men got up to. Certainly there were cults like that of Cybele, Atys or Aphrodite, whose largest temple (rumoured to have as many as 1,000 temple prostitutes) was in Corinth where Paul probably wrote this letter, and whose cult had recently been introduced into Rome. This cult had a very strong cross-dressing element. Not only that, but the rites involved orgiastic frenzies in which men allowed themselves to be penetrated, and which culminated in some of those in the frenzy castrating themselves, and becoming eunuchs, and thus priests of Cybele, for whom, as was common with Mother Goddess

---

4. See especially Wisdom 14:23–8. Independently of Jewish sources, evidence abounds of the practices in the ancient world surrounding the cults of different divinities: Cybele, Mithras and so on, and their popularity. For a particularly interesting and useful compilation of the evidence see Jeramy Townsley's 'Romans 1:22–28: Paul, the Goddess Religions and Homosexuality' available on his website http://www.jeramyt.org/papers/paulcybl.html.

5. Clement, *Paedagogos* 2.10.86–7, 3.3.21.3, translation Jeramy Townsley.

cults, transcending gender was particularly important. Such
castrated devotees, sometimes called *galli,* would wander around,
as do the *hijra* in modern India, as festal eunuchs assumed to have
magic powers or prophetic gifts. The body of just such a castrated
Roman eunuch priest with ornaments showing devotion to Cybele
was recently uncovered by archaeologists in Northern England.[6]

Paul's listeners would not have needed any explanation of this
sort of thing: it was a regularly occurring part of the public life of
the Mediterranean world at the time. What it meant for *galli* to
receive in their persons the due penalty for their error might refer
to the castration, or to their general weirdness of demeanour and
appearance, but Paul's readers would have picked up the sort of
thing he meant. Because, as any self-respecting Jew could tell you:
this was just the sort of idiotic thing that Gentiles got up to as a
result of their idolatry.

At this point, please notice something quite subtle: Paul is
shading towards puncturing the pride of those he has been building
up for a fall. After the graphic depiction of a set of practices which
were self-evidently pagan, and would allow the Jewish listeners to
feel very much a 'we' against the silly 'they' being described (and
the words Paul uses are those concerning purity and shamefulness
rather than morals and evil which is why I use words like 'silly' and
'idiotic' rather than 'wicked'), Paul moves on – still talking about
'they' – to a list of much more serious things: deep internal attitudes of heart. And of course he would still have his listeners
absolutely on side:

> And since they did not see fit to acknowledge God, God gave
> them up to a base mind and to improper conduct. They were
> filled with all manner of wickedness, evil, covetousness, malice.

---

6. BBC News for Tuesday 21 May 2002: 'Archaeologists in North Yorkshire
have discovered the skeleton of a cross-dressing eunuch dating back to the
4th Century AD. The find was made during excavations of a Roman set-
tlement in Catterick, first started in 1958. The skeleton – found dressed in
women's clothes and jewellery – is believed to have once been a castrated
priest who worshipped the eastern goddess Cybele. Archaeologists say it is
the only example ever recovered from a late Roman cemetery in Britain.'

You can imagine that we are still in the realm where the listeners will have been able to say, 'Right on, Brother!' – this was still the sort of thing they were used to hearing. But Paul sweeps on, moving on from those deep attitudes of heart which the silly 'they' are full of, to what one might call a list of rather more banal, domestic, common-or-garden forms of wickedness:

> Full of envy, murder, strife, deceit, malignity, they are gossips, slanderers, haters of God, insolent, haughty, boastful, inventors of evil, disobedient to parents, foolish, faithless, heartless, ruthless.

We are skating on thin ice here . . . would his listeners have already picked up hints that this list, containing not a single reference to anything sexual, was coming dangerously close to home? So Paul gives one final blast to the traditional anti-pagan trumpet:

> Though they know God's decree that those who do such things deserve to die, they not only do them but approve those who practice them.

You can see why those who divided the chapters divided the argument here: it sounds like the end of a breath – and it is. It is the end of a breath, but not the end of the argument, because the sting is still to come, and without the sting the argument is not complete:

> Therefore you have no excuse, O man, whoever you are, when you judge another; for in passing judgment upon him you condemn yourself, because you, the judge, are doing the very same things.

You can see what the effect of this phrase is on the preceding argument. The effect is rather similar to what would have happened if Paul had said, 'We all know that the Gentiles do idiotic things, get involved in bizarre rites and frenzies, and guess what terrible consequences this leads to: they become *gossips*, disobedient to their parents! Behave foolishly! How unlike anyone *we* know!' and then paused for the first giggles of self-recognition to break out.

Now, of course, this rhetorical device of building up his listeners for a fall, and then puncturing their balloon, wouldn't work at all if Paul were claiming that his listeners had been doing the same things as the pagans – that is the bizarre cults and frenzied sexualised rites leading to castration. His point is not that his listeners have been doing these things, but that even though they haven't, and wouldn't dream of doing them, they share in exactly the same pattern of desire, and the ordinary banal wickedness which flows from that pattern, the really serious stuff, which they have in common with the pagans who do indeed do those silly things.

Paul confirms what he has been doing all along by moving, at last, from 'they' to 'we', and his use of 'we' is interesting:

> We know that the judgment of God rightly falls upon those who do such things.

Paul appears to repeat the anti-pagan charge – that 'they know God's decree, and still do these things'. His repetition of it here, but in the form of 'we', sounds awfully like, 'Whether or not *they* know about God's judgment, *we* certainly do.' And then he goes on to address 'you' – not just a Jewish you, nor just a Christian you, but the human 'you' that is any of us.

> Do you suppose, O man, that when you judge those who do such things and yet do them yourself, you will escape the judgment of God? Or do you presume upon the riches of his kindness and forbearance and patience? Do you not know that God's kindness is meant to lead you to repentance? But by your hard and impenitent heart you are storing up wrath for yourself on the day of wrath when God's righteous judgment will be revealed.

From here Paul will go on to develop his understanding of how the human problem is fundamentally one of desire, and it is at the level of a change in the pattern of desire that we are saved by and through Christ, a change in the pattern of desire which even the Law, which was good in itself, could not effect. It is this analysis which led him to work out what a later generation, following St Augustine, would call 'the doctrine of original sin'. The whole purpose of this doctrine is to keep alive the sense that all humans, from the very outset of humanity, suffer from essentially the same pattern of distorted desire, with the result that none of us is in a position to judge others, because, unlike God, none of us is free from having our capacity to judge distorted by our social belonging. This is absolutely in line with Jesus' teaching in the Gospels: if Pharisees can't judge prostitutes, then Jews can't judge Gentiles, and, of course, vice versa.

I hope that you can now sense that there is another 'obvious' reading of Romans 1. The moment you realise that the introduction of chapter and verse numbers is discretionary, and it becomes possible to see that the whole point of the argument is leading up to the central puncturing of judgmental group creation, then it begins to become possible to hear St Paul's voice in a different way. What I call 'bathetic' Paul rather than 'portentous' Paul. Witty, rabbinic, persuasive Paul rather than Paul the univocal, authoritarian, irony-free zone. His argument works by setting his hearers up for a fall, and then delivering the coup de grace. If you want to see this for yourselves, and that is really the only way to do it, try reading aloud to yourselves, or to friends, the version I have made available for you,[7] the one without numbers, in the tones of portentous Paul. It works fine until you get to the end of chapter 1. But then try to read chapter 2 verse 1 in the same tone of voice. It makes no sense at all. If you read in the tones of an Ayatollah, then you have to stop at the end of chapter 1 and regroup for the next chapter. However, if you read in the tone of Paul the Rabbi, then you can cross seamlessly from chapter 1 to 2 and appreciate the full subtlety of his persuasive style on the way.

Well, there you have a Catholic reading of Romans 1. The only thing extraneous to the text which I have brought in is some knowledge of the frenzied cults of the ancient world. This helps to restrict any tendency to uncharitable actualisation of the text, in the same way as does limiting the reference of $o\grave{\iota}$ $\ensuremath{'} I o \upsilon \delta \alpha \iota o \iota$ in John's Gospel to the local Jewish authorities in first-century Palestine. The modern 'obvious' reading of the text also imports

---

7. cf. Appendix III, p. 236.

into it something extraneous: an understanding of 'homosexuality' as something which it was Paul's intention to condemn, despite the evidence that the modern category was unknown in the ancient world. The modern 'obvious' reading then uses this as a political and religious weapon against a modern group of people. I hope that I am being more obedient to the Pontifical Biblical Commission in preferring the ancient and limited meaning.

One of the things which I hope this makes clear is that even if it could be shown (as I do not think it can) that it is obligatory to regard Paul as referring to lesbians and gay men in what we know as Romans 1:26b–27; even then, the one use to which his reference could not be put, without doing serious violence to the text, is a use which legitimates any sort of judging of such people. Their presence in the text would be as illustrations for an argument of this sort: 'Yes, yes, we know that there are these people who do these silly things, but that is completely irrelevant besides the hugely significant fact that these are simply different symptoms of a profound distortion of desire which is identical in you as it is in them, and it is you who I am trying to get through to, so don't judge them.'

If you want to see what I mean, then try this for yourselves: Let us suppose that the Jewish preachers of the ancient world had become convinced that one of the things which idolatry led to was the widespread practice of Extreme Sports. Let us imagine, consequently, that they had prohibited such things. Now substitute the words 'abseiling' and 'paragliding' in place of what has sometimes been taken to be 'lesbianism' and 'gay male sex'.

> Their women took up abseiling,[8] and the men likewise gave up natural modes of transport and took up paragliding, men shaming themselves by imitating mere birds and often enough, owing to unexpected updrafts, receiving in their own persons the due penalty for their error.

Can you imagine how easily the Christian world would have abandoned the supposed ancient prohibition against these clearly

8. In the USA this activity is called 'rappelling'.

insane activities? The prohibition would have been abandoned by pointing out that an argument which referred tangentially to abseiling and paragliding as part of the build-up to a point concerning the impermissibility of judging anyone cannot properly be used to judge those who engage in abseiling and paragliding. The only reference to abseiling in Scripture would, rightly, be regarded as of no moral weight at all.

It is my view that Romans 1 has quite simply nothing at all to do with what we call homosexuality. I hope I have shown that it is perfectly possible to read it in such a way as to respect the integrity of the text, to show appreciation for, and agreement with, St Paul, and to show how Paul's argument is an important step towards formulating a major doctrine of the Church, without saying or implying anything at all for or against so-called 'homosexuality'. It is not my claim that this reading which I have given you is *the* real reading of St Paul, that *exactly this* and no more and no less, is precisely what he meant. I don't think there is such a thing as *the* real reading of this text. I think that there are better and worse readings of the text, and, more importantly, that there are more Catholic and less Catholic ways of reading the text, because reading the text within the Church is an infinitely creative exercise in giving glory to God and creating merciful meaning for our sisters and brothers as we come to be possessed by the Spirit breathed into us by the Crucified and Risen Lord.

The Catholic Church is heir to an extraordinarily rich tradition of creative Jewish textual reading, and we read Scripture eucharistically. Because for us the prime source of authority is not the text itself, but the crucified and living victim, alive in our midst, who is the living interpretative presence teaching us how to undo our violent and evil ways of relating to each other, and how together to enter into the way of penitence and peace. For us the phrase 'The Word of God' refers in the first place to a living person, and only by analogy to the texts which bear witness to him. The living hermeneutical presence is more important than that which it is hermeneuting. This is what is meant by Jesus telling the Pharisees in Matthew's Gospel:

'Go and learn what this means, "I desire mercy, and not sacrifice."'

And:

'. . . If you had known what this means, "I desire mercy, and not sacrifice," you would not have condemned the guiltless.' [9]

Now *there* is an instruction regarding the Catholic reading of Scripture from an authority even more important than the Pontifical Biblical Commission. And I'm glad to say that the Commission's passage which I quoted for you at the beginning of this chapter is in complete accord with it.

It is time we learnt to read the words of our brother Paul, someone who wrote to us not from above, but on the same, fraternal, level as us, in a eucharistic manner. Let us imagine him as with us at the eucharistic gathering, bearing witness to the effect of the Crucified and Risen One on his and all our lives. And let us learn to have his words interpreted to us through the eyes of the Lord in the centre of our gathering, the eyes of One who so much liked us and wanted to be with us that he gave himself up for us so that we might become able to create, with him, and in great freedom, a world full of mercy where there are no 'they'; a world where we can look at each other with hearts unchecked by niggles of the sort 'But the Bible says. . .', and with eyes undimmed by sacralised fatality.

9. Matt. 9:13; 12:7.

good-faith learning and the
fear of god

The virtue of *fear of God* is little mentioned nowadays,[1] but I would like to bring it back into our discourse. I invoke it because typically those who enter into some sort of moral discussion imagine that we are starting off from the standpoint of the good guys. Those who are moved by *fear of God* fear lest our own irresponsibility, our own hardness of heart and defect of vision perhaps be carrying us down a route that is too easy, one that is ever more free of voices which question and challenge us. So *fear of God* obliges us to a certain athletic tension with respect to our own way, lest it lead us into disaster.

In order to situate more exactly the reason for this invocation at this time, I would like to bring to your attention Gitta Sereny's book *Into That Darkness: from mercy killing to mass murder*. In this magnificent text Sereny shows the slow route to moral corruption undergone by a local Austrian policeman, Franz Stangl, who went on to become the Camp Commander of the extermination camp at Treblinka. Stangl would preside over the death of about a million people without committing a single act of personal violence, convincing himself that he had no other option owing to the harshness of the situation. However, it is not because of the interviews with Stangl that I indicate this text now, but because of

---

1. For greater clarification of the relationship between *fear of God* and the virtue of Hope of which it is a formative part, cf. Josef Pieper, *Hope* and especially section V 'Fear as gift' in *Faith, Hope, Love* (San Francisco: Ignatius, 1997).

the author's study of what happened in Germany when Hitler was planning his programme of murdering mentally and physically handicapped people.[2]

A former priest, who had become a Nazi official, was charged with obtaining from a distinguished Catholic moralist a formal written opinion concerning the probable reaction of the Church towards the policy of forced euthanasia which was to be introduced by the government. The opinion, whose five copies have disappeared completely, was written by the very distinguished moralist, Professor Mayer of Paderborn. According to the sworn testimony of those who read it, it gave to understand that the killing of the mentally handicapped might be admissible. Apparently, knowledge of the tenor of this document reached high within ecclesiastical spheres. From the silent reaction of those spheres, Hitler deduced that his programme of the killing of such patients would not provoke an enraged reaction from the Church. Having feared that the Catholic population, at the instigation of their hierarchy, would rise up against these measures, he saw that this wouldn't happen, so he could begin his programme. Which he then did.

Now, after the war, when there was an attempt to clarify the circumstances of the opinion and of who knew what before the introduction of the euthanasia policy, there were many cases of amnesia and declarations of not having known what was going on. Such forgetfulness and ignorance were difficult to believe, because there had in fact been a few brave and isolated voices among the hierarchs of the time who preferred to go to prison rather than keep quiet.

Thus, seduced by the possibility of a détente with a hostile regime, some notable Catholic figures felt it appropriate to drop some links from the hermetic chain of a moral doctrine which had been implacably opposed to allowing any exception to the prohibition of the murder of handicapped people. The result of this seduction was the murder of thousands of utterly vulnerable and

2. I refer to pp. 60–77 of the London: Pimlico 1995 edition of *Into That Darkness*.

unprotected people, the loss of credibility on the part of ecclesiastical authority, and, at the end, the absolute professional shame of those who had allowed themselves to be seduced.

The reason for invoking *fear of God* is because of the possible symmetries which exist with what is going on currently. If I had been in Germany at that time and in those circumstances, it would be very rash of me to think that I am, or that we are, better than our brethren in the faith who let the links drop. That is to say, it is much more probable that I would have been of the conformist party, and not of the brave party whose members were, over the long term, fully justified. Well, here we have something similar. Nobody doubts the Church's traditionally implacable opposition in the face of any attempts to legitimise sexual and affective relationships between same-sex couples. Yet behold, encouraged by the growing good will shown by the civil governments in our own and other continents, some of us, amongst whom I count myself, are proposing that we let drop a link in the chain of that implacable opposition, and are suggesting that it is quite possible that the Church can, without any damage to its divine doctrine and mission, change its characterisation of gay and lesbian people, and, changing its characterisation, change also its position with relation to the civil laws which normalise the lives of such people.

Well, I would be very stupid if I were not to ask myself whether, should I reach the age of eighty-one, like Professor Mayer of Paderborn at the time of the 1967 Frankfurt Euthanasia Trial, I am not running the risk of being found to be in the most absolute shame and discredit through having made myself an accomplice and a partisan of something which might, over time, come to be seen as a moment when our societies headed off down an insidious and sinister pathway.

And of course, none of us knows now what exactly will be the effects of the proposed changes to the law or the civil code in our countries. Ecclesiastical voices, with prophetic tones, predict severe damage to our social life, and consider, along with the highest representatives of Islamic thought, that the very foundations of society are threatened by the extension of the category of civil marriage to same-sex couples. Other voices point out that there is no sign of any such damage being produced in those countries or states where the law has already been changed. Instead these voices affirm that not to extend the right to full civil recognition is to carry on producing an evil in the degree to which people are being condemned to the category of second-class citizens without any objective basis. And of course, where there is discrimination without objective basis, and those who do the discriminating begin to be aware of the baselessness of their discrimination, they have ever less excuse for the evil they are perpetuating. Whatever the case, should the ecclesiastical argument be right, we would need much more time to measure the social consequences of the extension of civil marriage, although it is very difficult to say how these consequences would be measured.

That's why *fear of God* is so important. Whether we like it or not, we are in new territory, and the one thing that is certain is that, whatever we do, there will be consequences. None of us knows what the consequences will be, nor which of us will emerge at the end like our poor brethren in the faith, Dr Mayer of Paderborn and the bishops and cardinals whose silence was death for some of the smallest and weakest of their brethren.

It is for this reason that I would like to work very slowly, showing step by step the links in my argument so that, where what I say is crazy, this be rectifiable before it is too late. That is to say: mine is an attempt to talk about matters gay in the midst of the Church in such a way that what I say is capable of discussion and of being contested.

I consider it important to signal in advance what it is that I think I am doing, since it is notorious that if the characterisation of gay and lesbian people upheld by the Vatican Congregations be true, then it is to be doubted that gay or lesbian people who accept themselves as such would be capable of rational discourse about the matter. According to the official characterisation, such a person would have accepted as part of their 'I' something which is nothing but an objective disorder. This would have corrupting consequences in their self-presentation and in their capacity for reasoning. A parallel would be trying to talk to someone who is drunk. While someone is in that state, none of us would think that

that person is capable of reasoning or of moral responsibility. In fact, we would show a marked lack of sanity ourselves if we were to speak 'to' such a person, trying to engage his 'I'. Rather, while the drunken state lasts, his 'self' is temporarily beyond being engaged by us, and we would do well to talk 'about' him so as to work out who gets to swipe his car keys, and who will take him home and put him to bed.

So I know in advance that, seen from such a perspective, this attempt of mine to speak in the midst of the Church is no more than an attempt by a drunk driver to show the traffic cops that he's able to walk in a straight line. Normally the very fact of having a go is a sign that the driver is not altogether there. I would merely ask those who maintain the perspective of the Vatican Congregations that they take my attempt to walk in a straight line as a sign of good faith, and treat it as some sort of cry for help. That is to say, I'm asking that I not be considered an enemy of the faith, or an infil-trator who is sapping the foundations of the Church, introducing weird heresies. In the worst case scenario, I'm a deranged fool attempting a piece of reasoning, but at least with nothing hidden, all in the full light of day. And if the perspective of the Vatican Congregations turns out to be true, then I dare say that there are many of us who are similarly deranged and we are going to need very well-developed pastoral help so as to enable us to return to our right minds.

Thus to my first premise in this attempt. Currently the Church, including its gay and lesbian members, finds itself in a situation where there is a serious conflict between two elements of Catholic doctrine which hadn't appeared to be in conflict before, but which for a few years now have been producing a very strong disturbance in the life of many of the faithful. The two elements are as follows: on the one hand the Church's traditional teaching about original sin and grace and, on the other, the traditional teaching about sexual acts between people of the same sex.

The first element is well known. The Church teaches that at the Fall, and therefore in the real living out of all of us, our human nature was very seriously damaged, but that this damage did not destroy our human nature. The distinction is important. If our nature had been destroyed, that is, if we are radically depraved, as is taught by some of the churches which are heirs to the Protestant Reformation, then salvation would come to us as something without any continuity with our nature, with our past, and there would be no organic continuity between 'who I was' before accepting salvation and 'who I will turn out to be' when all is revealed. However, since our nature was seriously damaged, but continues to be human nature, salvation does reach us in the form of a process of the perfecting of our nature. As a result of this, 'who I will turn out to be' has, according to the most traditional Catholic teaching, reaffirmed at the Council of Trent, an organic continuity with 'who I was'.

Thus, what is normal within the living of the Catholic faith, what is normal in the process of growth in grace, is always starting from where one is, knowing that no part of human desire or living out is *intrinsically* evil, that is to say, incapable of being ordered or healed, only capable of being wiped out. Nevertheless, all our desire is damaged in the way we receive it and live it out: it is seriously distorted. But we can trust that even what is most base within a person's life is capable of being transformed into something which will be a reflection of the divine splendour. What is normal, then, in Catholic anthropology, is to regard no human desire, heavily distorted or addicted to evils of various types though it may be, as a radically perverse entity but rather to see it as something which can in principle be returned to flowing towards what is good.

This, I should say, is an essential part of the Catholic faith. Without this, the whole of Catholic teaching concerning grace, mercy, forgiveness and the sacraments would have to be altered radically. Furthermore, it seems to be part of that *sensus fidei* which Catholics have as an instinct that we understand that the mercy of the Church consists above all, and always, in starting from where one is, and not causing an obstacle to grace by insisting that one has to become something else before being able to receive grace.

The second element in this conflict is the teaching about sexual acts between people of the same sex. Until fairly recently it did not appear that there was a conflict between this teaching and the doctrine of original sin and grace, since the teaching about sexual acts was just that: a teaching about acts and nothing else. It was taught that what were forbidden were any sexual acts whatsoever between people of the same sex, with different reasons brought forth, in different periods, to justify the prohibition. However, what all the reasons took for granted was that such acts would be a perversion of a human nature which tended of itself, and always, towards what we would nowadays call some form of 'hetero-sexuality'. In prohibiting the acts, nothing was being said about the condition or being of the person, and it was understood that the prohibition didn't affect the *being* of the person, only the acts. That is to say, it used to be possible to say in good conscience to a person who had engaged in such acts that they should desist, and instead seek their flourishing, which they would only achieve if their desire were to return to its normal river bed. It was, for example, normal to suggest to young men who had confessed acts or thoughts of this nature that they should hurry up and get married so as to be cured. At a time when 'gay' hadn't yet been invented, and there were only 'sodomitical acts', there didn't seem to be a conflict between the teachings about grace and about those acts.

The problem is that over the last several decades these two teachings do appear to have entered into conflict. And the reason is a change in society which has come upon us all, Catholics or not. The change consists in the ever increased recognition during the second half of the twentieth century that it is really not possible to make such a clear-cut distinction between acts and being as had been traditional. That is to say, it seems that there exist some people, a minority which occurs more or less regularly in all societies and cultures, as well as in the groupings of other animals, who just are 'like that'. This doesn't appear to be an individual aberration, but it just appears to be the case that there is a class of people with the common and recognisable characteristic of a lasting and stable emotional and erotic attraction towards the members of their own sex. At the same time, it seems to be the case that if you remove from the psychological profiles of a hundred people only the detail concerning each one's sexual orientation, there is absolutely nothing in the profiles which would allow you to indicate in a regular and accurate way what the orientation corresponding to the profile in fact is. That is to say, the presence of an orientation towards a person of the same sex does not appear to bring along with it any emotional or psychological configuration, even less any deformation, which is not found equally among people of the majority orientation.

The conflict between the two elements of Christian teaching raises its head, then, because while the discussion was about *acts* and not *being*, it was thought possible to say to someone at the same time, 'Don't do that!' and 'Flourish, brother!', because it was thought that the acts didn't flow from what the brother was. However, it has become ever more problematic to bring together in the same phrase 'Don't do that!' and 'Flourish, brother!', since if it is understood that someone is just 'like that' then in part, at least, his flourishing will be discovered starting from what he is.

Now this conflict is by no means a merely academic matter. It is lived, very intensely, by many young people for whom working out whether it is a matter of 'I'm just like this, and so I must be this in the richest way possible' or whether it is rather a matter of 'I'm not like this, but I suffer from very grave temptations which in some way I must overcome' is a severely tortured experience. Evidence suggests that more and more young people are overcoming this conflict by working out that they just are 'like that', and it is starting from this that they are going to risk constructing a life.

Faced with these conflicts, the Vatican Congregations decided to respond. If they conceded that 'being like that' is simply part of nature, which is to say, part of God's creative project, then it is evident that the acts which flow from that way of being could not be *intrinsically* evil, but that they might be good or bad according to their use and circumstances, as is the case with heterosexual acts. So, they were faced with one of two possibilities: either we recognise that 'being like that' is neutral, which means, in the case of everything created, positive, in which case the absolute prohibition of the acts falls; or we deny that 'being like that' exists, except as a defect of a radically heterosexual being, and because of this the traditional absolute prohibition of the acts can be maintained.

Please notice that there are two logical barriers which the ecclesiastical argument cannot jump without falsifying its own doctrine. The first is this: the Church cannot say, 'Well, being that way is normal, something neutral or positive, the Church respects it and welcomes it. The Church only prohibits the acts which flow from it.' This position would lack logic in postulating intrinsically evil acts which flow from a neutral or positive being. And this would go against the principle of Catholic morals which states that acts flow from being – *agere sequitur esse*. The second barrier is this: the Church cannot say of the homosexual inclination that it is a desire which is in itself intrinsically evil, since to say this would be to fall into the heresy of claiming that there is some part of being human which is essentially depraved – that is, which cannot be transformed, only covered over.

Faced with these two barriers, ecclesiastical logic did a backward double-flip worthy of an Olympic gymnast so as to arrive at the following formulation: **'The homosexual inclination, though not itself a sin, constitutes a tendency towards behaviour that is intrinsically evil, and must therefore be considered objectively disordered.'** With this phrase, the Vatican Congregations sought to maintain the absolute prohibition of the acts without describing the desire as intrinsically evil. Nevertheless the price of this definition is very high. It obliges its defenders to insist that the homosexual inclination, independently of any acts flowing from it, is something objectively disordered. And the kind of objectivity they have in mind is deduced not from what can be known through experience, but is an a priori which depends on the Church's teaching concerning marriage. That is to say, the a priori of the intrinsic heterosexuality of all human beings. In other words, from the presupposition of the intrinsic heterosexuality of all human beings, it is deduced that the person whose inclination is towards those of the same sex is a defective heterosexual.

Well, let us not delude ourselves here. This characterisation of the gay or lesbian person as a defective heterosexual is absolutely necessary for the maintenance of the prohibition, as the authors indicate with the 'must be considered' of their phrase. The problem is that, for the characterisation to work properly within the doctrine of original sin and grace, it would have to be the case that the life of grace would lead the gay or lesbian person to become heterosexual in the degree of his or her growth in grace. That is to say, in the degree to which grace makes us more patient, faithful, generous, capable of being good Samaritans, less prisoners of anger, of rivalry and of resentment, just so would it have to change the gender of the persons towards whom we are principally attracted. The problem is that such changes do not seem to take place in a regular and trustworthy way, even amongst the United States groups which promote them with significant funds and publicity. As the senior representatives of such groups indicate: at most, and in some cases, a change in behaviour is produced, but the fundamental structures of desire continue to be towards persons of the same sex.[3]

This then is the conflict: for the prohibition of the acts to correspond to the true being of the person, the inclination has to be characterised as something objectively disordered. However, since the inclination doesn't alter, unlike desires which are recognisably vicious, the gay or lesbian person would have a desire which is, in fact, intrinsically evil, an element of radical depravity in their desire. And we would have stepped outside Catholic anthropology. Or, on the other hand, the same-sex inclination is simply something that is, in which case grace will bring it to a flourishing starting from where it is, and with this we would have to work out which acts are appropriate or not, according to the circumstances, and we will have stepped outside the absolute prohibition passed on to us by tradition.

What I want to underline here is that this is a conflict *between elements of Catholic doctrine* lived by many people. That is to say: when people say to gay and lesbian people, 'You should just be obedient to the teaching of the Church' it is no frivolity to reply, 'Sure, but which one? To the uninterrupted teaching about grace

---

3. I am basing this judgement of mine on my own experiences with such groups, on conversations with Jeremy Marks and other leaders of the formerly ex-gay group Courage (UK), and on Wayne Besen's book *Anything but Straight* (New York: Harrington Park Press, 2003).

and original sin? Or to the recent characterisation which the Vatican Congregations now consider necessary in order to maintain the traditional prohibition? Because both together, at the moment it's not clear how that can be done.' And since all parties to the discussion are in agreement that the teaching on grace is the most important, the conflict is reduced to one concerning the characterisation. Either it is true to affirm that the homosexual inclination is objectively disordered, or it is not.

That is to say, one side has got it wrong, and one side has got it right. And the field of possible error is in the area of what really *is*. The whole argument turns on the veracity or otherwise of the characterisation of what is. Either being gay is a defective form of being heterosexual, or it is simply a thing that just is that way.

And this brings us to the next step. If it were the case that the homosexual inclination truly were a disfiguration of a fundamentally heterosexual structure of desire, then there would be no conflict between the two teachings. There would only be a conflict between the truth and the grave disfiguration of desire in people who don't want to recognise their perversity, a very deeply rooted conflict, of course. However, if it were the case that the homosexual inclination is simply a thing that just is 'like that', and is not a disfiguration of anything, in that case the official characterisation, and along with it the absolute prohibition, is false. And the deeply rooted conflict would be one between the truth and the grave disfiguration of the intelligence and desire of the forces which do not want to recognise this emerging truth.

And here I return to the fear of God. I consider that it is very dangerous to say, 'One of us is wrong, and since it is certainly not I, it must be you.' Instead of this I would like to delineate a position which would allow us to seek the truth together and in good faith. I propose it for your consideration, so that it can be seen whether or not what it postulates be legitimate. I do this through some theses, along with some accompanying observations.

My first thesis is this: **I consider that the Catholic doctrine of original sin offers in principle the possibility that, over time, we come to learn something about our being human in such a way that a change is undergone *not by*** *the doctrine of grace but by its anthropological field of application.* Let me explain: if we were to follow the position which Trent regarded (rightly or wrongly) as the Reformed one, human beings are so depraved in our nature that we cannot learn anything true from ourselves, from what is around us, or from waves of change in society. The unique access we have to truth is through Revelation, and wherever there is a conflict between the apparent truth known naturally and Revelation, then it is Revelation which wins out, since our corrupted nature cannot serve as a criterion for truth.

If we were to follow the Catholic position, however, then even though human beings are gravely damaged in our natures, yet something can indeed be known, even though it be with much difficulty and by sorting through many misconceptions, concerning what is true starting from ourselves and what surrounds us. Furthermore, when there is a conflict between apparent truth known naturally, and Revelation, the apparent truth known naturally is indeed capable of acting in the role of criterion for our knowledge of divinely revealed truth. It is for this reason that Catholic theology speaks of a 'natural law', because we consider that creation and the new creation have an organic continuity between them which is in principle knowable by the exercise of reason.

From this we deduce the following: if the teaching of the Church were the position labelled 'Reformed', then there would be no possibility of our learning anything authentic concerning, for example, whether the homosexual inclination is a defect in an intrinsically heterosexual being, or whether it is something which just is like that. The only thing we could do would be to insist on the characterisation deduced from Revelation. However, since the Church's teaching is not this, but is subtly different, then in fact we cannot reject, on purely a priori grounds, the possibility that we human beings might reach, through a difficult path, one interwoven with many false leads, the understanding that what seemed to be a defect in something is not. Rather it is merely a normal occurrence within created matter, with its own tendency to flourishing.

This means that there are no reasons *of faith* which stand in the way of our carrying on in our search for which of the two positions be closer to the truth, and both parties can participate in the discussion and in the process of learning in good faith.

My second thesis, which follows on from the previous one, reads thus: **Authentic objectivity about what human beings are can be reached by means of careful study and discernment of the lives of people over time**. Since what is *now* is not totally bereft of continuity with what we *shall* be in the new creation, then in principle, and with due attention to circumstance, the tendency to corruption or to flourishing which can be detected by means of study and discernment of the lives of people over the long term, does indeed point towards what the person really is. That is to say, if it were true that all humans are, by the mere fact of being human, intrinsically heterosexual, then there would be detected in those who, not recognising this, live as if they were gay or lesbian, a growing corruption of their human nature which would affect all the areas of their lives. In the same way there would be detected in people who are apparently of homosexual inclination, but who hold fast to their intrinsic heterosexuality, a growing flourishing in all areas of their life.

Given that we are questioning pathologies of desire, let us take an analogy from the same field: by means of study, we have come to distinguish between people who steal, and people who are kleptomaniacs; between people who take measures to slim, and people who suffer from anorexia; between people who consume alcohol, and people who are alcoholics. In each case we know how to distinguish between those acts which, good or bad as they may be in themselves, are not part of an objectively disordered inclination, and those acts which are part of an inclination which we would call objectively disordered. We punish the thief, but we seek treatment for the kleptomaniac; we congratulate the person who goes on a diet, but we seek to help the anorexic. And we know, furthermore, that our distinction is *objective*: that kleptomania, anorexia and alcoholism are not only minority behaviour patterns, but conditions which, if they are not controlled, put the health and flourishing of the person into danger. In the same way it should be possible to detect if self-acceptance as gay tends to put in jeopardy a person's health and flourishing, or if, in the case of people who have these desires but do not accept them as part of their being, it is rather this non-acceptance which puts their health and flourishing into danger.

With this I am discounting the following possibility. This would be to affirm that, 'however much we study, human opinions are always so relative that we will never be able to demonstrate anything, so we must stick with Revelation, which is the only source capable of objectivity. Besides, Revelation in this area would concern a future created heterosexuality which would only be brought to fruition in the heavenly wedding banquet, so any signs of homosexual flourishing now are not revelatory of anything at all.' To discount this is to accept *in principle* the possibility of saying that belief in the intrinsic heterosexuality of all the members of the human race does not form an obligatory part of the foundations of the Catholic faith, however much it may have been a common presupposition until recently.[4] This is because we are in principle capable of reaching objectivity about the matter without depending on a doctrinal a priori. We may indeed discover over time that all human beings are intrinsically heterosexual, and that any appearance to the contrary is an illusion. But should we find this not to be the case, then there would be no problem for Catholic doctrine as such, since Catholic doctrine doesn't depend on what might turn out to be a false or uncertain anthropology.

And of course, if it were the case that not all human beings are intrinsically heterosexual, then extending to same-sex couples the opportunity to enter into civil marriage would present no threat to the existence of heterosexual marriage, and there would be no logical reason why same-sex couples should be deprived of that opportunity.

Well, I think that both parties could come to accept these theses *in principle*. Which would allow me to advance a third thesis: since we are in a field where reality is greater than the positions which are currently held as certain, that is to say, where truth is ahead of

---

4. This is not, of course, to question that as a matter of common sense, human *reproduction* is intrinsically dependent on the biological complementarity of the sexes.

all of us and obliges all of us to allow our perceptions to be expanded by study and knowledge, **there remain to be established the criteria which would allow a common agreement concerning what might constitute flourishing in the case of people of homosexual inclination**.

For example, there are things which are no longer in question. There is no sort of empirical evidence to suggest that a person of homosexual inclination be, for that reason, either more or less capable of exercising whatsoever profession. A person's excellence as pilot, gardener, nurse, teacher, surgeon, accountant, postman or priest seems to be in no way affected by their sexual orientation. Nor is there any evidence to suggest that the habitual sexual practices corresponding to the inclination affect those exercises of excellence except in cases of compulsive behaviour, which are certainly no monopoly of those of homosexual inclination.

One would have to say that the fact that 'the children of this world', normally so astute at perceiving the sort of excellences which would allow them an advantage over others, have not detected that the presence of gay people in their companies, their armies, or their professions, lessens their competitive advantages begins to speak strongly in favour of 'being gay' making no difference at all in the field of professional, economic and social viability. This would suggest that there begins to be a strong probability that the homosexual inclination of itself does not lead to any diminishment of human flourishing. However, it would, in my view, be insufficient to allow the matter to be considered resolved on this evidence. It might be the case that social and economic forces were happy to use a characteristic, let us say, of personal instability, or a habit of maintaining appearances, so as to have a strong and loyal employee who could be used in the service of a profession for a certain time, but who could finally be sacked as he or she burns out through lack of a healthy basis of personal living.

For it is not only social and economic flourishing which must be considered, but personal flourishing. And it is here that we would have to work out what are to be the criteria for flourishing. My suggestion, some more or less adequate questions, would be of this sort: does a person of homosexual inclination who accepts himself as such tend, because of this, to be more capable of personal responsibility, of developing interpersonal relationships in a serene manner, of truthfulness, of compassion, of acting in a non-possessive way, of overcoming rivalries, and of generosity extended over time, or less?

There would be two fields of comparison. The first would be between those of undoubted heterosexual inclination on the one hand, and those of a homosexual inclination, whether accepted or not, on the other. If it could be demonstrated as a stable, repeated and consistent result that people of homosexual inclination tend to be less capable of responsibility, of serene interpersonal relationships, of truthfulness, of compassion, of acting in a non-possessive way, of overcoming rivalries, and of generosity extended over time, then, given equality of social circumstance (a big 'if' for a group which will always and inevitably be a minority group), there would at least be a strong suspicion that there is something defective in the inclination itself. Up till now, I have not seen a serious study which demonstrates this, but this should not rule out the possibility of closer examination.

The second field of comparison would be between people of homosexual inclination who *accept* that their inclination is part of their being, and that their flourishing flows from this, people who in a certain technical language were referred to as 'egosyntonic', on the one hand; and on the other, people who *deny* that their inclination is part of their 'I', being rather a heavy yoke to be borne and the cause of severe temptations which must be overcome, people who in that same technical language were referred to as 'egodystonic'. If it could be demonstrated as a stable, repeated and consistent result that the former tend to be less capable in all the previously described areas than the latter, then we would have very good evidence to suggest that the homosexual inclination, far from being a thing which just is 'like that', is instead some sort of defect, and when it is treated as such, then the true nature of the person tends to flourish. And if not, not.

Now of course there may be other suggestions about the type of criteria which should be employed, and I welcome their being raised. My thesis is precisely that the appropriate criteria **are yet to be established**.

What is clear, however, is that for anyone who is interested in the truth, this matter can no longer be put off. It seems that when the Vatican Congregations discussed among themselves the criteria for admission to seminaries, one of their points of interest was exactly this one. If it is true that those who are 'egodystonic' are those most capable of flourishing, because they correspond more closely to the reality of being human, then it would be worthwhile to undertake a massive education campaign concerning this among young people, clearly demonstrating all the evidence so that those who have allowed themselves to become 'egosyntonic' either become dystonic or do not present themselves as candidates for the priesthood. But if it is not true, if it is the case rather that the egosyntonic are more likely to flourish, then it is very much in the interest of the whole Church, which traditionally has a considerably higher proportion of men of homosexual inclination among its clergy than that which appears in the general population, that its own employees dwell in truth.[5]

So my fourth and last thesis is simple. It is that **we can no longer put off seeking the truth of this matter in the Church**. I turn for support to some words of John Paul II:

---

5. In the event, when the Vatican Instruction barring the admission of gay men to seminaries came out in November 2005 (see Chapter 14), its authors had moved from the 'egosyntonic/egodystonic' distinction to one between 'transitory' and 'deep-seated' homosexual tendencies. This seems to me an improvement which opens up some interesting possibilities. The oft-quoted strictures in Scripture all refer to acts resulting from what we can now call 'transitory' homosexual episodes – Abu-Ghraib style gang-rape, cultic prostitution and the like. Church authority would be entirely right in calling such things evil and insisting that they never be approved. Just as it would be right in insisting that those who have been caught up in such things in the past, provided they are suitably penitent, should not be barred from the priesthood. Perhaps a way is opening out which will enable the traditional teaching to be maintained intact by referring it to its proper object, while recognising that the appropriate discovery of shapes of flourishing for those who are gay is an altogether different issue.

[Many] cases of 'social' sin are the result of the accumulation and concentration of many **personal** sins. . . . It is a case of the very personal sins of those who cause or support evil or who exploit it; of those who are in a position to avoid, eliminate or at least limit social evils but who fail to do so out of laziness, fear, or the conspiracy of silence, through secret complicity or indifference; or, of those who take refuge in the supposed impossibility of changing the world, and also of those who sidestep the effort and sacrifice required, producing specious reasons of a higher order.[6]

Now the validity of this teaching is independent of what turns out to be the truth about the homosexual inclination. If the inclination is an objective disorder, then those who are certain that it is must consider that the fact of hiding this reality, going along as if it were not the case, tends to produce a very grave social ill. They should provide both funds and human resources in setting up a convincing educational programme, starting from well-elaborated and well-trusted empirical data which demonstrate the truthfulness of their position and make it more and more difficult to ignore. They will have, as a matter of urgency, to exclude from seminaries and houses of religious formation all those people, whether 'formators' or 'formandi' who are not fully convinced by the true character-isation, since it would be very cruel to allow people who believe that their way of being is compatible with Christian living to remain in their delusion, wasting their time and their life uselessly. The traditional ecclesiastical ambiguity in this sphere, the usual 'don't ask, don't tell', will have to be changed into something much more rigorous. The fact that there seems to be a growing conviction everywhere that this position is wrong should encourage rather than discourage the desire to make truth resplandescent in the world.

If, on the other hand, the homosexual inclination is something that just is 'like that', nothing more, the late Holy Father's phrases are no less urgent, and have a special field of application within

---

6. John Paul II, Post-Synodal Apostolic Exhortation *Reconciliatio et Paenitentia* 1984 (para. 16).

ecclesiastical structures. For there can be very clearly detected within them dishonest social realities which are the fruit of many personal sins, situations of evil where many people have failed to tell the truth through fear of its consequences. People who have more than a strong suspicion that being gay is not an objective disorder, and who might well have committed themselves to building up the common good in their respective societies, but who fail to face up to the lie *'out of laziness, fear, or the conspiracy of silence, through secret complicity or indifference'*, the attitude *'of those who take refuge in the supposed impossibility of changing the world, and also of those who sidestep the effort and sacrifice required, producing specious reasons of a higher order'.*[7]

The enemy of the truth in this matter is not so much the stridency of voices opposed to change, but the silence of those who have more than a strong suspicion that the official position is nothing more than the production of a 'specious reason of a higher order'. I pray that we be gifted with both fear of God and with mercy towards the cowardice in our own and others' hearts so that we may have the courage to seek the truth together, and the charity to leave no one in the place of shame in which Professor Mayer, and the ecclesiastical superiors who knew his opinion, dwelt in complicity and silence.

---

7. *ibid.*

human sexuality . . . or ecclesial discourse?

I would like to share with you something that I have been coming to understand, as recent rows which touch on life in the Catholic Church, other churches, and gay-related matters, have rumbled on. That something is perhaps best pointed to by asking whether the rows are really to do with human sexuality. Or whether they haven't much more to do with our capacity, or incapacity, to talk ecclesially.

The first point I would like to make is a little provocative, setting up a distinction between the thought of Freud and the thought of René Girard, whose disciple I am. Imagine a Freudian or a neo-Freudian looking at a rugby scrum. We can hear such a person commenting, after a bit: 'Hmmm, lots of latent homo-sexuality around here.' Now imagine a Girardian or neo-Girardian gazing at the goings on at a gay sex club. Such a person might say, after a bit: 'Hmmm, an awful lot of latent rugby playing going on here.'

Funnily enough when I have talked to gay male audiences on retreats and made this comparison, they've always smiled and got it immediately. The Girardian comment rings much truer to our experience than the Freudian. And this is not, I think, because it is ideologically more flattering to us. But because you can't hang around in such circles for very long without realising how much of the apparently sexual activity which is going on is to do with touching, with bonding, being with the tribe, with affection and with playing games.

Now I think that this is more important than meets the eye,

because it is suggesting that the sexual drive is not, if you like, the key psychological impulse, the key drive, the centrepiece of desire, as a good deal of our discourse implies. Rather it suggests that the sexual component of desire is comparatively symptomatic of other things which precede it and inflect it this way or that. Or to put it another way: it is not the sexual drive which makes us into rivals. It is dealing with rivalry which shapes how we are sexual.

My assumption is that Girard has it basically right. And one of the consequences of this is that I'm not sure that it is appropriate to spend much time discussing human sexuality. For to do so is to go round and round forever discussing a very malleable, rather fluid set of symptoms, rather than engaging in the real discussion about their prior socialisation. The real discussion involves, therefore, our looking at how we talk about things, which is a very large part of how they are humanised and lived.

If you are with me on this, you may not perhaps be surprised when I say that it gives a quite different reading of the controversy surrounding the systemic failure of the clerical culture of my own Church in dealing appropriately with the percentage of its own members in the United States who perpetrated sexual abuse against minors. One of the readings we heard, and which was common enough, was that the problem was clerical celibacy. In this view, clerical celibacy leads to emotionally repressed, sexually immature, males who are then at a particular risk of acting out inappropriately with the children or youths who come into their responsibility.

This emphasis on the sexual, and the chance of a swipe at celibacy, seems to me to do no service to understanding at all. It ignores the fact that the percentage of clerical offenders against minors is pretty much exactly the same as in any other profession or walk of life. The trouble with the clerical culture was not in the greater percentage of offenders, but in the greater success in the cover-up. It was the extent of the cover-up, not the incidents of abuse, which caused real scandal to the faithful. And it is here, it seems to me, that you have the bitter fruits of an obligatory celibate culture (and this is not a criticism of celibacy itself at all, but of the culture formed by its obligation): the bitter fruits are not in the sexual acting out, but in the group-think and the club culture which couldn't talk about these things in an adult way, and so which went into knee-jerk group shame-avoidance mode.

Think of it this way: one of the curious things about the Catholic Church, with the hugely homophobic public discourse of its central officials, is how very few and far between are the genuinely, personally, homophobic members of the episcopate (as opposed to those who will occasionally make publicly homophobic utterances to signal their suitability for higher office). And this I suspect is for a fairly simple reason. There are hardly any Catholic bishops in the English-speaking world, if any at all, who haven't been socialised since their youth into a significantly, but discreetly, gay culture. Whether or not they are themselves gay, they have grown up in a world where the presence of gay people, and the malaise concerning honest talk about them, has been thoroughly normal. Furthermore, and properly, part of their socialisation into that world has been learning not to throw stones in the glass house.

I suggest that it is this combination of a discreetly but thoroughly gay socialisation, and a malaise about open speech which has contributed to the systemic failure surrounding the child abuse issue. It has meant that the clerical group was significantly slower than the rest of society in being able to make the distinction between 'gay' and 'paedophile', because 'gay' was all around, but as something not to be talked about, and yet as something towards which the clerical culture was, and is, generally rather merciful. I wonder whether part of the problem wasn't that the all-male, obligatory celibate culture with a strong gay element set itself up for a failure of intelligence: it was the fact of being accustomed to turning a blind eye to others' indiscretions and trying to avoid scandal for them and for the group which led people to be unable to tell the difference. The difference in question being that between adults who had occasional consensual sexual relationships with other adults which may or may not have led to mutual flourishing, and adults whose occasional 'falls' were part of a pathology which could lead to no flourishing at all, only repetitive damage to their victims and themselves. Group-think, and a defective official definition which maintained the culture of that group-think, meant that too often its members couldn't tell the difference until it was far too late.

If you want to check this out, just ask yourself how much more difficult it would have been for the culture of cover-up to flourish if there had been a significant number of married women in positions of real responsibility in the personnel offices of Diocesan chanceries.

Well, so much for my first point, which is to explain why I am scarcely going to be talking about sexuality at all, and consider it something of a red-herring. How we humanise desire has very little to do with talking about sex per se, but a very great deal to do with how we socialise talking. And that is what I want to major on.

So my second point is about shifting patterns of discourse in the Catholic Church. And again, I can only be provocative rather than exhaustive. As you all know, the clerical culture within the Catholic Church is an all-male affair. Until fifty years ago, it was, and had been for over a millennium, an all-male affair whose members were socialised into thinking in a language other than the maternal language of any of them, and who learned to debate and to discuss things in that language. Elaborate rules regarding the agonistic structure of discourse were observed. Debates were syllogistic fencing matches and so on. I don't think we have any clear idea of our current difficulties in the Catholic Church if we don't have some sense of the consequences of the astoundingly speedy collapse of Latinity in the west.[1]

One of these consequences is, I think, that we don't yet know how to talk as Catholics. Latin is a splendid legal language stressing objective reality in a way that is useful for governing. It came into its own as a language of Empire. It is much poorer at a whole lot of the forms of discourse which have become common since the late Middle Ages. In particular, it can't begin to match up to the languages which have flourished since the novel appeared and began to make available to people another way of truth-telling and story-sharing. It helped shore up a world, long past its sell-by date, in

---

1. The best guide to this that I know is Walter Ong's book *Fighting for Life: contest, sexuality and consciousness* (University of Massachusetts Press, 1989).

which a strong distinction was made between the objective (good, reliable) and the subjective (bad, prone to error). But it has become increasingly clear that too strong a distinction in this area is unhelpful. Our subjectivity is an objective fact about us, and we cannot be objective except in such a way as works through our subjectivity. And our subjectivity comes from what is outside us and precedes us. We ourselves are largely functions of public desire.

One of the key factors relating to the collapse of Latinity and the world of discourse which came with it has been the emergence of women as protagonists in the same world of discourse as men, on a greater and greater level of parity, everywhere except the clerical culture of the Catholic Church with its monosexual priesthood. But now, that monosexual priesthood is without a special language, and the deliverances of those formed in the world of Latin and its supposed objectivity, even when they appear in a vernacular tongue, are increasingly incomprehensible to a younger generation.[2] In other words, our monosexual priesthood is without a language of its own, and has had very little access to ease and fluency with the changing shape of the language of everybody else, given how much of that language has developed over the last century or so precisely in the areas of emotional and sexual honesty.

This I think has been part of the problem in being able to talk about these things at all in my Church. There is a huge stress for people caught between two entirely different ways of talking, the one corresponding to the clerical culture, where an ability to avoid emotional and sexual honesty and the language of subjectivity is necessary for survival, and certainly for promotion, and one where

---

2. If you pray the Office, it is increasingly the case that you need to make an ideological choice *not* to alter 'men' to 'humans' or 'men and women' since the obvious and natural thing is to see 'men' as an unfortunate leftover from an earlier generation and change it quite unconsciously. Or then again, take the Vatican's claim that 'the homosexual inclination, though not itself a sin, constitutes a tendency towards behaviour that is intrinsically evil, and therefore must be considered objectively disordered'. Now try to explain to someone that this is a clean piece of philosophical language, rather than violent and unchristian name-calling.

an ability to be transparent and honest, to be seen to be vulnerable and to be able to tell a story, are the sine qua non for being thought convincing.

Here an example could well be differing reactions to *Humanae Vitae*. I think that the people for whom Paul VI did the least favours by his 1968 encyclical were not the married people who were directly affected by it, but rather the celibate caste which was not directly affected by it. Notoriously one of the effects of *Humanae Vitae* on the Catholic laity, especially in Northern countries where a Protestant-style conscience has been pervasive even in the Catholic Church, was a great crisis of conscience as a generation of lay people learned to disregard the papal teaching. And one of the ways this happened was that a generation of the Catholic faithful learned to talk about their experience, their feelings, their bodies, their commitment and so on in a way which simply sidestepped the rhetorical world of the encyclical. In short, it speeded up the effects of the schism of discourse which is currently operative in the Catholic Church, turning even Northern Jansenists into something much closer to Italian Catholics in their ability to love the Holy Father and pay very little attention to him especially when he's on about sexual matters.

My point is that an unintended consequence of *Humanae Vitae* was to give the clergy a thirty-five-year indult from reality. The encyclical was particularly likely to affect married heterosexual people. These people are scarcely represented at all in the clergy, since hardly any of the clergy are married, and the proportion of the clergy that is non-heterosexual is considerably higher than that in the population at large. Whereas the laity had to work through the issues of conscience and start to develop other ways of talking, including facing up to the demands of honesty and authenticity which the struggle to recover the link between the objective and the subjective brings to the fore, the clergy as a group were able to carry on for thirty-five years with a fictional teaching and without having to work through the issues of conscience for themselves in the same way.

It seems to me that the current malaise over the gay issue in the Catholic Church is more than anything else a malaise produced by a clerical crisis of conscience concerning being able to talk. And more specifically, to be able to talk about being gay in a natural and adult way, and to relate as such, whether in a genitally active way or not. I refer to a thirty-five-year indult, since that is the time it has taken for what was, as Paul VI knew, implicit in *Humanae Vitae* to come full circle. While he was mulling over preparation for the encyclical, Paul VI was told that if he permitted a separation between the unitive and the procreative function of sex in the case of heterosexual married couples, he would be depriving the Church of any realistic reason for making same-sex acts intrinsically wrong. And so it has turned out to be. The vast majority of the faithful has not accepted *Humanae Vitae*, and sure enough, since we are quite logical animals, over time the percentage of straight Catholics practising some form or other of birth control who are willing to judge gay people negatively for acts which are no different from their own in respect to what the Vatican refers to as their 'indispensable finality' has diminished steadily.

The thirty-fifth anniversary of *Humanae Vitae* coincided almost to the day with the Vatican's release in 2003 of its document concerning legislative proposals for same-sex marriage. And I suspect that in the future it will be seen as something of a turning point, because the document was so bad that not even conservative commentators were able to do much to salvage it. Furthermore, it does seem that at last it has had the effect of encouraging a few members of the clergy to begin to say publicly that they will not go down the route of pretending that this form of discourse is acceptable.

The pain and anguish behind all this in the clerical life of the Catholic Church is, as far as I can see (and I have met many priests from many countries talking about exactly this sort of thing) the anguish of men who want to be honest, but don't know how to be so without exploding and losing everything, and yet who scarcely dare to be able to say that 'the teaching of the Church is wrong and it is wrong to be complicit with it'.

So, my second point has been one concerning the loss of a language and the emergence of different ways of talking from which the members of the clerical culture have been largely excluded. It seems to me that the malaise to do with honest talk concerning sexuality, and in the clerical culture, especially gay sexuality, is a perfect symptom, a flashpoint if you like, of the way these huge linguistic and cultural changes have been working.

My third point is an attempt to be a little bit more explicitly theological in envisaging a way forward. And to do this, once again, I'll be a little provocative. I can't get it out of my head that behind all our rows, our arguments, our passion, our anger and our righteousness is a huge giggle.

I mean, just think of it like this: who on earth would have the temerity to try and save us? Who on earth would think it worthwhile to take us so seriously as to help us to be less serious? The very idea is ludicrous! And yet we are committed to it. Of all the many ludicrous things which we have got up to as humans and as Christians over the last couple of millennia, surely to have got ourselves in a mess over the theological status of gay people must qualify as one of the most ridiculous. I wonder whether all those mediaeval scholastics whom we loved to ridicule for their mathematical ability when it came to angels dancing on the heads of pins aren't splitting their sides in raucous cacophony at our extraordinary seriousness and anger in dealing with something which is rather obviously of limited importance.

And yet, what is behind it all? A huge, risky, audacious, crazy undertaking by God to produce something fun, something that can share in God's life and God's joy, out of nothing at all. But to produce it in such a way as to allow the nothing at all, who have no right to be there, to act like customs officials or immigration officers, filters examining what is allowed in, getting all pompous at supposed breaches of our immigration rules. Taking our tasks terribly, terribly seriously and not noticing the hidden outbursts of radiance and delight from those who escape our vigilant attention and are smuggled into, and become the treasures of, the land whose frontiers we patrol, though we ourselves scarcely ever step beyond the immigration posts which we maintain at such expense.

Well, I wonder whether, if we can concentrate a little on this ludicrous giggle, we mightn't see it disguising its mirth at our

seriousness so as not to humiliate us while all along getting us to try
and lighten up. So I'd like to say that for me being Catholic is being
at a huge and very spacious party at which there are an awful lot of
people, most of whom are not at all like me and with whom I don't
have much in common. Furthermore this is a party to which I have
been invited not because I'm special, or any of the other people are
special, but because the host invited me, part of his little joke, a
joke whose full sense isn't yet clear to me. And yet I'm beginning
to get the sense that it is a good joke, that the intention behind it is
benign, and that if only I can let go of taking myself too seriously,
then I'll get it and will really enjoy the dance.

One of the things about this party is that quite a lot of us spend
quite a lot of time trying to work out who should be at the party
and who shouldn't, even when the evidence is that the host is
pretty promiscuous in his invitations. Right now we're faced with
the growing possibility that a bunch of people who it has long been
agreed by almost everybody shouldn't be at the party can take off
their masks and be at the party as themselves. And this means
facing up to the possibility that a lot of us have been very cruel and
nasty to a lot of people over a long time, thinking ourselves quite
right to be so.

Here's where we are at: there is a fundamental disagreement
about an issue of truth. Either the host does welcome gay people
into his party, or the host does not. Here is the trouble. The host
notoriously gave it into the hands of humans to decide who was in
and who was out, to bind and to unbind. And how that power to
bind and unbind operates has from the outset been a matter of a
squabble. Scarcely surprising when you consider the ludicrous
project which the host has, of getting us to become the agents of his
party when he knows that we are much better at saying 'no' to
people who are not like us, than at saying 'yes'.

It seems to me that the place where we are at is this. The
capacity for party seems to be grinding to a halt because of the
question of whether, after all, the promiscuous host isn't once
again trying to smuggle a new bunch of people past the bouncers
and get them into his party; or whether it is not the promiscuous
host who's doing the smuggling at all, but some evil agent who

wants to destroy the party by infiltrating evil people into it, people incapable of partying.

Now, let me be quite clear: it is one or other of these possibilities. One or other side is deceived. There is a question of truth at stake here. And I personally think it would be very dangerous if I were to translate that into 'One of us is wrong, and it isn't me'. The question seems to me to be a different one. Given that none of us is the host, and given that all of us are in this by accident, have been invited thanks to the generosity of someone else, isn't the real issue *not* the question of who is right or wrong, but rather how we talk to each other in the interval while we wait for the host to make it clear? This is back to the question of discourse again. What runs the risk of destroying the party is much more *how we talk to and about each other* than it is *what conclusions we reach*. And this is for the obvious reason that the conclusions we reach are entirely dependent on how we talk.

So here is my point: the proper place for the discussion about this issue is where Our Lord told us it is:

> "Make friends quickly with your accuser, while you are going with him to court, lest your accuser hand you over to the judge, and the judge to the guard, and you be put in prison; truly, I say to you, you will never get out till you have paid the last penny."[3]

My own hunch is that God *is* revealing to us that gay people, just as we are, are part of humanity and that it is as such that we are invited to share in the party. But I may be entirely wrong. Nevertheless of this I am sure: that being right or wrong is not so very important. Being so grateful to be invited at all that I am quite determined to be as warm, charitable and friendly as I can learn how to be towards those who completely disagree with me is terribly, terribly important: for it is by this that I will be judged.

If what I am saying is true then it is a fundamental theological point in this discussion that it is not how I defend my own, but how I imagine, portray and engage with my adversary which is the only

3. Matt. 5:25–6.

really important issue at hand. It may even be important to lose the argument, as only the really serene and confident can, if that is the only way to win him over. After all, our example is One who was happy to be counted among the transgressors so as to get across the power of God and the wisdom of God to those who couldn't understand it.

If this is the case, then the really hard work in Christian theological discourse lies in the ecclesiological sphere: creating Church with those whom we don't like. Or to put it another way: as a Catholic, the only way I could conceivably be right in what is recognisably a new theological and moral position is if I show how that being right is nothing to do with me, and how it includes an account of how we have all been wrong together in which I too am on the side of those with whom I disagree as someone undergoing a change of heart along with them.

Now can I say how one of the things which delight me in my own Church is how much easier this is made by my own church structure. One of the things which are impossible as a Catholic who thinks about theological matters is to get by for long without thinking about how church order impinges on creative thinking and activity. Or, in other words, no flights of fancy about heavenly gradations or celestial emanations are ever able to get very far without the sheer fact of the Vatican knocking us back into what I call 'Realkatholicismus'. And I am utterly delighted by this. It means that I am always going to have to be in communion with fundamentalists as a condition for staying at the party. Any tendencies I might have to belong to a group of people like me, who think like me, agree with me, and with whom I could form a nice friendly like-minded clique, are constantly being smashed. And the wonderful thing about this is that there are only two ways of dealing with the sheer fact of the Vatican. One is to be scandalised by it, go into rivalry with it, let it be the hidden or not so hidden 'double' in all my thinking – perpetually there as the bad guy over against whom I make myself good: in short a stumbling block.

And the other is to regard it as an extraordinary grace to have such a large and visible mirror over against which I can gradually learn to let go of my self-importance, my need to be right and so on. It is as I gradually undo my own paranoia, my own fear of my own fundamentalism, my own dictatorial tendencies, all of which it is terribly easy to project onto the Vatican and thus think of myself as good by contrast, that I become able to see what it is really like to be at this extraordinary party. In short, the Vatican becomes something much closer to being a rock on which there is built a hugely spacious edifice where others are burdened about responsibility so that I can be free to experiment, confident that between us we won't get it too wrong over time.

If I may make this point: now, at this time, in all our Churches one of the things which the 'gay' issue has exposed is gaps between so-called liberals and so-called fundamentalists, and about the near impossibility of dialogue between them. I want to say, as a Catholic: never, ever let go of your fundamentalists if you wish to stay at the party. It is of course terribly dangerous for them to be left to a world of their own creating. But it is no less dangerous for those who do not share their expressed opinions to leave them. Because we are almost invariably run by the same patterns of desire and so forth, but displaced onto something else. If you want an example, then think of this, told me by an Episcopalian in the US the week after the consecration of Gene Robinson. He said, 'Well, it's simple. They're wrong, and we've got the money.' In fact, this was told to me by someone who was in favour of Bishop Robinson's consecration. But you can easily see that exactly the same sentiment could have been uttered by someone opposed to the same consecration. Down this route lies the mutually incorrigible umbrage of mirror-image sects.

But we'll never work through our own fundamentalisms and our own anger and small-mindedness, our own longing to be safe in a group of people like us, and so come to all truth, unless we find ways of hanging in with those whom we think of as unlike us. Especially since their 'unlikeness' is usually a projection of the bits of ourselves we don't like onto someone we feel safer about fearing than ourselves. It's only when we can relax about God wanting *them* at the party that we really will be able to get over our hidden fear that he can't really want *us*.

So, my third point is about how the gratuitous nature of the party should nudge us into seeing the importance not of being right, but of being reconciled.

My fourth point attempts to develop from this. If what I have been saying is true, then we will be judged not by how excellent we were at putting forward our own rightness and the wrongness of others, but by how excellent we were at creating space for those we consider to be wrong. By how easy, in fact, we made it for them to repent.

I take it for granted that we would agree that the whole purpose of repentance is not God wanting to humiliate people because of our pride and wickedness, but God wanting people to be able to be in on the party, which means having all that stuffy narrowness of heart and self-righteous heroism which makes us stand-offish at the prospect of such a common and plebeian festivity, undone. And that means our learning to lose face, and not to mind losing face. Well, it is extremely difficult and unpleasant to lose face, and often enough we have a queasy feeling somewhere just beneath the surface of things, upon which we can't lay our finger, that we are going to have to lose face in order for things to get better, and we both long for it and dread it at the same time. The one thing we hope is that, however it happens, it will be less dreadful than we fear, and we will not be completely humiliated by it. We hope that whoever, or whatever the agent of our uncovering is, they will be a great deal more merciful than we sometimes imagine – the sort of person who will be able to chuckle afterwards and say something like, 'There, that wasn't so bad after all, was it!'

Well, if that is what we hope for, for ourselves, then it is obviously the case that we will be fulfilling the law and the prophets if we act towards others as we wish others would do to us.

I may well be wrong on the gay issue. That is to say, wrong in my belief that the discovery that there is just such a thing as being gay is part of how the gospel has worked in our midst, teaching us to discover what God's creation really is by teaching us how to detect our lies and violence in ganging up on scapegoats. I may well be wrong about this. But I do not think I am wrong to trust that God wants to make it easier for me to discover how wrong I am, not more difficult; and he longs for me not to head up paths that do me no good, rather than capriciously leading me into them.

But this means that there is a very serious obligation on *me* to make it easier for those I consider to have got it wrong, not more difficult. To reach them, not to provoke them. It means, for instance, that it is a very grievous ill when I use what I regard as their wrongness in a self-indulgent manner, to make me feel better about myself.

And this means that a considerable part of the theological effort which I think is called for is the courtesy of constructing bridges for the benefit of others, being vulnerable on their turf, exercising magnanimity towards foes. It is for this reason that I think that the patient work is not engaging in debates in the here and now, since the agonistic structure of such things almost invariably seduces us into the need to win, but slowly trying to construct ways of talking into which people will be able to relax when they tire of the current fights.

This is why I have concentrated on the doctrine of original sin. It seems to me that, within the framework of Catholic doctrine, this is the way those who may need to save face will be able to. If I were speaking to a Catholic audience on the subject of a way ahead in this area, it would be the doctrine of original sin which I would major on. Where I have had the opportunity of doing this, I have tried to emphasise how what this doctrine does in its Catholic version is make room for us all to be wrong together, and yet all able to be rescued together, and all able to learn together.[4]

Of course, neither I nor anybody else can force people to come to the table and talk about things. What we can do is help to create ways out of their current situation such that they may be less afraid to go down that route when they finally lose confidence in their current rhetoric and way of doing things. And this creation of loopholes for others is perhaps best done by people who don't need to be in the front seat at the banquet, who don't need approval, recognition and so forth. Only those who are at the lower seats at the banquet and whose absence won't be noticed can take time out

---

4. cf. Chapters 8 and 9 of this book.

to run off and start to plan the menu and fetch in the provender for the next banquet, since the food for this one seems to be running low.

So, my fourth point turns out really to have been a question: what forms of discourse can we engage in which will make it less difficult for others to lose face, bearing in mind that if we are wrong, what we most hope for is that someone will make it easy for us to lose face, give us a soft landing?

My fifth and final point is the beginnings of a sketch in a direction of a way of talking about this, and I don't want to pretend that this is anything other than extremely tentative. It is what I call: 'navigating wrath'. If it is true that what Jesus did was to knock out the centrepiece of the mechanism by which humans make anything sacred, that is, by offering himself up to death in a typical sacralised lynching so as to show that the victim is innocent, and that what appeared to be sacred had nothing to do with God; if that is true, then it is not surprising that one of the consequences of the arrival of the gospel in our midst is, as Jesus predicted, 'wrath'. If you take away something sacred from people you are taking away part of the principle by which they have identity, togetherness, security, life. And one of the natural reactions of people who have lost, or are in the process of losing their identity, their security and their togetherness, is wrath, scrabbling about for a new victim to give them a new unity, identity and togetherness.

I take it that the reason behind giving us the Christian Church is to enable people to navigate the wrath that has been released by the gradual loss of belief in the violent sacred. If this is true, then one of the things we should expect at a time like this is an outburst of wrath. After all, another piece of how a violently sacred world was held together is being taken out of circulation – gay people are just becoming ordinary humans. And we are indeed getting the outburst of wrath. The wrath is nothing to do with God, and it is not desired by God. It is how the beast reacts to losing another bit of his prey, and we are all caught up in it to a greater or lesser extent.

I rather think that part of the way that the mercy of the gospel works is by making available a safe place, especially to those who feel most threatened by the shifting of order, togetherness, goodness, the loss of a world where the good is good and the bad is bad. This place, the Church, is where we can work through our wrath over time. It is for this reason that it would be terrible if the Church were not structured around something apparently and immovably part of the world of wrath. That is to say, if church authority did not give comfort to those who are distressed by the loss of the sacred by apparently offering a bulwark to hold onto in the midst of their loss of identity, then it would make salvation possible only for those of strong conscience, which would be elitist and un-Catholic. It is not that church authority is part of wrath. It is that it is a shock absorber for wrath. Part of what a rhetoric of immovability, of the impossibility of change, achieves is the creation of a safe space for the brethren of weak conscience.

In this sense I would like to share with you my naval theory of the papacy. My view is that the Pope's job is to be the figure of unity by being the last man off the sinking ship. It is only when everyone else has moved on, has accepted that change has happened irreversibly, and is happy with it, that the Pope can leave that old world behind, with no one left to scandalise by doing so (though more and more people will have been scandalised by his refusal to give it up, but they will be doing so from a position of strength, of growing confidence in the new world they inhabit). Then Peter can declare that episode over.

Well, where I would like to take this, but cannot do so now, is in the direction of re-imagining church history in the way that the book of Revelation seems to suggest: as something which is to do with being saved from wrath, and which therefore includes how we learnt to be wrong. But this, in the book of Revelation, is a synchronous, liturgical account of history, which is very, very difficult for us to grasp. This seems to me to be the real challenge for us now: what account can we have for how we have been wrong, and are still wrong now, and are yet being saved infallibly by One who loves us and is much more merciful than we?

How can we learn to talk about the discovery of things which show quite clearly that strictures which we once regarded as sacred are not so, but which respects the fact that in just the same way as we must be reconciled with our brothers and sisters now with whom we disagree, so we can show no superiority to our brothers and sisters of past generations whom we regard as having got something wrong, because we hope that others yet to come will extend the same bridge of merciful discourse to us? The rhetoric of immutability has its place, but is obviously not a true description. The notion of development of doctrine is a nice try, but cannot cope with the fact that the Church has held diametrically and exactly opposed teachings at different times. I wonder whether 'navigating wrath' doesn't offer us a better chance of creating the Catholicity of being saved together across time, which is what our host is trying to give us.

—◄◦►—

honesty as challenge, honesty as gift: what way forward for gay and lesbian catholics?

I would like to talk with you about honesty, not as about something obvious, but as about something problematic. This is not merely because it is difficult for me to be honest — and it is as difficult for me as for anyone else — but because I think that the notion is too important for us as Catholics, now, to be left without examination.

That honesty has been important for those of us who are gay and lesbian is something which, while it is resoundingly obvious, has not perhaps been examined as closely as it might. The reason why I want to talk about it is that I think we are so close to finding ourselves in an entirely new space in the life of the Church as gay and lesbian Catholics, that I'm very keen that we don't stab ourselves in the foot, thus slowing down our getting there.

There is a tale told about one of Abraham Lincoln's generals during the Civil War in the United States. The general in question was called Burnside, and he was, by several accounts, famously incompetent. As the Civil War drew towards its conclusion, and in fact shortly before the final victory of the Union, Burnside managed to lead his troops to yet another resounding defeat. Lincoln is reputed to have said, 'Only Burnside could have snatched one last catastrophic defeat from out of the jaws of victory.' My fear is that by treating honesty as something obvious, we may do a Burnside, and I want to avoid that.

Let us start with something which *is* obvious, and then try to examine it. We've reached a stage in the life of our Church where it is not at all unreasonable, or uncommon, for people to say something like this: 'Why should we believe our bishops, priests or church leaders when they talk about big things which really matter, like God, the resurrection of the dead, or the presence of Jesus in the sacraments, if we can't trust them to talk honestly about little things that don't really matter, like their own or other people's sexual orientation?' One of the reasons for this sort of question is that it is increasingly common for fourteen- or fifteen-year-old kids to be able to 'come out' in their high schools and not only not to be attacked for it, but to earn the respect of their peers as having moral credibility for having come out. These kids, both straight and gay, understand perfectly well what moral courage looks like, and understand, as do most people in practice, that the earliest and most fundamental moral questions in anything to do with things gay as they actually affect gay and lesbian people have very little to do with sex and everything to do with peer group honesty, rejection, acceptance, fear, hatred, courage, solidarity and friendship. The kids are of course quite right. The contrast between this and the lifestyle of people for whom the gay question is reduced to a discussion about sexual acts in a way which lets these same people off the hook of dealing with peer group honesty about who they are, and which rewards not courage but cowardice, is as obvious as the Emperor's new clothes.

Twenty years ago it might have been considered scandalous for a priest or a bishop to speak honestly as a gay man. Now the burden of what gives scandal has shifted. It is vastly more scandalous that such people *cannot* speak honestly when so many others can, given that truth, transparency and coming into the light are central to the gospel whose ministers many of us are ordained to be.

Well, so far, so obvious. But now I'd like to stand back from this familiar picture of honest gay and lesbian people and dishonest clerical structures and question it a little, not because I think it is basically untrue, but because I think it is basically unhelpful, and pursuing it constitutes a failure of magnanimity, of nobility of soul. If I may use a military image, it is as though some soldiers had, with enormous bravery and in the face of astounding odds forged across an apparently impenetrable river or canyon which was part of their enemies' defences, and once they had got to the other side, rather than carrying on their battle against the enemy, had turned round and sat down on the heroically conquered farther bank and proceeded to jeer at those on their own side for their cowardice in not managing to get over the obstacle. In truth, the point of bravery is not to make cowards feel bad about themselves, but rather so to change the situation that the cowardice of others no longer matters.

As I see it, the problem is this: while I think that it is true that one of the principal problems we have in the Church at the moment is a lack of honesty, this is not, and can never be, a matter of some people who are 'honest', for instance, out gay and lesbian people, or straight adults who refuse to beat about the bush, using their honesty as a weapon against other people who are 'dishonest' – most notably the denizens of the clerical culture. I think honesty is too important a matter to be allowed to be cheapened by its use as a weapon, as a means of comparison against some other group, or as a form of accusation against others. And the reason that I think it is too important is because honesty is absolutely indispensable for one of the most pivotal realities of the Church, which is the reality of witness. Without the apostolic group giving credible witness to the effects on them of the crucified and risen Lord there would be no Church. And without that witness being kept constantly alive and credible, there will be no Church. Though, as Our Lord indicated, under the circumstances of a mass failure of witness, even the stones will cry out.[1] So I'd like to explore how we can move ahead in developing a more honest Church. And this will necessarily be a very tentative expedition, since the pronoun corresponding to the word 'Church' is not, in my lexicon, 'they', but 'we', so the question is how can we be more honest?

Now I'm not going to start by giving a definition of honesty. This is really because I don't have one. I hope I'll get closer to one by the end, because I hope you will share with me a sense of how much stranger a thing honesty is than we had imagined. I want to

---

1. Luke 19:39–40.

start by making a simple contrast between honesty as a challenge and honesty as a gift. As gay and lesbian people we know easily enough that honesty has been a challenge for us. Most of us have had to struggle to be honest with friends, with relatives, with employers and with ourselves. Many of us will have taken long detours prior to coming to some sort of honesty – journeys away from home, flights into depression, sexually compulsive behaviour or some sort of chemical dependency. Many of us may still be circling the airport hesitating about aiming for the runway rather than touching down. So we all sense what honesty as a challenge looks like.

And those of us for whom honesty has been a challenge are highly likely to be those most tempted to want to use honesty as a challenge for others – the image I gave you of the heroic troops standing on the bank and jeering at those of their own side who hadn't made it across the great divide. And this is scarcely surprising, especially if our experience of coming to honesty has also been an experience of loss – loss of job, of reputation, of security, of friends. However, I think we are going to get stuck at a level of honesty as cheap weapon if, when we start to get honest, we also start to be particularly vexed by the dishonesty of others. The real challenge, I want to say, is for us to begin to imagine honesty as a gift, something of which we are so massively the recipients that we can't really be its brandishers as if it were our own.

So, in order to begin to sink into the possibility of imagining honesty as a gift which we are receiving, let me try and say what I think honesty is not. Honesty is not the same as sincerity, and it is not the same as holding fast to the truth. Let me try and explain what I mean. Someone who is sincere believes that they are telling the truth, and the sincerity is supposed somehow to underline the truthfulness of what they are saying. It means that it is not so much what they are saying, but the passionate guarantee of their good faith in saying it which is the point of the communication. They want to get across to you that, whether what they are saying is true or not, they really mean it, and are completely implicated in what they are saying. From the official Catholic perspective, being 'out' as a gay or lesbian person is a form of mistaken sincerity, a passionate identification with something which it is a mistake to believe really exists.

And of course, it is not for nothing that sincerity is a virtue particularly appreciated in cultures strongly marked by the Reformation, since it is the virtue of the one who is justified by faith. If you believe it strongly enough, passionately enough, then the belief itself makes you good. The object of the belief is less important than the force of the conviction itself. The danger with this, of course, is that it can reward self-deception. The more conviction we can muster up, the more we can do what we want, and convince ourselves that we are right to do so, and so to want. Even when this requires us to engage in a very selective approach to what we know to be true of ourselves and others, and encourages us to iron out precisely those wrinkles in our own and others' stories which might give us real insight into what is really going on. Those elements are presentationally dangerous for brandishers of sincerity, and so are censored out. For the truth is that we can never really know ourselves well enough to be able to present ourselves as completely implicated in what we hold to be true.

Then there is the traditional Catholic opposite of sincerity, which would be belief in the importance of holding to the truth about what is objectively so, without paying any attention to your subjectivity. And this of course has its cultural consequences as well. Until recently it was taken for granted, for instance, that the very best sort of Catholic prelate was one who was absolutely rigid in his adherence to the teachings of the faith as they concerned moral matters in public, and absolutely merciful and tolerant with those who could not live up to them in private. Just because no one can live up to the demands of this or that virtue doesn't mean that you try to re-write the rule book. You keep the rule book exactly as it is, and are extremely merciful to all those who can't keep the rules, which probably includes yourself.

Well, the Catholic Church in the United States has recently been witness to the collapse of this whole way of approaching things. Whether fairly or not, by the end of 2002 Cardinal Law had come to symbolise the way in which a hard-line witness to a certain objective understanding of holding to the truth was seemingly wedded to a private complacency both with individual cases of delinquency and with systemic dysfunction.

Just as, in the case of sincerity, the truth is that we can never really know ourselves well enough to be able to present ourselves as completely implicated in what we hold to be true, so in the case of the 'holding to truth' model, the truth is that we can never efface ourselves so completely as to be completely un-implicated in what we hold to be true.

Now, I want to suggest that honesty is neither of these, neither sincerity nor holding to the truth, for an interesting reason. And that is that honesty cannot be possessed. It involves instead a certain being possessed, a certain undergoing. Both sincerity and what I call holding to truth involve an act of possession. The person who is being sincere is taking hold of themselves and aligning themselves with what they see as true as though that act of self-possession was in itself a virtuous thing. I think of Tony Blair's protestations of sincerity in his belief in the pretexts for the war in Iraq, a display of sincerity which appears to have been supposed to stand instead of any objective evidence which might have justified him making the decisions he did. Given that he didn't have any weapons of mass destruction to brandish, he brandished himself as sincere, as though this were some sort of consolation prize, or perhaps was itself a fact as objective as the objective lack of any other convincing evidence.

Old-style Catholic protestations of truthfulness also involve an act of possession: given that, in that view, we can't rely on the vagaries of human nature, and given the inability of humans to live up to anything for any length of time, we need to lay hold of a form of truth that is not subject to those vagaries, to that inability, and so we have these objective truths which are held by the Church, and we need to hold firm to them, even if we can't live by them. In doing so, in fact, in holding to them particularly heroically when they most completely contradict who we are and what we do, especially then are we being good. So what is possessed here is possessed by the 'Church' which thus becomes an objective form of collective sincerity, and is able to possess truths entirely inde-pendently of the lives of any of its members. And of course, under these circumstances, it actually becomes rather important not to know too many truths about the lives of its members, because only while not much is known can manifest failures to live what is claimed to be true be regarded as 'so many bad apples' in a barrel of a silent, but heroically faithful majority.

Well, now I am going to try and venture something about honesty. I think that what is particularly striking about honesty is that it is something that can never be laid claim to. When someone presents themselves as honest, we are right to suspect that they are trying to pull a fast one over us. Were I to have made out that my presentation was going to be something like 'an honest gay man talks honestly about the Catholic Church', I very much hope that the aroma of snake oil would have kept you all at home, or sent you to a good honest leather bar, the sort of place where people get their pretence out of their systems and into their uniforms, the sort of place where people can be relaxed and self-mocking about the disjunction between their self-presentation and their reality.

Honesty is something perceived as attractive by the onlooker, and noted by the listener, not brandished by the person who is being so described. And this is for a simple reason: honesty is perceived in someone's undergoing something in a way which tends towards truthfulness. And it is particularly related to this sense of them *undergoing* something. It is precisely that they are not laying hold of something, but are working through something outside their control having happened to them. In short, they are being possessed by a truthfulness which is coming upon them. It is not the case that they are laying hold of and wielding a form of truthfulness, whether individually or collectively.

What is being undergone is a certain becoming honest, usually in spite of oneself. And this presupposes something rather odd, and which we ought not to have to remember as Catholics, since it is part of our fundamental theology. It presupposes that someone is bringing us into the light from a dark place. Or, if you like, that our normal condition is a certain sort of dishonesty, and that becoming honest is a gift. And it is a gift given to us as we become capable of self-criticism.

This seems to me to be absolutely vital. The frightening thing about someone who is sincere is that they are incapable of self-criticism, and thus liable to be dangerous to themselves and to others. The frightening thing about the holding to objective truth model of Church is that it cannot allow *reality as undergone* to act as a way of learning about who we really are. It sets up self-knowledge to be the enemy of truth.

But it seems to me that what is coming upon us as Church now is precisely the growing inability to be able to regard self-knowledge as the enemy of truth. In other words, we are learning to be self-critical as Catholics. And this is something new and rather remarkable. It is no longer a question of there being the two positions which have informed church discussions since the Reformation: the position of the innocent outsider so scandalised by the awfulness of the institution that they just leave it, shaking the dust off their feet. And on the other hand the position of the heroic defender of the institution, refusing all criticism of it. We actually find ourselves undergoing a refusal to be so scandalised by the institution that we head off into some romantic sunset. We find ourselves actually developing a sense that it is in and through even the corrupt institutionality that we know that we are capable of being reached, and that this is what it is like to undergo salvation: that God likes us so much that he comes into our midst to undo from within the various forms of enclosure and darkness which we are inclined to prefer to the adventure of living in the light.

In other words, self-critical institutional living, a sense of sociological suspicion towards all and any institutional claims but without a rejection of how we are in fact dependent on institutions seems to be coming upon us as a normal way of living the faith. What some people have described, somewhat dismissively, as 'defecting in place' seems to have a far more positive quality to it than we have attended to.

Now this, it seems to me, is very important for us to consider as gay and lesbian Catholics. Being gay or lesbian is not something we grasp and hold onto, even though we may do just that at a particular stage, when coming out, or whenever. I think it is rather the case that being gay or lesbian is something which we find ourselves caught up in as humans coming of age in a quite particular social climate. That is to say, we are far more undergoers of something than creators of it, let alone protagonists in it. And we don't know where it is going. It does appear to be a human discovery, being made in our time, that there simply are a certain percentage of people of both genders who just are principally attracted at a profound emotional and erotic level to people of their own gender. And that this is not a moral issue, something that should be or shouldn't be, but is much closer to being something which just is.

What is more, we don't know where this is going. It isn't at all clear yet 'what gay and lesbian people are for', or if indeed that is an appropriate question to ask. Certainly that question can only be asked when the existence of such people is considered as something that just is, rather than considered to be some sort of moral defect from some norm which *should* be the case. And we don't have to have answers to these questions. We do need to be aware that this discovery which is being made is exactly that: a discovery, which means uncharted territory.

I rather think that here we need to be honest as gay and lesbian Catholics. We are not making a piece of special pleading concerning human rights treatment by church authorities. We are not asking people who have traditionally been nasty to us to be nice to us. We are not brandishing incontestable scientific facts against some bunch of obscurantist ideologues. We are finding ourselves caught up in taking part in an adventurous creation of something which has never been done before: something like a redefinition of being human, for which words like gay or straight are insufficient, but which affects both gay and straight alike. As silly as the notion of 'Queer eye for the straight guy' is, its stereotypes and its humour mask something very remarkable: a suggestion that straight and gay are *for* each other in some way yet to be understood as mutually enriching, as leading to flourishing.

Now that sounds like a red rag to the bull of conservative commentators: 'You see, the wicked faggots are out to change human nature, which is impossible, and they know very well what they're trying to do.' But it isn't, because the point is not that we are out to do anything, but that we find ourselves involved in something which is bigger than us, and which is just happening, at a greater or lesser speed, all over the planet. Other commentators have indicated that the possibility of regularly effective and cheaply accessed means of contraception has in fact produced a huge change in human understanding of what it is to be human. And I suspect that the developing understanding of what it is to be gay is part of the same change.

The old way of talking about what was true or not true made a distinction between objective and subjective, such that truth was objective, and self-perception was subjective, and was therefore inclined to be wrong. But we are gradually learning that people's subjectivity is an objective fact about them, that the pattern of desire which forms how we relate to each other is not, and can never be, simply an individual mistake. It is always the starting point from which it becomes possible to make mistakes or not. In other words, whatever being gay or lesbian is, there is a reality here which is bigger than us and of which we are more or less symptomatic, and which we can't simply avoid by some intellectual sleight of hand, or some act of will. To attempt to avoid it feels more like a refusal to undergo being created than it feels like a bearing of a heroic witness to an unreachable form of sanctity.

Because of this sense that we are undergoing something, we can also begin to be quite honest about the various forms of life which this change has spawned which aren't so wonderful, or are of limited usefulness. While we were under attack, and felt ourselves having to be defensive, we were very incensed when people attacked our health record, our higher than average smoking, our higher than average use of 'party drugs' and so on. Well, we needn't be. These are not things that are to do with 'being gay', they are a sign that we haven't yet allowed ourselves to be so reached by the One who loves us that we can take responsibility as gay people for each other and start, self-critically, to create new forms of community and social life. I think David Nimmons' book *The Soul beneath the Skin*[2] is quite right to be trying to get us to change our typical

---

2. David Nimmons, *The Soul beneath the Skin: the unseen hearts and habits of gay men* (New York: St Martin's Press, 2002).

message to ourselves about ourselves, which is an adolescent message, rather buying into the picture of ourselves as hedonistic sex pigs, and being both proud of and ashamed of this at the same time. Instead, as he shows, we have good reason to be becoming aware, at a sociological level, of the changed nature of our societies. Particularly our large urban societies, where hints are beginning to emerge of what positive contribution being gay might make to the wider human landscape.

But here is the truth of this: it is in learning to do this honestly, to develop this self-critical reception of who we find ourselves becoming, and not being dependent on the approval or the disapproval of others – both the need for approval and the need for disapproval are equally strong drugs –, that we are in fact going to be more Catholic, and more capable of helping to create and sustain Church in the century which is beginning.

It seems to me that one of the major problems we face as gay and lesbian Catholics is that we live in a puritan society. By a puritan society I don't mean one which is morally restrictive, I mean one which is morally schizophrenic. It is a world where good is boring and where naughty is fun. But this is the reverse of the Catholic world, where sin is boring and we are being summoned into becoming something much bigger, more creative and fun than we can imagine.

And yet this puritan world diminishes us all. What would it be like for us to find ourselves creating, together, as gay and lesbian Catholics, ways in which good is creative and playful, if you like, where we are able to refuse the fears of those who linger on the bank we have left, and take forward the creation of a safe space for others to nest in? What would intentional communities of care for each other, starting from where we are, look like? What sort of shape can we imagine for new places which would be multipliers of volunteering and the invention of new apostolates? In short, what would 'parish' look like? Curiously, I think that this quiet re-imagination of parish is in fact happening all around us, and will continue to happen, though many of us won't even notice that it is this that is being Catholic. And that it is this that is creating the future of urban living for the Church.

What I would like to ask us to avoid is stabbing ourselves in the foot! Stabbing ourselves in the foot looks like refusing to believe that we could possibly be being pushed into being a gift for the renewal of the Church simply by learning how to respect and love each other as gay and lesbian people, and instead engaging in perpetual sniping with those of our brothers whose approval we do not need, but who will depend on us creating gentle bridges for them to be able to join us in this adventure.

yes, but is it true . . . ?

Thank you for inviting me to speak as part of this panel.[1] Initially I turned down the invitation for two reasons: in the first place I've just come back from a week's teaching and so haven't got my act together; and secondly, I felt that it would be more appropriate if the theological issues were addressed by someone who is them-selves in a partnership, which I am, alas, not. Nevertheless the invitation resurfaced, and so, at the risk of the classic clerical trap of a straight celibate priest giving untested marriage advice to straight couples, I find myself, an unpartnered gay priest, speaking to this issue from a position of similar ineptitude.

Since the government announced its proposals, and this meeting was set up, the Vatican came out with its document last Thursday, which was supposed to cast light on, or a shadow over, any deliberations such as these, so I'd like to start by asking us to consider our reactions to this intervention.

In the first place, I would like to say this to you: don't allow yourselves to be provoked. This sort of document and the language

---

1. In both this chapter and Chapter 14 I have decided to keep the format of a pastoral response to a particular situation at the invitation of a particular group of people. In this case, the situation was a 2003 meeting of a group of Catholics to discuss the UK government's legislative proposals for same-sex civil partnerships which became, with minor alterations, the law of the land in 2005. Between the meeting being set up in June 2003 and its taking place in August, the Congregation for the Doctrine of the Faith published its *Considerations regarding proposals to give legal recognition to unions between homosexual persons* (31 July 2003), thus giving our meeting quite a new dynamic, and one to which the panel of which I was a member attempted to respond.

it uses hits us in the gut, and then we find ourselves reacting in ways which are not reasoned. In fact, part of the provocative nature of such documents is that they tend to take people out of their capacity for reasoned response, and then we lose it, and any subsequent argument becomes heated and hateful. Let us take a little time to stand back from the intervention and allow ourselves to be set free from being knee-jerked into reaction.

In order to do this, I would ask you to accompany me on an imaginative exercise which might help us put things in perspective. Let us imagine that we are in Germany in 1933, and the Vatican has just come out with a document full of just such absolutist language. It tells us that there are certain legislative proposals afoot to discriminate against Jewish people; that however mild and benign they seem, these proposals are in fact a grave moral evil which attack the root of the possibility of a just human society; and that if the proposals flourish, untold damage will occur to the fabric of our humanity. Bishops are to speak out against such proposals, no Catholic politician is even to contemplate supporting them, since that would be to approve evil. Where such legislation exists already, Catholic politicians must work for its abolition, and may only support legislation which does not abolish it in as far as this tends to reduce its scope.

I put it to you that if such a document had come out in 1933 or 1934, rather than the somewhat muffled statements which did emerge, we would all be very proud of it now. At the time, various people might have said that this was an unwarranted intervention in democratic process and so on, others might have commented unfavourably on the harshness of the tone, the absolutist language, or the infelicity of the translation. But in retrospect, it would have turned out to be exactly right.

I say this because I have absolutely no objection in principle to the Vatican coming out with a document such as the present one. I have no objection to the Vatican shouting at us or our bishops or our elected officials, nor to the harshness of tone, nor to the infelicity of the translation. It is not stupid to imagine that we may need such a shout. The appropriate reaction on our part to a document of this sort concerning the Jewish question in 1933, if we had been blessed with such a thing, would have been 'Yes, but is it true?' And would to God that we had found it within us to ask such questions, to answer them affirmatively and to prevent our society from going to hell in a handcart.

The Vatican officials who published this letter clearly think that the movement towards legislative proposals for same-sex partnership or marriage which is growing all over the world is a sign that we are going to hell in a handcart. And the only response that is worthy of us is not to get worked up about the tone, the style and so on, but simply to ask, 'Yes, but is it true?'

So that is what I would like to look at with you. Is it true? In the first place the intervention has no new doctrinal point in it. It is an entirely logical intervention, starting from a familiar a priori position. This is the view of the Roman congregations that there is no such thing as gay and lesbian people as a class, merely individually defective heterosexual persons with a more or less strong tendency towards certain gravely immoral acts. Starting from this point, the position of the intervention is entirely logical and correct. If there were no such thing as gay and lesbian people as a class, then of course any legislation which tended to treat those deluded enough to think they are such people as though they really were, would be compounding madness and would represent a grave social threat.

Just because a number of regularly hard-drinking motorists were to get together and form a lobby demanding specially permissive driving licences and elastic speeding laws for their group would not mean that there is a class of people called 'alcohol-fuelled drivers' with special rights and responsibilities. We would all agree in treating alcohol-fuelled drivers as defective sober drivers, and would all agree that legislation, far from making life more permissive for them, ought, while extending compassion to them, to make what they do illegal, and to protect society from the consequences of what they are inclined to do.

So, the only question before us is: 'Is it true that lesbian and gay people are defective heterosexuals?' According to how we answer this question, everything else follows. I myself, and I guess all of us here, take it for granted that it is not true, and that we are discovering that there just is such a thing as being lesbian or gay, in itself a matter of no great significance, something capable of properly human flourishing or of dehumanising corruption – you can be a good gay man or a bad gay man, but it is not that you are gay, but how you live your life including how you develop and exercise being gay, that determines your goodness or badness. In this I am quite simply in disagreement with the Congregation of the Doctrine of the Faith on a question of truth.

I would like to point out how everything else in the document flows from the same starting point: all the observations about the common good of human society make no claim to be reasoned deductions drawn from the evidence of what we have learned in places where same-sex marriages or partnerships have a track record capable of being studied. They are the necessary outworking of the view that, since their protagonists would be self-deluded defective heterosexuals, same-sex partnerships can't contribute to the common good, or help build up human society.

There is one place in the document where, curiously, reference is made to experience, to empirically measurable fact. I say 'curiously' since, although evidence of experience is absolutely indispensable for any real 'natural law' argument, such appeal to experience is very rare in Vatican documents in this sphere:

> As experience has shown, the absence of sexual complementarity in these unions creates obstacles in the normal development of children who would be placed in the care of such persons. They would be deprived of the experience of either fatherhood or motherhood. Allowing children to be adopted by persons living in such unions would actually mean doing violence to these children, in the sense that their condition of dependency would be used to place them in an environment that is not conducive to their full human development.[2]

Well, of course, all the attention has been directed to the word 'violence', with some condemning it and others alleging an unfortunate translation. In fact the word 'violence' is instantly qualified

2. *Considerations,* para. 7,3.

in a perfectly proper way, and going on about it is a complete red
herring. The important point here is that an empirical claim is
being made. At last!

Yes, but is it true? Is it true that experience has shown that kids
brought up by same-sex partners fail to flourish appropriately because of this? There are long-term studies concerning this. As far as
I am aware, most such studies have indicated that there is no
measurable defect in flourishing in such children. I have read that
children brought up by lesbian couples are particularly likely to be
stable and well balanced. But I may be wrong about this: there may
be a wealth of evidence to the contrary, to which many of us may
have been blind. In which case the Vatican certainly should bring it
forward and make a fuss about it. If it were true that experience
(measured study over time, undergoing proper peer review) has
shown it to be the case that to entrust infants to the care of same-
sex partners has a deleterious effect on their upbringing, and is thus
a form of violence, then of course we should fight tooth and nail to
prevent this from happening. But is it true? (I note that there is no
footnote at this point in the Vatican's document to indicate the
source of the claim 'As experience has shown . . .'. Should not
someone expressing serious concern about what might happen to
infants do better than that?)

Another point worth mentioning here is that, completely in line
with their own logic, the Vatican officials do not treat us, lesbian
and gay people, as subjects who can be addressed, or who are
capable of reasoned speech ourselves. In this document we are only
a 'they', objects referred to. Again, this is not simply a cosmetic
failure. In the official view, people like us, gathered here to discuss
our government's proposals concerning partnership legislation, are
not strictly speaking reasonable subjects who might have something
to say on a matter affecting us. We are not capable of being subjects
by virtue of our having 'come out', our having come to regard
being gay or lesbian as part of our lives to be welcomed. The only
'homosexual' persons who might be subjects in such discourse are
those who accept that their inclination is a more or less strong tendency towards acts which are intrinsically evil, and must therefore
itself be considered objectively disordered.

Well, several weeks ago, before this document came out, and before we even knew that it was in the offing, the steering committee of the Roman Catholic Caucus of the LGCM[3] came out with our own initial response to the UK government's proposals and to the cautious and moderate statement of the Catholic Bishops' Conference of England and Wales. Halfway through our response we said:

> The Bishops' Conference statement prompts us to ask, at this stage, a fundamental question: Is the Church's hierarchy able to recognise unambiguously that lesbian and gay people exist as a class of people with rights and responsibilities just as we are? If the Bishops are not able to do this, for whatever reason, then any attempt to make the civil sphere adjust itself to their a priori non-recognition of lesbian and gay people as a class of people with rights and responsibilities just as they are, must be coherently challenged.

So, our question has been answered quite unambiguously by the Vatican document. The Church's hierarchy does not recognise lesbian and gay people as a class of people with rights and responsibilities just as we are. It can recognise us as humans, but not as humans who are humans *as gay or lesbian*. Let me explain why this is important. If someone were to say, 'Do you believe that Muslims in Britain should have human rights?', you could say, 'Yes, of course they should have human rights, as humans, but not special rights as Muslims. So they should be protected from being attacked, harassed, and so on, as any human should, but on the other hand, they shouldn't be allowed to set up mosques, madrassas, practise marriage according to their laws, or follow their own dress or dietary regulations, including specific animal slaughter techniques. That would be to treat them as a class just as they are. Allowing them to live according to Muslim tenets and customs would not contribute to the good of society.' You could of course have asked the following question in seventeenth- or eighteenth-century

---

3. The London-based, but UK-wide Lesbian and Gay Christian Movement.

England: 'Do you believe Catholics should have human rights?' And received just such an answer.

So, our hierarchy can say, 'Yes, of course we recognise gay and lesbian people as humans, and they should be protected from attack, harassment and unjust discrimination, but, No, we can't recognise them as a class capable of living in a way which might suggest that they have typical patterns of behaviour and living which are either no threat to society, or may, given peace and development, be positively beneficial.' In fact, the hierarchy cannot recognise us as a class of people with rights and responsibilities just as we are without *in that act* showing that they do not agree with the truth claim underlying the Vatican document.

This means, I'm afraid, that the Vatican has boxed in our bishops, who, as many of us know from experience, are a thoroughly decent, moderate and warm-hearted bunch of people many of whom, off the record, are at least sympathetic to the notion that the underlying Vatican truth claim in this area may simply be wrong. But they have been boxed in because any intervention they make in the political arena without distancing themselves from the underlying Vatican truth claim is instantly open to the charge that they are only fictionally a part of the debate, since their starting point is the a priori one that gay and lesbian people don't really exist as a class with rights and responsibilities just as they are. After all, why should any elected representative, or body of Whitehall mandarins, pay any attention to the details of a contribution to a discussion when the contributor's underlying principle is that the discussion shouldn't be happening in the first place?

Part of our role as Catholics in this will be helping our bishops, informally, get out of this embarrassing position in which they have been put. Though we must probably recognise that they cannot even openly ask for our help in considering these matters since to do so would be to recognise us as reasonable participants in discussion, something which they can only do at their peril in relation to their own command structure. Any approaches from them should be treated as the friendly advances of brave men.

However, I'd like to suggest that we should treat this business of our not being considered reasonable subjects of discourse not as a burden to be groaned about resentfully, but as an opportunity. It is, indeed, our place of freedom. Given that from the official point of view, we are simply not reasonable people, they cannot of course object to this or that bit of our unreason, but must simply treat us as 'they'. In fact they have fallen into the age-old trap of being able to say to us nothing at all since 'where everything is a sin, nothing is a sin'. So now we have an enormous freedom to develop our understanding of what a specifically Catholic culture of same-sex partnerships might look like. And this is what we should be doing. After all, no one else is going to do it for us.

May I suggest that instead of arguing about 'Should the Church allow gay marriage?', we should instead be asking a more classic question. Given the existence, present and future, of committed, long-term partnerships recognised by civil law between adults of the same sex who happen to be baptised, what should we call these? To what forms of flourishing can they contribute? What might their relationship be to the creation of forms of hospitality to the vulnerable, whether children or other precarious people? Please remember that in the classic understanding of marriage, it is the fact that the two partners are baptised which is what gives the marriage its sacramentality. They are living out a secular reality, marriage, in a way which is elevated by the fact that each is acting out the role of Christ loving his Church by giving his life, even unto death, for the other.

What is that going to look like for us? We are going to have to develop rites and forms of ceremony to mark important moments in such lives within extended communities of Catholic friends. And again, may I suggest that we take our lesson from many centuries of history. We can develop forms of ceremony and rite entirely without clerical intervention: let us remember that in the marriage ceremony it is the couple who marry each other, and only since the Council of Trent in the sixteenth century has church authority insisted on the presence of an ecclesiastical witness, a priest or deacon, and that was to protect the freedom of couples who might make their vows in private, consummate them and declare them, only to be dragged promptly apart by angry relatives – think of the role of Friar Laurence in *Romeo and Juliet*.

That the clerical witnesses to our ceremonies are likely to be invited friends rather than official signatories should not put us off from developing the rites. We are also in a much freer position from which to start than many straight people. They are not able, legitimately, and officially, to cohabit for several years before coming up to the altar. Officially, they should not have cohabited or had intercourse before marriage. Yet the whole question of what an appropriate culture of courtship looks like in our society is currently up for grabs – the whole process of socialisation and emotional development by which people of whatever sexual orientation reach sufficient maturity to be able to make partnership commitments in which the sexual element has its proper place.

So, we have both a carte blanche and a lot of work to do in developing our understanding of what seems like an appropriate period of solidification of partnerships, creating the space in which people who may not have had a chance to develop the habits of fidelity which make commitment possible, are empowered to do so before their partnership is celebrated in a liturgy. And this is of course relatively independent of whatever civil celebration might have been undergone, of whether or not civil society calls it a marriage. But this is an area where we, lesbian and gay Catholics, can slowly develop a culture over time, together. And that, I think is what we should be thinking about: what will it look like to create and nourish a strong and responsible culture of same-sex partnerships, including the elements of ongoing care for each other, and availability for the vulnerable, which will be specifically Catholic?

I have a fanciful suggestion here, my own name for what some of us are looking for. I would like us to talk not about the sacrament of matrimony, but about a 'Pax'. I thought of this word from the French term 'PACS' which as you know was set up a couple of years ago as their form of civil partnership available to same-sex couples (but not them alone). But I want to spell this with an 'x' so that it is the Latin word meaning 'peace' and at the same time a reference to the passing of a symbol of peace amongst the congregation during the mediaeval rite of Mass. May I suggest that what we look at are ways in which same-sex couples can form and develop a 'Pax'. This would not be matrimony (the 'munus' of the 'mater'), but a way of creating and sustaining little outbreaks of peace and creativity. Can we develop a culture of same-sex part-nerships which is a flourishing of myriad paxes?

I'd like to conclude by going back to the beginning. We are all of us, over the next few weeks and months, likely to be in con-versations with friends, family, press, church officials and others about this issue. May I beg you not to yield to the temptation of being provoked, not to allow yourselves to be fascinated by the violence of the language in the recent document, not to indulge in the easy critique of the Vatican which our culture and our press offer us, but instead to keep raising this little question: 'Yes, but is it true?' The only issue at stake for the Church in discussions of gay and lesbian anything is the issue of truth. Thank you.

CHAPTER THIRTEEN

the place of shame and the giving of the Spirit

In the Introduction to my book *On being liked*[1] I gave an account of how the Holy Spirit fell upon the Gentiles as described by Luke in the Acts of the Apostles. My aim was to open up the story in such a way that it makes sense to gay and lesbian people who are discovering ourselves on the inside of the Church in a way that leaves much of ecclesiastical officialdom either perplexed, angry or speechless. However, that is not the only account of the giving of the Spirit in the New Testament. Paul, for instance, points towards the same process by means of a quite different set of resonances. These resonances also seem to me to offer gay and lesbian people very fertile ground for coming to understand how loved we are.

So I'd like to look with you at a fairly basic piece of Christian theology concerning the giving of the Holy Spirit. And to do this, I'm going to start with a rather odd phrase of St Paul's in his Epistle to the Galatians. It comes at Galatians 3:10:

> For all who rely on the works of the law are under a curse; for it is written, 'Cursed is everyone who does not observe and obey all the things written in the book of the law.' (NRSV)

It appears that some Jewish Christian teachers had been telling the Galatian Christians that now that they have been baptised and have come to know the God of Israel, they should also keep the Law of Moses, since those who don't keep it will be cursed, as it says in

---

1. London: DLT, 2003/New York: Crossroad, 2004.

199

Deuteronomy.[2] The chunk of the Law which these teachers probably quoted to their listeners was Deuteronomy 27:26. Paul, on the other hand, is arguing against this insistence that the newly baptised Galatians should be circumcised, inducted into the people of Israel and made to obey the Law of Moses. His position is that it is those who *rely* on the Law who are under a curse.

What is curious is that, at first sight, the text Paul quotes seems to be exactly the reverse of helpful to his argument, since his version of the passage from Deuteronomy says quite straightforwardly:

> 'Cursed is everyone who does not observe and obey all the things written in the book of the law.'

This presupposes that everyone who *does* observe and obey all the things written in the books of the Law will be *blessed*, and only those who *fail* to observe and obey them will be cursed. Paul himself has talked about how he used to be zealously obedient to the Law, so he did not doubt that it was possible to observe and obey all the things written in the books of the Law. Why then would he use a verse in which the Law formally curses those who do *not* obey it to back up his claim that those who *rely* on works of the Law are under a curse? It does not seem to be a logical argument.

Well, one of the things we mean when we say a text is Holy Scripture is that it knows more than we do, and that when it doesn't fit into our logic, it is good for us to wrestle with it until it yields its logic to us, until, that is, we can allow its logic to open us up, rather than think that we can dominate it. And for me, this is one of those 'aha!-moment' texts where we can get an insight into a different order of thinking from the ones we are used to, a moment where that different order of thinking can cast a new light onto a widespread array of concerns.

For Paul is quoting the text not, as we would usually imagine it, as a proof text, a way of saying 'you see, the text agrees with me'.

---

2. I follow J. Louis Martyn's magnificent *Galatians*, in The Anchor Bible series 33A (New York: Doubleday, 1997).

It doesn't agree with him. Rather he is quoting it as internal evidence of an anthropological structure. He quotes the verse so as to show that *because it curses those who don't obey the Law* the text of the Law itself shows that it is part of a system of goodness which divides between good and bad, and thus that even those who uphold it, who are apparently blessed by it, are in fact dwelling in the sphere of a curse. In other words he is quoting the words in a way that stands back from them and says: 'Look at what this sentence gives away about the sort of system of which it is an integral part.'

Now this, dare I say it, is a subtle point, and one which, once we begin to get it, makes everything Paul then goes on to say about Jesus becoming a curse for us, and how it is from this that the Holy Spirit flows to us, luminously intelligible. Paul is in fact showing signs of a stunning structural intelligence. If the Law curses some-body, then it creates a world of good and bad, and this means that the 'good' in that system is fatally dependent on the 'bad'. If I rely, for my goodness, on holding onto, and obeying, everything in the system, then that means my goodness is 'over against' someone else's badness, and thus, being dependent on it, is part of it.

Furthermore it means that for as long as I am beholden to the system of goodness, I will never in fact be able to obey the commandment which all agree to be a simple summation of the whole Law: 'You shall love your neighbour as yourself',[3] because the Law as system of goodness will prevent me from recognising the neighbour who is *as myself* and who needs loving, because often enough it will hide that neighbour under the veil of being a 'cursed other'. In other words, the lived anthropological effect of the system of goodness is, in practice, that of nullifying the goodness towards which the commandment points.

So we have the classic Pauline insight that no system of good-ness, precisely because it sets up a world of good and bad, blessing and curse, can be from God, since God is only blessing, only promise, and that the real danger to moral life in any given society comes not in the first place from people who are 'bad', since they

---

3. Gal. 5:14.

are in a sense too obvious to worry about, but rather from systems of goodness, which, since they are dependent on a 'wicked other', are terribly dangerous. They are dangerous in an obvious sense to those who are their necessary bad guys, since goodness becomes a matter of zeal in persecuting such people, as Paul himself had done. But systems of goodness are especially dangerous in a less obvious sense to the 'good' guys as well, since the 'good guys' are unlikely to perceive that, far from worshipping God, becoming dependent on God and being given their identity by God, who is not over against anything at all, they are in fact being given their identity by that violent 'over against' by which they build themselves up. In other words, they are the ones most prone to become violent nihilists, thinking themselves servants of God.

Well, where would Paul's insight leave us, if there were not more to say? It would leave us in a world in which we only have a religion of law, of belonging to an insider group, and of sacred texts. This anthropological structure would leave us in the terrible situation of being permanently divided against ourselves, since even when we want to be good, we find that our very being good is over against others, and leads us to treat them in a way that makes it impossible for us to be good. In fact it makes us haters of our neighbours, and reduces us to the level of our hatred, however little we want it to. That would be the world of the permanent scandal, the inescapable double-bind, of dangerous goodness, and there would be no escape from the 'other' over against whom I define myself so as to receive goodness.

Every system of goodness would be a sacred trap, pronouncing itself a culture of love, of peace, and so on, but in practice building up walls of difference so that it is able to give the impression of being loving and peaceful to those who are within, while being run by a totally different pattern of desires towards those who fall into the category of the necessary wicked other. After all, it is mob action against their 'sacrileges' which makes my goodness 'sacred'. In fact of course, such a split between 'good to those within' and 'fierce to those without' never works quite like that, and those nearest and dearest to zealous 'insiders' often pay a very high psychological price for their proximity.

However, what has enabled Paul to see how this works is something really very odd indeed, and it is central to every aspect of our faith. Paul has understood something about what Jesus had been doing by going voluntarily to his death on the cross. And he refers to it in Galatians 3:13 by saying:

> Christ redeemed us from the curse of the law by becoming a curse for us – for it is written, 'Cursed is everyone who hangs on a tree' . . . (NRSV)

Now this is not simply a word game for Paul – as though he'd managed to find a suitable text to quote back at his adversaries who had brought up the question of the curse of the Law. As always with Paul, any debating skill with the words or texts which he had up his sleeve is used to point to something bigger than the words, bigger at the level of fundamental anthropology.

Paul is indicating that one of the true ways of understanding what Jesus was doing in going voluntarily to his death is to see God as making habitable the space of the cursed one for us. Now let me try and expand that notion a bit, since as it stands it is sometimes understood as though God had set things up so that someone needed to be cursed, then God got Jesus to stand in for being cursed, and now that that has been done, the curse has been lifted.

However, Paul is very far from such a notion. We can tell that, because Paul does not think that the Law came from God – in fact he specifically refers to it as given by angels through a mediator, thus denying it a divine origin.[4] For Paul, the promise of a *blessing* came and comes directly from God to all people because of Abraham and has no duplicity, no ambivalence and no double-binds involved in it. The Law, however, was something that was not part of the divine promise, but was an angelic crutch added through Moses to contain violence. The fact that the Law contains violence in both senses of the word 'contain' – that is it holds violence back (limiting revenge), and it harbours violence within itself (author-ising curses) – is part of the proof that it is involved in ambivalence, and double-bind, and therefore cannot itself come from God.

---

4. Gal. 3:19.

No, for Paul it was not God who had set it up for Jesus to be cursed at all. The sphere of the curse is what it looks like to live in a world in which good and evil are defined over against each other – in other words, it is a strictly anthropological – human – reality. Occupying the space of the cursed-one for us, which is how Paul depicts Jesus – and Paul always portrays Jesus as crucified – is an extraordinary anthropological act empowered by God, and one which makes perfectly good sense to us from any number of lived experiences.

The example I use most frequently, because it has resonance with so many people, is the example of the class fairy. Hardly anyone can get through the education systems of our world without coming into contact with groups where someone gets to occupy the space of the class fairy – and this has nothing in particular to do with sexual orientation or gender, though words like 'fag' and 'sissy' as well as 'geek' and others tend to get bandied about a lot in what we might call the do-it-yourself 'class fairy' construction kit. Nor is it only boys who construct their unity this way. Several women have shared with me similar stories from within girl-only classes.

We all know how it works: being good, being cool, being on the right side, in with the right crowd and so on depends fundamentally on not being the class fairy. It is as if we all know that the finger is hovering, and is going to point to someone, and we'll do all the manoeuvring we have to in order for the finger not to point to us. But point it will, at someone, and that means that they get to bear the burden of the curse. And that means that we get to be good and cool and so on, and they get to be miserable and bullied, and maybe traumatised and suicidal, and in some cases armed, murderous and 'postal'.

Now, nobody goes voluntarily into that space of being cursed. The person who is put there feels all the pain and shame of ostracism, of being cast out, of loss, of different forms of death. It feels like being destroyed, and that's exactly what it is. There is absolutely nothing redeeming about such suffering, pain and loss: the identity which the group is giving that person is one of nothingness and death. Any of us would do anything we could to avoid such a fate, including making damn sure that it's someone else who occupies that space in our group, and if that fails, then we are pushed kicking and screaming into that place and are destroyed by it.

Paul's insight is that Jesus did go voluntarily into that space and occupied it peacefully, knowing full well that it constituted the psychological space which the Law, backed by crowd psychology, designated as 'cursed by God'. And he was seen by his disciples having occupied the space, coming among them still peacefully, not vengefully, and as clearly having achieved something for them which they could pass on to others. He is described in other places in Scripture as standing as a Lamb slain,[5] or going outside the camp as did the scapegoat from the Levitical rite,[6] and we are urged to join him there. It is as if by his living in the midst of the curse and refusing to regard it as a curse, or be run by it as a curse, or react to it as a cursed-one does, the trap door of the trap got permanently stuck just, just, open, so that it could never close again. And with that, the curse lost its power, and the system of goodness became powerless, or moot.

It is as though the class fairy could be glimpsed, unperturbed, glad to have occupied, and to be occupying, the space of shame, and happy to be doing so. He does this because he knows that the class will fatally choose a fairy, because that is the only way they know to keep themselves together, to keep good 'good' and bad 'bad', which is the only way they have ever structured their bonding, their jockeying for prestige and their playing. But if someone could occupy the place of shame, the place of the curse, without being in reaction to it in any way, then the moment some in the class begin to glimpse him or her doing this, they can see that the place of shame, the place of the curse, is survivable, its toxicity quietly evanescent. From the moment they perceive this, then their system of goodness starts to fall apart, and they are left with the task, both delightful and wrenching, of starting to be given an identity that is not over against any wicked other; in other words, they are given

5. Rev. 5:6.
6. Heb. 13:13.

the vocational project of inventing an entirely new way of playing, an entirely new script.

We can imagine the physical elements of the act of occupying the place of the curse, but it is more difficult for us to spend time trying to consider the spirit in which it was done by the one who was moving voluntarily into it. What was the spirit, the attitude, the set of desires, with which this human being, Jesus, was able voluntarily to enter this space of the curse, allowing himself to be killed?

Let us consider the question of power. We all know what power looks like: it looks like being strong enough not to be in the place of the curse, but rather to put others in the place of the curse. Power is to do with winning. But the sense of power behind entering the place of the curse is a power unimaginably stronger than that, since it is the power to be peaceful and creative in the midst of non-being, which is a power no human has. The power to 'lose' voluntarily is the power of someone who is so much stronger than the winner as not even to be in rivalry with them, not even at the same level in any way, not over against them at all.

The spirit with which this was done was one of unconcern about being blessed or cursed by the system of goodness, because not relying on the system of goodness to be given identity, and only concerned with showing that it is possible to be held in a blessing by God that is in no way defined, either positively or negatively, by that system of goodness. In other words, the intention with which this space was occupied was to benefit others who had no notion of how much they depended on the system for their goodness, and therefore were very unlikely indeed to be able to appreciate what someone was doing for them. Imagining that this was done 'for me' is one of the most difficult things to be able to grasp. And this is because this sort of gift is not part of some human reciprocity, some give and take, which we can imagine. In fact it is the opening up of an entirely new sort of reciprocity, a capacity for receiving and giving which is not within the normal human parameters of systems of gift.

Let us consider the question of imagination. What on earth must it be like to be a human being for whom everything in every system which gave him identity and strength was telling him that he was a failure, cursed, not going anywhere, was abandoned by God, had been leading people astray, with everything he hoped for crushed and snuffed out, himself betrayed and abandoned by friends? And what was it like yet to have had an imagination empowered by a trust in another 'Other', utterly outside the order within which we live, inviting him to imagine his being a dead man as a place from which he would be given-to-be creative, so that dwelling in the desert of shameful death, dwelling in non-being, peacefully, would become the place of springs for himself and for others?

Well, of course, with every one of these questions we are dealing with something which we can't put into words properly, but we are dealing with the shape, if you like, of the giving to us of the Holy Spirit. The only breath that can bring down systems of goodness, and of course 'closets' in our modern sense are parts of systems of goodness, is the breath of the Lamb who is standing in the midst of the collapse as one slain. The Synoptic Gospels show this graphically, with Jesus on the cross handing his Spirit back to the Father, in preparation for the Spirit to be breathed on us thereafter.

Now, for Paul as for us, none of this is accidental to, or secondary to, Christian life – something we know about as well as being good Christians. This goes straight to the core of how we come to be Christians at all. The Holy Spirit, the Spirit of God, was made available to us in the first place by a particular creative human acting out on the anthropological level, a particular human creative acting out that was run, if you like, by a set of attitudes, parameters of desire, which are normally off our screen, but could just about be glimpsed after Jesus had lived out 'becoming a curse for us'.

What happens to us, as Paul was at endless pains to remind people, when we hear this story, when Jesus is portrayed before our eyes as the rejected one, as the destroyed class fairy; and what happens when we believe that God himself, the Creator of the universe, was fully involved as the generosity behind Jesus' 'becoming the curse', is that we find ourselves undergoing being set free from being run by any system of goodness and badness over against others, any system of belonging which blesses by cursing.

After all, the Law, the system of goodness, has done its worst, and is survivable; the jaws of the trap are stuck open. We find, that is, that the Law has become moot for us, it has no further use, and can just be gently let go. We also find that we are empowered to desire to enter into the same dynamic ourselves, confident that the One who held Jesus in being, not over against anything at all, will hold us in being, not over against anything at all, and give us new being and a new identity as we are so held.

This is why we are baptised into Christ's death, as Paul points out.[7] It means that we have agreed to join the party of the cursed one, to swim with the ugly duckling. We have agreed to undergo death in advance, to occupy the place of shame and curse voluntarily, to be forever linked to the class fairy. And enabling us to do that, we find that the same set of attitudes, patterns of desire and imagination that enabled Jesus to do what he did, are given to us. This giving is called the Holy Spirit, and by it we can inhabit, dwell in, the same space of shame, of the curse, of death, but as if these things were nothing, thus contributing to keeping alive the possibility of the goodness and vivacity of God being made available to us humans here on this earth.

This is, if you like, the shape of the gift of the Holy Spirit. It is the power and wisdom which enabled Jesus to do what he did, occupying the place of the cursed one, occupying the place of shame, the place of toxicity, so gently, and with such a total lack of rivalry, or of vengeance that all the powers which hold places of toxicity, of shame and of curse together have the sting removed from them, and they gradually begin to deflate like so many paper bags. In place of those frightening simulacra of power and of meaning, there begins to become luminescent, very slowly, quietly and gently, the unfrightening, untrapped, 'not-out-to-get-us', good-for-us sense and meaning of what the Creator of all things has been bringing into being all along.

The gift of the Holy Spirit to us, transforming our pattern of desire, and enlightening our imagination, empowers us to dwell in the same space, with the same gentleness, thus letting the simulacra

7. Rom. 6:3.

gradually deflate and what is real become attractively resplendent, so that we can participate with ever less self-concern in the adventure of making all things new. It is because it is able to move us not from without, as group pressure, and crowd psychology does, but from within, without displacing us, that this Spirit has properly been recognised as being in no sort of rivalry with us, or with any power in this world and, thus, it too has been recognised and confessed as God.

Well, this wasn't only a quick class in catechesis. I want to take it further by opening up with you some ways of looking at the collapsing 'closet' in our Church and our society. The 'closet' can be looked at as a literary reality, as a political reality, as a socio-logical reality, and it is interesting enough under any of those headings, and a queer theorist, a political analyst or a sociologist would have much to say. However, I aspire to be a Catholic theologian, and it seems to me that part of the claim of theology is that it has a different, and a more profound and complete, way of telling the truth about even such worldly realities as these. And part of what I consider to be an essential avenue of theological exploration is how we are to learn to tell the story of what is happening to us in the sphere of matters gay and lesbian *as an intrinsic part of the Christian story*. And this means as something which is part of exactly the same dynamic as the opening up of heaven made possible by the death and resurrection of Jesus.

Please note that this means something rather different from much of the discourse around LGBT[8] issues which we often hear in religious circles. Because it means that I am inviting you to consider something which is not the same as saying, 'LGBT issues are a human rights issue, so the Church must learn to respect human rights.' Nor is it the same as saying, 'Well, Christianity is tough, particularly tough for gay and lesbian people, and we know that God is merciful, so we want to be let off the tough bit as it applies to us, we want to be given permission to have a "lite" version. Just as Microsoft gives us the option, with its XP operating system, of

---

8. The now traditional acronym for Lesbian, Gay, Bisexual and Transgendered.

the "Home Version" or the much heavier "Professional Version", so we'll leave the "Professional Version" of the Catholic operating system to the hard disk drives in the Vatican, and we'll settle for the nice, user-friendly "Homo Version" instead.'

What I am suggesting is something rather different. I am suggesting that the full whack of the Catholic operating system enables us to discern what is going on with matters LGBT *as intrinsic to what Jesus was about*, and thus something which is affecting all believers, and ultimately all humans.

You see, I think that the very existence of, and our awareness of, the 'closet' is a sign that the 'curse of the Law' has been undermined. Before Jesus stepped into the place of shame, thus removing the sting from the system of goodness, showing that the space which it designates as cursed is liveable, there was no 'outside' the system of the Law, no way of looking at it and perceiving that it was a place of double-bind, of futility, of ambivalence and did no good to those who hoped it would make them good. What Jesus offered, and offers, by being amongst us as cursed-one-made-alive is that view on the system of the Law from the 'outside', such that it begins to be possible to deal with it rationally, rather than merely to be driven by it irrationally.

Well, the very fact that we have started to notice that there is something called 'the closet' is because of a comparative novelty in our history: people who have started to say, 'I just am gay, or lesbian. It's not that big a deal. You can heap on me what you will, but it does no good, since I'd rather be dead than pretend.' In other words, there has begun to be an 'outside' from which it can be seen how those who are not prepared to say 'I just am' live. And this 'outside' has been produced by people who are prepared to occupy the place of shame, from which voices shouldn't be allowed to be heard, and which tended to be linked to death, depression, dishonour and loss.

The interesting thing, of course, is that it was not necessarily to be expected that there *is* a survivable place of shame that can be lived in this sphere. It might have been the case, as was certainly thought when our societies' definitions presumed the intrinsic heterosexuality of all humans, that the attempt to stand in the place of shame and just 'be' gay or lesbian was a completely fatal and mad move, since if someone claimed to be gay, rather than merely repenting of their evil behaviour, over time the manifest wickedness of their ways would catch up with them. An alcoholic who claimed that being alcoholic meant that, in his case, as opposed to that of occasional social drinkers, heavy consumption of alcohol was good for him, would eventually find that his liver gave the lie to his claim. Someone who thought that the fact that she had lost feeling in the nerves of her hands meant that she was the sort of person who could stir-fry manually, or put her hand in flames with impunity would fairly quickly discover the disadvantages that attached to her belief.

However, the curious thing is that while societies tended to treat being gay as some form of objective disorder, and some similarly self-destructive outcome was expected, in the degree that people started to occupy the place of shame, it did indeed begin to become evident that it was survivable, and that being gay is just something that *is*, more comparable to left-handedness than to alcoholism. Or, if you like more biblical language, the society which threw gay people into the fiery, fiery furnace, as Nebuchadnezzar did with Daniel and his two companions, began to sense to their amazement that the fire was not consuming the gay people, and some wicked theologians began to point out that there appeared to be a fourth man walking with the other three, in the midst of the fire: 'and the appearance of the fourth is like a son of the gods'.[9] This for me is one of the reasons why I am delighted to be Catholic, because the Catholic operating system allows for exactly this reality to become clear. The Holy Spirit is what enables us in the Church to live through the collapse of the system of goodness and yet find that what emerges, refined as if by fire, is what we really are becoming. Or, in more classic language, the collapse of the extrinsic religious Law is accompanied by the painful emergence of the discovery of the Natural Law, inscribed into our very being by our Creator who calls us to himself.

And I notice that this is exactly how the Holy Spirit seems to

9. Dan. 3:25.

have been operating as it collapses the closet, and opens the door. What for many long years was a characterisation of people as necessary 'bad guys' within a system of goodness, has been collapsing with astounding speed over the last fifty years or so. What has enabled it to collapse has been people living and dying, often enough with enormous bravery and through great loss, in the place of shame. And the result of this has been twofold, the beginning of the discovery that there just are people who are what we now call gay and lesbian, and that who they are to become will start from, and work with, what they are, that the Natural Law is our friend. And that all this is a genuine anthropological discovery about what it is to be human, and one which once discovered, can never be gone back on in good conscience.

At the same time, this increasingly peaceful occupying of the place of shame has created an 'outside' from which some look back at the system of goodness and see those who rely on it as trapped within double-binds and scandal. This place of double-binds and scandal affects all who depend on it for their goodness, whatever their own sexual orientation. Just think of all those hard-line straight people who have lined up in recent years with the most closeted of gay political and religious leaders to shore up the system of goodness against necessary enemies, apparently in ignorance of the sort of company they are keeping. However, those who are most directly affected are those whom the peacefully occupied place of shame reveals as wedded to their own destruction, wrath and double-binds not by their nature, but by a cultural system which only fear prevents them from leaving. These are the denizens of what we call 'the closet', and of course, more than anyone else, these people have a stake in trying to keep alive the system of goodness and its wrath against those who dare to survive the 'outside'.

The question, then, before us, is: what can we discover of who we are called to be as we dwell in the midst of this process of collapse and recreation, discovering our new being as the Holy Spirit brings us to life?

Now, curiously, I don't want at this point to rush in and give you definitions and political projects. I want to say something very old-fashioned and apparently inappropriate. Because our vocations, our life projects within the calling into being of the *Ecclesia*, are such a serious matter, our new direction is inseparable from our undergoing. It is only in the degree to which we find ourselves slowly dwelling in the undergoing which I have been describing that we will find ourselves able to construct patterns of living in the midst of what seemed until recently to be impossibility.

It is as we find ourselves empowered by the Holy Spirit to dwell peacefully, and without resentment, in what is slowly becoming a space of evanescent toxicity, but which is still for some a powerfully dangerous place of shame, that new vocational directions will become clear. In other words, it is by prayer and contemplation over time that we will discover ourselves on the inside of what we are to become.

For instance, any discussions about 'family' in current cultural circumstances are marked by toxic attempts to designate the family as a system of goodness, and gay and lesbian people and their needs and aspirations as somehow the enemies of this system. Typically we fight the political battles of votes and causes first, and the real battles of psychological involvement and pain only later. I would urge us to keep our minds on the real battle at the same time as we find ourselves, whether we want to or not, involved in the political battle. In the real battle, many of us have found that the very notion of 'family' is a frightening reality, something which threatened us, and within which we would have no space because of finding ourselves to be gay. But now, as we discover the Holy Spirit empowering us to live in the place of shame, without reactivity, without resentment, at last we can begin to imagine that even our own experience of undergoing family, which has sometimes been an experience of having to live in dependence on a hostile reality, is being shifted, such that both our families and we can begin to work out what it is to live together, be for each other, support each other, correct each other, take care of each other starting from what we really are, rather than from false premises about what we should be. Those premises diminish us all, and create as much misery among those heterosexuals who find that the system of goodness condemns them to a deep ambivalence towards their gay children and siblings, as it does among those children and siblings for whom 'family' is turned by the system of goodness into a synonym for 'annihilation of being'.

It has been, as some cultural commentators have begun to notice,[10] the particular strength of the Catholic family, and the family in majority Catholic cultures, that it has proved relatively resilient in the face of hierarchical attempts to shore up systems of goodness, and has typically opted for the hard work of learning how to love its gay and lesbian offspring over time, including being pleased with and protective of the legal protections which their offspring and siblings are beginning to receive, rather than go along with the easy morality of absolute definitions and consequent hatred and separations which the system of goodness has sought to reinforce.

The same pattern can be seen with the question concerning the proper shape in the public sphere of same-sex coupledom. There is the political battle, concerning access to civil marriage and its rights and responsibilities, and there is the real vocational battle which goes along with, underneath, and beyond that, which can only be dwelt in over time by those undergoing it. This looks something like: 'What on earth is the shape of healthy socialisation into the possibility of courtship, of adolescence lived at the same time as my heterosexual peers instead of put off until much later? What forms are to be taken by adolescent hopes, fears and dates shared with family and friends instead of hidden or skirted around out of a surfeit of delicacy, shame and fear? What is it going to look like as those who 'just are that way' become able, from their childhood on, to aspire uninterruptedly to a shared life with a same-sex partner without having to go through the huge psychological battles of wondering whether this would ever be possible, whether such happiness was even imaginable at all, and thus without the scars of a long battle with impossibility being etched into their soul?'

Even more than this: what sort of gift to family, Church and

---

10. cf. the August 2005 column by Michelangelo Signorile entitled 'Could Catholicism be Good for the Gays?' www.signorile.com/articles/nyp144.html.

society are same-sex couples going to be? What sort of sign of divine blessing and creativity are they going to be? In what ways are gay and straight couples and families going to be 'for' each other in the future, beyond the little hints offered by *Queer Eye for the Straight Guy* of a heretofore unimagined outpouring of fabulosity and fashion sense among straight males? It seems that gay couples find themselves having to create, imagine and negotiate every area of their togetherness, because they cannot rely on some tradition of what seems 'natural'. Just so, might not such couples be found to have something to offer those for whom the apparent naturalness of their heterosexual togetherness actually makes it more difficult for them to become viable creators of coupledom and family? This seems to be happening as it becomes clearer all over the world how much less 'nature' has to do with forming the basis of opposite-sex coupling than was thought to be the case, and how much more it is shifting patterns of power, desire and money that are at work. It will, I suspect, be only over time that, by dwelling in the place of shame without reactivity, and without resentment, letting go of superficial bids for approval and short-term solutions, that we will begin to glimpse the shape of our vocations to create living signs for each other in this sphere.

Finally, let us turn to the issue of vocations to the presbyterate.[11] As you would expect, given what I have been telling you, I approach the matter of gay men and the presbyterate in a slightly different way from many commentators. In the first place, I would like to indicate that in dealing with the current state of the clerical formation system in regard to the gay 'thing' it is not a matter of 'It ain't broke, so don't fix it'. It is broke. It does need fixing. The clerical world, and its seminary feeders, are a classic example of

---

11. This chapter was written very shortly before the Instruction 'Concerning the Criteria for the Discernment of Vocations with Regard to Persons with Homosexual Tendencies in View of Their Admission to the Seminary and to Holy Orders' was issued by the Congregation for Catholic Education (Nov. 2005). I have edited what I say here to avoid repeating material which is either now irrelevant or included in my response to the Instruction after it finally came out. That response is to be found in Chapter 14.

what it is like trying to live a double-bind in the midst of a collapse of a system of goodness, with all the fear of shame, and the outbursts of wrath that you would expect. The clerical world is deeply structurally dishonest concerning the gay issue. And I don't think that I am being an apologist for right-wing pressure groups when I say that I wouldn't encourage someone I like and value as an honest gay man to enter the seminary at the moment. The chances of them being able to develop as a mature human being without having to play absurd and demeaning games of pretence, emotional blackmail and worse are, I would guess, minimal. Until the whole issue of being gay is able to be dealt with publicly and honestly in the Church (and that will depend on those who are already in the clerical system being a great deal more courageous in standing up for what they know to be true about being gay than they have been heretofore), I don't think that there is much mileage in making out that it is hurtful to gay men to ask them not to join the seminary for the moment.

Given this, I would like to make some suggestions for reading current events positively. I believe fervently in the Ignatian principle that one should read all church documents in the best possible light – seeking to imagine a benevolent intention even where there may not be one. And this is not only for reasons of mental hygiene. It is because imagining and interpreting something positively is actually a creative act which tends to make it more likely that things develop that way.

I take it that well-intentioned people in the Vatican have worked out for themselves that the current official characterisation of homosexuality espoused in recent documents is not a matter of faith, is open to change and, indeed, appears to be changing such that while in the old characterisation homosexuality was assumed to be a serious personality disorder, and this remains the default position, it is certainly not heretical to imagine that modern understandings of same-sex attraction, as being no more of an objective disorder than left-handedness, may well turn out to be right.

The moment that it becomes clear that what has up till now been the official position is fast en route to becoming an 'opinion' alongside other possible opinions, then in fact we are a long way down the road towards the ability of the Church to live rationally with reality in this sphere. However, such a change can't be promoted from on high without causing scandal to those of weak faith, typically those who hold most rigidly to an un-nuanced image of Church Teaching as absolute and immutable. So the change must be allowed to permeate through gradually, as in fact is already occurring. However, with this there comes a realisation that what is essentially good news for the laity, as the possibility of honest life and straightforward pastoral initiatives opens up, may come over as rather bad news for the clergy, and especially those clergy who, over the last thirty or forty years, have been socialised into a culture of dishonesty which was cemented in place by the old official characterisation.

Please remember that the old official characterisation effectively made a big distinction between 'being' and 'acts' such that clergy were encouraged not to come 'out', not to accept themselves as gay men, but to agree that they were severely defective hetero-sexuals and all would be well so long as they were chaste. Under cover of this officially favoured distinction, many closeted priests could conduct witch hunts, whether ideological or, in the case of seminary formators and bishops, actual, against gay people more honest than themselves, talking about how terrible 'those homo-sexuals' were and so on. One of the least edifying dimensions of the whole clerical world is the frequent presence of anti-gay per-secutors whose own homosexuality, furtively acted out on, appears to be known to everyone except themselves. Yet these people can scarcely ever be effectively confronted, since their own pathology has up till now been backed up by the 'teaching of the Church'.

Well, it seems that the Vatican is dropping the gulf it had erected between being and acts, to which I can only say 'hooray'! That gulf has been one of the biggest bulwarks against honesty and mental and spiritual health in clerical life. Of course the dropping of the distinction is cast in terms of the Vatican having reached a negative opinion about gay people, such that they have so serious a personality disorder that they can't really be expected to live celibacy properly, and therefore have no place in the priesthood.

But this negative *opinion* shouldn't be allowed to overshadow the more significant fact that at last the *distinction* which launched a million lies is now being laid to rest. It is 'who we are' that is the real question, not in the first place 'what we do'.

I think it was no accident that the anonymous official from the Roman Curia who leaked to *The New York Times* in September 2005 some details of the Instruction which eventually came out in November commented that 'the very definition of homosexuality is not fixed'. He was as good as saying that what used to be *the* characterisation of gay people as objectively disordered, trumpeted by many as the unchanging teaching of the Church, has become an opinion. This means that in time, as new understanding becomes commonplace, and honesty and balanced socialisation from childhood upwards become normal for gay Catholics, so the current negative opinion can be changed, and there will turn out to be a place in the seminary for that very small proportion of gay men, as for that very small proportion of straight men, for whom celibacy is a gift and a calling, rather than an obligation forced by a mixture of taboo and pre-scientific psychology.

My view then is that the Instruction is probably best regarded as an administrative intervention marking a proper pause in a system which it knows to be in deep trouble precisely because of the systemic dishonesty which has characterised the living out of this issue. It is not even clear how rigorously those proposing it expect the document to be applied: the moment a Vatican document spells out that there is room for exceptions to its own rule – an assumption which is normally very much there, but not stated – you can take that as a green light to those who will drive no mere coach and horses, but entire cavalry divisions, through the doors of the exception. However, the main point is that the Vatican effectively recognises that it cannot yet offer gay males an honest home within church structures, so it would be immoral to tempt them to join the seminary. It can't say publicly, but merely hints, that of course, as the definition of homosexuality shifts, and the shape of healthy gay lives becomes clearer and more visible, so the question can be looked at again.

Now, personally I think that this process, awkwardly handled as it no doubt will be, is very good news for the vast majority of gay Catholics. I rather suspect that the changes which have been happening in society are going to be dealt with rationally by church authority, and that we are on the cusp of very significant developments. The principal beneficiaries will be gay and lesbian lay people, since it will become possible to implement pastoral work that is not run by the weird double-bind of the old characterisation, and eventually the fruits of this will feed into a healthier clergy. But we should not be surprised if things appear to be going backwards rather than forwards. The captain of a very large ship turns the wheel a very few degrees, and the prow swings into the new direction. The stern, meanwhile, appears to swing in the opposite direction. However, all the stern is doing is aligning itself with the new direction of the prow as both move forward.

And with this swing, any number of impossible, taboo issues in the Church may suddenly find themselves the subjects of rational discussion! So let us, as we discover ourselves on the inside of our callings, allow ourselves to receive the Spirit of One who, able to imagine the joy which he was going to bring about, gave himself to undergoing the cross, occupying the place of shame as if it were nothing, and because of this makes alive the place of unimaginable honour and approval given by God the Father, Creator of us all.[12]

---

12. Heb. 12:2 – my rendition.

a letter to friends

Cari amici,

Various of you have asked me for a considered reaction to the recently released Vatican instruction[1] concerning the non-admission of gay people to seminary formation. I accept your challenge and am putting a few thoughts down. Please allow me to reply first as someone who aspires to be a theologian and then later as a priest. I hope that the reasons for my making this distinction will become clear.

My reaction on first reading the text was complex. I was relieved by how short and clear it is, much pared down from whatever has been going the rounds of the Roman Congregations these last eight years; I was moved to giggles of fond sympathy as I thought of priests I know, both straight and gay, in the light of the wish list of desirable qualities concerning affective maturity, ability to relate well to both women and men, and capacity for spiritual paternity; and I was struck by how much effort had gone into making the tone softer and more muted than in other recent Vatican pronouncements on gay-related matters.

Nevertheless, the text is quite straightforward. It wisely sets out that it is basing itself on what has been the normal public expression of church teaching on matters gay in the years since the Second Vatican Council. It then gives a very brief précis of the key points

---

1. 'Concerning the Criteria for the Discernment of Vocations with Regard to Persons with Homosexual Tendencies in View of Their Admission to the Seminary and to Holy Orders' issued by the Congregation for Catholic Education on 29 November 2005.

of that teaching as represented in John Paul's Catechism. These are first: that all gay sex acts are gravely sinful; and second: that being gay is an objective disorder.

Having set this out, the instruction then makes a distinction between men who are gay, and those who are not gay but have engaged in same-sex acts at some time or other. This is a perfectly reasonable distinction easily grasped by common sense (and usually especially clear to gay people): the same-sex horseplay of adolescents, or the circumstantial 'homosexuality' of long-term same-sex confinement in prison, on shipboard, or during military service is not the same thing as being gay.

The document then goes on to indicate that the fact of such transitory episodes in the life of a straight male should not be an impediment to admission to seminary provided it is clear that the candidate has long given up being involved in such things. However, those whom most of us would nowadays call 'gay' are not to be admitted.

Because the instruction refers to people with 'deeply-rooted homosexual tendencies', rather than saying 'gay people' or 'homosexuals', some commentators have claimed that the authors are only referring to a particular sort of troubled or obsessive gay person, but this is, in my view, wishful thinking. The terminology is the logical extension of the view that there is no such thing as being gay. From this point of view, it is merely the case that some ontologically heterosexual people live with deeply rooted homosexual tendencies which constitute an objective psychological disorder. These are what you and I would call gay people.

The remainder of the document is taken up, as it should be, with comments directed at those responsible for priestly formation. The accompanying letter to bishops, which was not released at the time of the Instruction's publication, makes clear that this is really where the emphasis of the text is: all religious superiors must apply these norms. No gay men should be admitted to the seminary, and nor should any gay men be teaching those who are in formation in seminaries or religious houses.

The instruction is clear, straightforward and logical and I don't think any service is done by anyone attempting to represent it as saying other than what it does. If they are tempted, then Cardinal Grocholewski's elucidations on Vatican Radio and Mgr Anatrella's commentary in *L'Osservatore Romano*[2] should give them pause for thought.

So let me set out what I think is the way forward in receiving and interpreting this text. First, it is an administrative document from a mid-level Roman dicastery. It chooses to set forth its instructions within the current ordinary teaching of the Church. To that end it bases itself on the Catechism, which is, in this sphere, a mutable compendium of recent teaching rather than anything more authoritative.

I think it does this for two reasons. In the first place, the teaching about who is to be admitted to the seminary has obviously got to be in line with what can clearly be understood to be the ordinary teaching of the Church as it applies to everybody else – this is not a discussion of an arcane teaching reserved to a priestly caste.

And secondly, the Catechism is not supposed to be part of a theological argument. There is a proper sphere for theological argument, and a rather more significant Vatican dicastery which oversees its development. However, it is not the proper place of an administrative instruction from a lower office to be other than a reflection of the current doctrinal status quo.

The Instruction's reference to the Catechism is interesting. It resumes its teaching that same-sex acts are always wrong (a very traditional teaching) and then it paraphrases the Catechism to the effect that deep-seated homosexual tendencies are objectively disordered (a very recent teaching). It doesn't bother to quote the link phrase from previous documents to the effect that it is *because* the acts are intrinsically evil, that the inclination *must be considered* objectively disordered. The two teachings are quoted in un-coupled form, and the second, more recent, teaching is quoted without any attempt to back it up.

---

2. Anatrella's 'Riflessioni sul documento' were published at the time of the Instruction's release and republished in the *Edizione Settimanale in Lingua Italiana* of 9 December 2005.

Now here is the crucial point: it is from this premise of the free-standing second teaching concerning the objective disorder of what you and I call being gay that everything else in this document flows. And yet that teaching is here presented in the most muted form I have seen it in a recent Roman document. It is almost as if some of the many higher authorities which have reviewed this document before allowing this particular dicastery to publish it might be saying something rather like this:

'Look, we know that there are a lot of us, priests, bishops, cardinals, seminarians, seminary teachers and religious superiors who are gay; and there are many of us, whether straight or gay, who don't in fact buy the line that being gay is an objective disorder. We know that there are many of us who regard being gay as no more pathological than being left-handed. Yet the fact remains that the current ordinary teaching is that being gay is more akin to a personality disorder than to left-handedness. There are improper ways of dealing with the disjunction between that widely held, if rarely expressed, opinion and the current teaching, and there is a proper way. We want to close off one of the improper ways of dealing with this in the hopes that we can all move together toward finding the proper way.

'The improper way is to pretend in public that you go along with the teaching while in fact, and in your private life, you do not. The result of going down this route has been many of us encouraging people to join the seminary and priesthood just so long as they become inducted into playing the sort of game that too many of us have been playing for too long. That is, letting it be perfectly clear off the record that being gay is fine, just so long as we don't say in public that we're gay, and just so long as we agree not to challenge in public the teaching that being gay is an objective disorder.

'Well, treating people in this way is to do something terrible to them: it makes them live a lie as a condition for becoming a minister of the gospel. And it is to do something terrible to the people whom we are supposed to be serving: it creates a clerical caste which has its own, tolerant rules and structures for life within the club, the price for whose maintenance is that its gay members agree not to challenge those who are publicly harsh and intolerant about matters gay whenever these surface in the public arena. In other words, the Catechism teaching is for the plebs, while we have our own hidden teaching, our own safe space, for the elite.

'Even a cursory acquaintance with the gospel reveals that if this is how we have been living, then we should fear for our salvation, and we should be deeply penitent for having gone along with and contributed to this mess. So let us please close down this culture of dishonesty and agree only to accept candidates and form them in the light of the current teaching of the Church rather than in the light of what we think the current teaching of the Church ought to be, but are not brave enough to say so.

'For this to happen we have to agree that there is a proper way to deal with the disjunction between the current definition of gay people as defective straight people and the opinion of many of us that this definition is simply not true. And there is such a proper way: finding constructive avenues of raising the question of whether the teaching as it stands *is true*. This would mean studies and questions being formulated by theologians and by experts in the relevant human sciences concerning what is really true in this field, with the open-ended study process backed up by bishops and universities who are brave enough to say that such study is necessary. Such studies and questions would obviously respect and adhere to the major teachings of the Church and yet be able to indicate how commonly held opinions thought to be definitive may in fact be more contingent than was thought, and how perceiving this does not put into danger the integrity of the Catholic faith or the holiness of life into which we are being inducted.

'One such area might very well be the question of whether the characterisation of the homosexual tendency in recent official documents is a matter of faith, or if it is a more or less well-founded opinion based on a currently available anthropological and psychological understanding which might indeed yield to a more complete understanding of how it is that some people are "that way". It is certainly extremely unlikely, despite some of our more hot-headed curial brothers, that any church document should be read as trying to make a matter of faith out of a highly contingent empirical judgement – we do remember the Galileo case! But a strongly international Church, with many members in many different cultures, is also unlikely to accept the changes in its anthropological presuppositions which new contingent empirical judgements might provoke until such a time as the case for their objectivity is very well made by those who know how to bring together theological discourse, scientific expertise and the simple ring of truth-telling. And that takes time, and study, and bravery.

'So this proper way can only be engaged in by those who are prepared to be in a minority position, not have their views respected initially, and have the faith and trust that if what they say is true, then its truth and value for the life of the Church will emerge eventually, however discouraging things might seem now. There is no short cut to this way. It is the way that is proper to the gospel we all seek to live by.

'It is only when the case is made in such a way that it is obviously held as normal by the sane majority of the Catholic laity – and this may be fast happening in many countries already – that we can reconsider the question of who is to be admitted to the priesthood. The question before us is primarily an anthropological one, affecting all of us as humans, and only secondarily a clerical one, affecting the life of the clergy. So we must prevent the inevitably scandal-ridden discussion of clerical homosexuality becoming a substitute for the real discussion concerning what is true about humans, which also has obvious consequences for civil legislation in all our countries. What we certainly cannot tolerate is what has happened over the last decades, which is that the priesthood has run ahead and quietly allowed its members to live by a quite different understanding of what is true in this area than that which they are expected to uphold in public as the teaching of the Church for the laity.

'Because we all know that this is a particularly difficult and delicate area, in which so many of us are involved: so many of us have skeletons in our closet, and so many of us are frightened of blackmail or of being "outed", we are going to bend over backwards to lower the barrier on this one. So we are setting out the current teaching in its most muted form in the hope that some of you will dare to raise the truth question in a way that will enable us all to move forward. We are also publishing a commentary by a psychologist (with whom we do not expect you necessarily to agree) to underline the fact that the truth in this area is one which is ultimately going to be worked out with relationship to what is empirically true in the disciplines of the human sciences. Please remember that one of the signals we are all getting from the pontificate of Papa Ratzi is that things can be talked about. John Paul's bar on adult discussion has gone. So we beg you, don't run and try to protect the old dishonest "don't ask, don't tell" game we've all been playing, and which has had such catastrophic results. Instead, obey the instruction and find ways of enabling us to advance in truth.'

This is how I make sense of the document as a theologian, regarding it as a small-scale administrative intervention within a much broader argument concerning what is true, the proper parameters of which are only now beginning to become imaginable.

Many people will now have to work out for themselves whether to obey the Instruction or not, and if so, in what way. My own sense (and I am no ethicist) is that there is a circumstance which would justify a gay seminarian not leaving or a gay seminary professor, or formator within a religious congregation, not re-signing. This is if the bishop of the diocese with his priestly council, or the religious superior along with the support of his provincial officials, were to state publicly that they will not apply this in-struction. And this is because, as a matter of conscience, they do not believe the anthropological premise of current church teaching in this area to be true. And until the truth of the matter is more clearly elucidated by the proper study of the human sciences they are not going to put the future of the portion of the Church which has been entrusted to them in jeopardy by mortgaging it to such uncertain science as underlies this instruction. Some recent public statements made by bishops and religious orders seem to be heading this way.

However, there will no doubt be dioceses or religious con-gregations which are not prepared to take such a public stance, but merely want the gay seminarian or professor to stay. These will say something like this: 'Whatever the document may say, we think that what is important is affective maturity, not sexual orientation. So those gay seminarians or priests whom we judge to be affectively mature, capable of celibacy, and upholders of the teaching of the Church are welcome to stay.' They are apparently unaware that they are inducing the seminarians and professors into duplicity. Such bishops and religious congregations are effectively saying, 'We don't really believe in the Church's teaching in this area, but are not prepared to subject it to rational public questioning, so you are welcome, provided you grow up to be like us, and learn to say in public that you uphold the Church's teaching in this area, which we all know that you, like we, do not.' Such apparent kindness without courage and conviction leads to the death of souls. In such a case the seminarian or teacher would do far better to heed the Vatican instruction, leave that particular institution and find a more honest sphere in the life of the Church within which to pursue their ecclesial vocation. The Vatican instruction has the merit of clarity and consistency, even if it is entirely mistaken in its empirical evaluation.

Now, if I may turn to my personal response to the Instruction as a priest. For me, as for many of us, this document was long expected. Many priests were severely buffeted by the deeply irresponsible public remarks of papal spokesman Dr Joaquín Navarro Valls a few years back claiming that gay priests were invalidly ordained. This seemed to me a nonsense at the time, and I am glad to see that that issue has formally been laid to rest: being gay does not impede the validity of ordination. I am also somewhat relieved by the obvious statement of reality, implicit in this document and explicit in the accompanying letter: that there are priests who are gay. It is not so long ago that it was thought to be the gripe of weird troublemakers to say so. I hope that this will have the effect of giving a certain freedom to those priests who are psychologically strong enough to be able to say, at last, that this is who they are. After all, there's not much that can be done about it any more.

I should say that I am not remotely offended by the obvious implication of the document that I should not have been ordained.

All those involved in my ordination knew me to be gay, and yet I was ordained during a period when we as a Church were weighed down by a systemic inability to raise the question of whether the anthropological premises of the teaching were true. This obviously had deleterious consequences for the ability of many of us to make psychologically valid vows or promises of celibacy. Official teaching was (and is) that gay people had no choice but to be celibate anyhow, so what did it matter if I had any sense of calling to be celibate or not? It is of course true that the systemic weight of dishonesty is not merely the fault of dishonest individuals, but has a dishonesty-producing dynamic of its own. Yet, even so, we are many, many men who went along with this system, benefited from it, and bear guilt and confusion through it. And I am one such and in no position to complain if someone says I shouldn't have been ordained.

Nor am I offended by the implication that I am deficient as regards affective maturity. As it happens, this is clearly true. One of the advantages of having been living as a priest who is a juridical non-person over the last ten years is the increased sense of the gap between the generosity of the One calling and the inappropriate-ness of the ones called. It is quite clear to me that the sacrament of Orders is from God, and works relatively independently of both the affective adequacy and the canonical systems of those upon whom it is bestowed, and I've learned to trust that more and more. I've also been aware that when people have reported a flow of power through my ministry, this has scarcely been related to personal qualities of my own, let alone to any canonical approval of my role. Like most priests, I am experientially aware that the weight of glory is carried in earthen vessels. So I must confess that the Instruction's meditations concerning psychological appro-priateness for the priesthood did seem to me to emanate from *la Ruritanie profonde*.

However, as a priest thinking of my brother priests, I must say that I am most struck by something about which I've seen little comment. The Instruction appears to regard 'deep-seated homo-sexual tendencies' not only as an objective disorder (with which empirical judgement I disagree). Much more strikingly, and I think rightly, its authors appear to regard such tendencies as an objective *fact* about a person. But this means that someone who hides the fact that he is gay, instead loudly proclaiming his undying loyalty to the current magisterium of the Church, is no more suitable to be a seminarian or a seminary rector or instructor than the visibly gay person who expresses some reservations as to the sanity of agreeing with everything the magisterium says all the time.

In other words – and this does seem to me to be important – the document has bitten the bullet of the fact that we are talking about what people *are* and not about *their ideological position*. This means that the Instruction cuts at least as far to the right as it does to the left. I'm rather afraid that in recent years many, many young men of a conservative bent have been swept up into places of very conservative formation where piety and an ability to hold and defend implausible magisterial positions were the true hallmark of the John Paul seminarian. Such people were given the impression that the rigorous maintenance of ideological correctness would trump inconvenient details concerning who they might be.

Well, that impression was false. Who you are is an objective truth about you which, irrespective of your ideological standpoint or your delicacy of conscience in admitting to it, bars you from being a seminarian or teaching in a seminary. Heretofore a capacity for a certain dissemblance about who you are was a sign of suitability in conservative circles, as though being gay were properly a subjective matter of the internal forum. But that is no longer tenable. Now that same dissemblance about who you are merely compounds an already insuperable and objective unsuitability.

As a priest, my concern is this: I had the good fortune, ten years ago, to lose everything I held dear, to work through the sense of being stabbed in the back by the Church of my love, to learn that the consequence of thinking it worth telling the truth in this area is to lose all rights, and somehow to begin to make sense of it all and survive with faith intact and strengthened. But this is a devastating process, and it has taken me several years of clinical depression, unemployment and emotional paralysis to begin to work through it. This process is not something I would wish on anyone else at all. Since then, I very much hope that many other gay priests of a more flexible mindset than my own will have had plenty of opportunity to think about what they should do, how they should respond, work through issues of 'coming out' and so on – they will have lived, after all, through the wall-to-wall news coverage of the priest paedophilia cover-up. They will have become boringly used to hearing that it is all the fault of the gays, or the liberals, or dissenting theologians. And they will have had some chance to make psychological adjustments to the new realities that they are facing, and develop the new sort of capacity for honest discourse whose birth within them is a sign of great grace. I have had the privilege of meeting a good number of such priests and sharing retreats with them as they work through precisely these issues for themselves.

Those who will have had no chance to be properly prepared are those who were given the impression that the gay issue was an ideological one, part of a culture war, something to do with what people did (sex acts) or what people said ('coming out', challenging church teaching), not what people *are*. Seminarians and seminary professors in this situation, who are going to be among the least able to voice their pain and their protest, are the people who will have the hardest time dealing with feeling stabbed in the back by this Instruction's recognition that 'having deep-rooted homosexual tendencies' is a fact, a fact they have been given no encouragement or vocabulary to deal with; and that, if they are honest, they must therefore go.

I hope to God that proper financial and psychological resources for the long-term care and accompaniment of these exiled sheep, many of whom will not have even begun to discuss these issues with their own families, are going to be provided by those who, at least as much as the dishonest liberals they so ardently and publicly despise, have led people up the garden path of unreality. That too is a salvation issue.

Thank you for accompanying me through these ruminations. Let us pray for each other as we accompany each other through this surprisingly hopeful episode in the life of our Church.

Your brother,

James

2 corinthians 5:1-21

¹ For we know that if the earthly tent we live in is destroyed, we have a building from God, a house not made with hands, eternal in the heavens. ² Here indeed we groan, and long to put on our heavenly dwelling, ³ so that by putting it on we may not be found naked. ⁴ For while we are still in this tent, we sigh with anxiety; not that we would be unclothed, but that we would be further clothed, so that what is mortal may be swallowed up by life. ⁵ He who has prepared us for this very thing is God, who has given us the Spirit as a guarantee. ⁶ So we are always of good courage; we know that while we are at home in the body we are away from the Lord, ⁷ for we walk by faith, not by sight. ⁸ We are of good courage, and we would rather be away from the body and at home with the Lord. ⁹ So whether we are at home or away, we make it our aim to please him. ¹⁰ For we must all appear before the judgment seat of Christ, so that each one may receive good or evil, according to what he has done in the body. ¹¹ Therefore, knowing the fear of the Lord, we persuade men; but what we are is known to God, and I hope it is known also to your conscience. ¹² We are not commending ourselves to you again but giving you cause to be proud of us, so that you may be able to answer those who pride themselves on a man's position and not on his heart. ¹³ For if we are beside ourselves, it is for God; if we are in our right mind, it is for you. ¹⁴ For the love of Christ controls us, because we are convinced that one has died for all; therefore all have died. ¹⁵ And he died for all, that those who live might live no longer for themselves but for him who for their sake died and was raised. ¹⁶ From now on, therefore, we regard no one from a human point of view; even though we once regarded Christ from a human point of view, we

regard him thus no longer. [17] Therefore, if any one is in Christ, he is a new creation; the old has passed away, behold, the new has come. [18] All this is from God, who through Christ reconciled us to himself and gave us the ministry of reconciliation; [19] that is, in Christ God was reconciling the world to himself, not counting their trespasses against them, and entrusting to us the message of reconciliation. [20] So we are ambassadors for Christ, God making his appeal through us. We beseech you on behalf of Christ, be reconciled to God. [21] For our sake he made him to be sin who knew no sin, so that in him we might become the righteousness of God.

———◄O►———

wisdom 12:23–13:10 and 14:9-31

12:23 Therefore those who in folly of life lived unrighteously thou didst torment through their own abominations. [24] For they went far astray on the paths of error, accepting as gods those animals which even their enemies despised; they were deceived like foolish babes. [25] Therefore, as to thoughtless children, thou didst send thy judgment to mock them. [26] But those who have not heeded the warning of light rebukes will experience the deserved judgment of God. [27] For when in their suffering they became incensed at those creatures which they had thought to be gods, being punished by means of them, they saw and recognized as the true God him whom they had before refused to know. Therefore the utmost condemnation came upon them. **13:1** For all men who were ignorant of God were foolish by nature; and they were unable from the good things that are seen to know him who exists, nor did they recognize the craftsman while paying heed to his works; [2] but they supposed that either fire or wind or swift air, or the circle of the stars, or turbulent water, or the luminaries of heaven were the gods that rule the world. [3] If through delight in the beauty of these things men assumed them to be gods, let them know how much better than these is their Lord, for the author of beauty created them. [4] And if men were amazed at their power and working, let them perceive from them how much more powerful is he who formed them. [5] For from the greatness and beauty of created things comes a corresponding perception of their Creator. [6] Yet these men are little to be blamed, for perhaps they go astray while seeking God and desiring to find him. [7] For as they live among his works they keep searching, and they trust in what they see, because the things that are seen are beautiful. [8] Yet again, not even they are to be excused; ⁹ for if they had the power to know so much that they could investigate the world, how did they fail to find sooner the Lord of these things? ¹⁰ But miserable, with their hopes set on dead things, are the men who give the name "gods" to the works of men's hands, gold and silver fashioned with skill, and likenesses of animals, or a useless stone, the work of an ancient hand.

wisdom 14:9-31

⁹ For equally hateful to God are the ungodly man and his ungodliness, ¹⁰ for what was done will be punished together with him who did it. ¹¹ Therefore there will be a visitation also upon the heathen idols, because, though part of what God created, they became an abomination, and became traps for the souls of men and a snare to the feet of the foolish. ¹² For the idea of making idols was the beginning of fornication, and the invention of them was the corruption of life, ¹³ for neither have they existed from the beginning nor will they exist for ever. ¹⁴ For through the vanity of men they entered the world, and therefore their speedy end has been planned. ¹⁵ For a father, consumed with grief at an untimely bereavement, made an image of his child, who had been suddenly taken from him; and he now honoured as a god what was once a dead human being, and handed on to his dependents secret rites and initiations. ¹⁶ Then the ungodly custom, grown strong with time, was kept as a law, and at the command of monarchs graven images were worshiped. ¹⁷ When men could not honour monarchs in their presence, since they lived at a distance, they imagined their appearance far away, and made a visible image of the king whom they honoured, so that by their zeal they might flatter the absent one as though present. ¹⁸ Then the ambition of the craftsman impelled even those who did not know the king to intensify their worship. ¹⁹ For he, perhaps wishing to please his ruler, skilfully forced the likeness to take more beautiful form, ²⁰ and the multitude, attracted by the charm of his work, now regarded as an object of worship the one whom shortly before they had honoured as a man. ²¹ And this became a hidden trap for mankind, because men, in bondage to misfortune or to royal authority, bestowed on objects

of stone or wood the name that ought not to be shared. [22] After-
ward it was not enough for them to err about the knowledge of
God, but they live in great strife due to ignorance, and they call
such great evils peace. [23] For whether they kill children in their
initiations, or celebrate secret mysteries, or hold frenzied revels
with strange customs, [24] they no longer keep either their lives or
their marriages pure, but they either treacherously kill one another,
or grieve one another by adultery, [25] and all is a raging riot of blood
and murder, theft and deceit, corruption, faithlessness, tumult,
perjury, [26] confusion over what is good, forgetfulness of favours,
pollution of souls, sex perversion, disorder in marriage, adultery,
and debauchery. [27] For the worship of idols not to be named is the
beginning and cause and end of every evil. [28] For their worshipers
either rave in exultation, or prophesy lies, or live unrighteously, or
readily commit perjury; [29] for because they trust in lifeless idols
they swear wicked oaths and expect to suffer no harm. [30] But just
penalties will overtake them on two counts: because they thought
wickedly of God in devoting themselves to idols, and because in
deceit they swore unrighteously through contempt for holiness. [31]
For it is not the power of the things by which men swear, but the
just penalty for those who sin, that always pursues the transgression
of the unrighteous.

romans 1:14–2:5
(RSV, but without verse and chapter breaks)

I am under obligation both to Greeks and to barbarians, both to the wise and to the foolish: so I am eager to preach the gospel to you also who are in Rome. For I am not ashamed of the gospel: it is the power of God for salvation to every one who has faith, to the Jew first and also to the Greek. For in it the righteousness of God is revealed through faith for faith; as it is written, ''He who through faith is righteous shall live.'' For the wrath of God is revealed from heaven against all ungodliness and wickedness of men who by their wickedness suppress the truth. For what can be known about God is plain to them, because God has shown it to them. Ever since the creation of the world his invisible nature, namely, his eternal power and deity, has been clearly perceived in the things that have been made. So they are without excuse; for although they knew God they did not honour him as God or give thanks to him, but they became futile in their thinking and their senseless minds were darkened. Claiming to be wise, they became fools, and exchanged the glory of the immortal God for images resembling mortal man or birds or animals or reptiles. Therefore God gave them up in the lusts of their hearts to impurity, to the dishonouring of their bodies among themselves, because they exchanged the truth about God for a lie and worshiped and served the creature rather than the Creator, who is blessed for ever! Amen. For this reason God gave them up to dishonourable passions. Their women exchanged natural relations for unnatural, and the men likewise gave up natural relations with women and were consumed with passion for one another, men committing shameless acts with men and receiving in their own persons the due penalty for their error. And since they did not see fit to acknowledge God, God gave them up to a base mind and to improper conduct. They were filled with all manner of wickedness, evil, covetousness, malice. Full of envy, murder, strife, deceit, malignity, they are gossips, slanderers, haters of God, insolent, haughty, boastful, inventors of evil, disobedient to parents, foolish, faithless, heartless, ruthless. Though they know God's decree that those who do such things deserve to die, they not only do them but approve those who practice them. Therefore you have no excuse, O man, whoever you are, when you judge another; for in passing judgment upon him you condemn yourself, because you, the judge, are doing the very same things. We know that the judgment of God rightly falls upon those who do such things. Do you suppose, O man, that when you judge those who do such things and yet do them yourself, you will escape the judgment of God? Or do you presume upon the riches of his kindness and forbearance and patience? Do you not know that God's kindness is meant to lead you to repentance? But by your hard and impenitent heart you are storing up wrath for yourself on the day of wrath when God's righteous judgment will be revealed.

Earlier versions of all the chapters of this book, except Chapter 6, have appeared at one time or another on www.jamesalison.co.uk.

Chapter 1 is a very slightly modified version of a talk given to the Order of Julian of Norwich in Waukesha, Wisconsin in May 2003 and was subsequently published by the Order in booklet form.

Chapter 2 is a very slightly modified version of a talk given at the Ceiliúradh in Dublin in June 2003 and subsequently published in *Studia Liturgica* 34 (2004), pp. 133–46, and is published here by kind permission of the Editor.

Chapter 3 is a highly edited version of the transcript of the Felix Arnott Lecture given at the Australian Catholic University in Brisbane, Australia in August 2004.

Chapter 4 first appeared as an article in *The Tablet*, 19 March 2005, Vol. 259, No. 8580, pp. 10–11, and is published here by kind permission of the Editor.

Chapter 5 is a very slightly modified version of a talk given at the Conference on Evil held by The Metropolitan Center For Mental Health and The Metropolitan Institute For Training In Psycho-analytic Psychotherapy in New York City in April 2005.

Chapter 6 is a slightly modified version of a talk given at the Clergy Conference of the Society of Analytical Psychology in London in November 2005.

Chapter 7 is a slightly modified version of a presentation for the Conference entitled 'The anatomy of reconciliation: from violence to healing' held by the Trinity Institute in New York City in January 2006.

Chapter 8 is a slightly modified version of a lecture given at the Mount Saint Agnes Theological Center for Women in Baltimore, Maryland in January 2004 and was subsequently published by the Center in booklet form.

Chapter 9 is a translation of a public lecture originally given in the Universidad de Valencia in March 2005. In its English translation it first appeared as Chapter 6 of Filochowski and Stanford (eds.), *Opening Up: Speaking Out in the Church* (London: DLT, 2005), pp. 66–80, and is published here by kind permission of the Editors in a slightly revised and updated form.

Chapter 10 is a very slightly modified version of a lecture given at the Sarum Consultation on Human Sexuality and the Churches held at Sarum College, Salisbury in February 2004. It was subsequently published by Sarum College Press in a collection entitled *Human Sexuality and the Churches,* edited by Tim Macquiban and Danny Rhodes, pp. 69–86, and appears here by kind permission of the Editors.

Chapter 11 is a slightly modified version of a talk given at Fordham University, New York City in November 2003 and organised by the Catholic Chaplaincy at the University.

Chapter 12 is a slightly retouched version of a talk given in St Anne's, Soho, London in August 2003 and published thereafter in *The Furrow* (2003), pp. 538–45. It appears here by kind permission of the Editor.

Chapter 13 was originally given as a Cardoner Lecture in Creighton University, Omaha, Nebraska in October 2005 and appears here in slightly shortened form.

Chapter 14 was a response to a request from the Pastoral Communications Office of a Latin American Diocese and various friends and appeared originally as a letter sent by e-mail and published on www.jamesalison.co.uk in December 2005.